The Financial Sector and Economic Development:
The Mexican Case

THE FINANCIAL SECTOR AND ECONOMIC DEVELOPMENT

The Mexican Case

by Robert L. Bennett

THE JOHNS HOPKINS PRESS,
Baltimore 1965

This book has been brought to publication with the assistance
of a grant from The Ford Foundation.

To those who have influenced me most:
C. A. B., R. L. B., A. F. B.,
R. H. M., and C. E. A.

Preface

FORTUNATELY FOR THOSE interested in the role of financial institutions in economic development, during the past two decades a comprehensive and detailed monthly record has been kept of the activities of Mexican financial institutions. Few countries whose financial sector is not entirely government-owned can provide such comprehensive statistics for a comparable stage in their development. However, these available data and other data necessary for interpreting them are scattered in a number of publications issued in a number of years, and these publications are largely in the Spanish language. A useful task is accomplished, I hope, in bringing data on the Mexican financial sector into juxtaposition with data on the nonfinancial sectors, in presenting the data for two decades together in one place, in performing elementary statistical transformations so as to render the data more readily comparable, and in making this information available in English. In the present study, flow-of-funds tables are developed for a four-sector economy—business and individual, government, rest-of-world, and financial sectors—with the financial sector further subdivided by type of liabilities —monetary and nonmonetary—and type of ownership—government and private. Where possible, these statistics cover the period from 1940–1960, but the analytical portions of the study deal primarily with the 1945–1959 period.

The most important objective of the present study is to outline a theory of the role of the financial sector in economic development—a theory which recognizes important institutional differences between underdeveloped countries and advanced countries and between underdeveloped countries today and advanced countries during the early years of their development. Until recently only banks were financial institutions considered worthy of the special attention of economic and monetary theorists. The empirical work of Raymond Goldsmith and the theoretical work of John G. Gurley and Edward S. Shaw have resulted in an increased interest among economists in the activities of nonbank intermediaries. The theory of finance developed by Gurley and Shaw leads one to consider the entire financial sector important in economic development. However, Gurley and Shaw's application of their theory has been to an economy at a relatively advanced level of industrialization rather than to an economy during the early years of a development effort. During these earlier years of a development effort it is necessary to place greater emphasis on structural change in both the financial and nonfinancial sectors. It is also necessary to place greater emphasis on market imperfections in an economy in which the money and capital markets are relatively undeveloped. For these reasons, in the theory developed here attention is focused on the quality of the financial sector's assets more than on the quantity and quality of the financial sector's liabilities.

While the model developed here is designed specifically with reference to the institutional patterns of Mexico, it is hoped that other countries— particularly other Latin American countries—have sufficiently similar financial characteristics to give the policy conclusions of this study a wider relevance.

Among the many people who provided helpful suggestions and criticisms of various portions of this study, Professor Stephen L. McDonald of the University of Texas, Professor Murray E. Polakoff of New York University, Professor Rondo E. Cameron of the University of Wisconsin, Lic. Leopoldo Solís M. of Banco de México, and Professor Paul Wonnacott of the University of Maryland deserve special thanks. I am also deeply indebted to Robert Cuba Jones and his wife, Ingeborg, for invaluable bibliographical assistance and extraordinary hospitality during the research in Mexico. Editing the entire manuscript was only one of the innumerable ways in which my wife, Carol, made this work possible. She, Bill, and Patrice exhibited remarkable patience.

This study was made under a Ford Foundation fellowship in economic development and administration and under a post-doctoral grant from the Graduate Program in Economic History of the University of Wisconsin. The conclusions, opinions, and other statements of this study are those of the author and are not necessarily those of any of the individuals or institutions mentioned above.

Portions of Chapters I and V appeared in slightly revised form in the *Journal of Finance*, which has kindly permitted their use here.

Contents

LIST OF TABLES

TEXT

Contents

11. Government Sector: Analysis of Selected Real Sources
    and Uses of Funds 100

12. Rest-of-World Sector: Analysis of Selected Real Sources
    and Uses of Funds 103

13. Financial Intermediary Sector: Real Sources and Uses of Funds
    as Percentage of Gross National Product 106

14. Values of Variables, Mexico, 1945–1959 122

15. Relative Importance of Sources of Innovation
    Financing, Mexico, 1945–1959 123

16. Analysis of Financial Sector Flows of Funds to
    Businesses and Individuals, Mexico, 1945–1959 125

17. Percentage Reductions in Per Capita Output Increases
    under Three Assumptions: Mexico, 1945–1959 129

APPENDIX

1. Financial Intermediary Sector: Balance Sheet,
   Mexico, 1945–1960 146

2. Total Monetary Intermediaries: Balance Sheet,
   Mexico, 1945–1960 148

3. Total Nonmonetary Intermediaries: Balance Sheet,
   Mexico, 1945–1960 150

4. Total Government Intermediaries: Balance Sheet,
   Mexico, 1945–1960 152

5. Total Private Intermediaries: Balance Sheet,
   Mexico, 1945–1960 154

6. Banco de México, S. A.: Balance Sheet,
   Mexico, 1945–1960 156

7. Government Nonmonetary Intermediaries: Balance Sheet,
   Mexico, 1945–1960 158

8. Deposit and Savings Banks: Balance Sheet,
   Mexico, 1945–1960 160

9. Total Private Nonmonetary Intermediaries: Balance Sheet,
   Mexico, 1945–1960 162

10. Total Financial Intermediary Sector: Selected Real Sources and
    Uses of Funds, Mexico, 1944–1960 164

Contents   xiii

Introduction

THIS BOOK ON the role of the financial sector in the process of economic development is both a theoretical and an empirical work. The theory of the role of the financial sector presented here is an extension of the Gurley-Shaw theory of finance developed by John G. Gurley and Edward S. Shaw.[1] The application of this theory is to the Mexican economy during the 1945–59 period. These were years during which Mexico was passing from a subsistence agricultural economy to one in which rapid economic development was becoming self-sustaining. During this period the Mexican economy was experiencing rapid and far-reaching structural changes which influenced and were influenced by structural changes in the financial sector. Mexico's economic development experience during this period was so successful that other countries, particularly other Latin American countries, can profit from careful analysis of the causes of this success. A theory of finance which fits the Mexican experience well can be helpful as a background for policy decisions in countries wishing to follow Mexico's example.

In the present study we follow Gurley and Shaw in analyzing the activities of a financial sector which includes all financial intermediaries, both bank and nonbank intermediaries. We also follow Gurley and Shaw in considering the liabilities of the financial sector, both money and nonmonetary liabilities, to be similar for analytical and policy-making purposes.

However, since Gurley and Shaw have emphasized those portions of their theory which are of particular relevance to the United States economy, the theory used here departs in several important respects from the assumptions of Gurley and Shaw. First, whereas Gurley and Shaw explicitly assume an absence of market imperfections, we emphasize

[1] John G. Gurley and Edward S. Shaw, *Money in a Theory of Finance* (Washington: The Brookings Institution, 1960).

1

imperfections in the money and capital funds markets. The highly developed money and capital funds markets of the United States might permit a meaningful analysis which assumes absence of market imperfections, but in countries beginning the process of economic development it is necessary to recognize the relatively undeveloped state of these markets. Where Gurley and Shaw assume markets quite responsive to changes in interest rates and financial institutions quite efficient in allocating the available loanable funds among alternative demands, we assume market imperfections and are thus forced to give more attention to the particular asset preferences of individual financial intermediaries.

Gurley and Shaw discuss the financial sector's activities under several different assumptions as to the degree of control over the financial sector exercised by the financial authorities. In this study a financial sector regulated in its entirety by the financial authority is assumed. This institutional pattern is assumed, first, because we are interested in analyzing the contribution which the financial sector can make to an economic development effort if all of its flows of funds are planned with a view to their contribution to this effort. A second reason for this assumption is that Mexican financial laws and many Mexican financial practices already reflect detailed regulation of the activities of the entire financial sector. Gurley and Shaw conclude that the activities of unregulated financial intermediaries necessitate greater restraints imposed by the financial authority on the group of regulated intermediaries. By discussing a completely regulated financial sector, we give little attention to this aspect of the Gurley-Shaw theory, which has provoked much controversy in the United States.

A final major difference in emphasis in the theory used here from that of Gurley and Shaw concerns the budget restraint of individual financial intermediaries. Gurley and Shaw usually assume that any financial intermediary other than the central bank obtains funds only as the nonfinancial sectors increase their holdings of its liabilities. Thus in the Gurley-Shaw analysis the preferences of the public for the liabilities of particular intermediaries, together with the reserve requirements and interest rates imposed by the financial authority on these liabilities, determine the quantity of funds allocated by particular intermediaries to the nonfinancial sectors. In the present analysis we permit the central bank and other financial intermediaries to hold as assets the liabilities of other financial intermediaries. Thus some financial institutions can specialize in receiving funds from the nonfinancial sectors and other financial institutions can specialize in providing funds to the nonfinancial sectors. In the United States we are familiar with the practice of nonbank intermediaries' holding deposits in commercial banks. But in Mexico the commercial banks' and central bank's holdings of the liabilities of nonbank intermediaries are greater than nonbank intermediary holdings of deposits. These inter-intermediary funds flows and control of these flows play an important role in our theory of how the financial authority can overcome rather quickly some of the obstacles to development imposed by financial market imperfections.

Having pointed out major differences between the theory used here and the Gurley-Shaw theory, let us specify some further institutional conditions explicitly assumed in our model. We assume that all money is credit money rather than commodity money and that the central bank provides for an efficient medium of exchange—that any form of the medium of exchange at the discretion of the holder can be exchanged at a fixed ratio for any other form.[2] The central bank is further assumed to provide a secondary market for financial intermediary assets to meet the liquidity needs of the intermediaries.[3] These assumptions, which are realistic for underdeveloped countries generally, permit us to reject any assertion similar to the real-bills doctrine that the peculiarities of the liabilities of a particular financial intermediary require that intermediary to hold particular types of assets.

This book contributes nothing to an understanding of the role of inflation in the economic development process. Many authors have emphasized the possibility of beneficial effects of inflation through increasing the rate of saving or through permitting fuller utilization of existing capacity to produce. Many other authors have emphasized the possibility of deleterious effects of inflation through lowering the propensity to save in the long run or through distorting demand patterns. The ways in

[2] Where only paper money, deposits, and token coins are media of exchange, caches of unused paper money and coins (both of which are relatively free goods to the society as a whole) are sufficient to ensure an efficient medium of exchange. It might be impossible to ensure an efficient medium of exchange in countries whose citizens hoard coins with relatively high commodity values. However, the effects of coin hoarding might be minimized through a reduction in the commodity value of coins or through the provision of legal-tender paper money in small denominations.

[3] These liquidity needs result from the possibility that the public would shift its liquid asset holdings among intermediaries, thus reducing the liabilities to the public of some intermediaries.

which the activities of the financial sector can induce inflation are sufficiently well understood to require no further elaboration here. We accept, of course the proposition developed by W. Arthur Lewis[4] that in a closed economy production financed by money creation is desirable if its opportunity cost is zero. But we wish to avoid the controversy over the extent to which production at zero opportunity cost is possible, as well as other controversies over the desirability of inflation. Little attention has been given to the noninflationary ways in which the financial sector can promote economic development. This book points out ways, short of promoting inflation, in which the financial sector affects and is affected by economic development.

We do not trace out the implications for this analysis of the Lewis assumption that production is possible at zero opportunity cost. We assume that both capital and labor are required in production, that capital is specialized rather than a homogeneous commodity, that the fully employed capital stock is a bottleneck factor strictly limiting increases in aggregate production, and that reductions in the real wage rate are not possible. Together these assumptions amount to assuming full employment of capital in the sense that increases in production are contingent on increasing the stock of capital or on improving techniques.

The theoretical basis of this analysis of the role of the financial sector in economic development is presented in the chapter which follows. Emphasis is on the allocation function of financial intermediaries. In addition to relying heavily on the Gurley-Shaw theory, the analysis utilizes the Schumpeterian theory of the role of innovation in economic development.[5] Underlying the entire theoretical structure is the institutional theory of economic development presented by C. E. Ayres in *The Theory of Economic Progress.*[6] This last theory presents the institutional arrangements, including the financial practices, of a society as at best only permissive of economic development. The process of economic development in the institutional theory is largely a process of technological innovation breaking through institutional impediments to economic development.

---

[4] W. Arthur Lewis, "Economic Development with Unlimited Supplies of Labour," *The Manchester School* (May, 1954).

[5] Joseph A. Schumpeter, *The Theory of Economic Development* (Cambridge: Harvard University Press, 1934).

[6] C. E. Ayres, *The Theory of Economic Progress* (Chapel Hill: The University of North Carolina Press, 1944).

Mexico was chosen for the empirical portion of this study for three reasons. First, Mexico's transition from a relatively stagnant agricultural economy to one of rapid and self-sustaining economic development occurred quite recently and in a short time. After two decades of relatively constant and low per capita output, Mexico in the 1940's and 1950's attained more than a two per cent per year increase in per capita output while population was growing approximately three per cent per year. Second, during the last two decades Mexico has boldly and imaginatively used the financial sector in a program of economic development financing. Private financial intermediaries, under government regulation, have made significant contributions to development financing—particularly toward the end of the 1945–1959 period—and nearly a score of government-owned, special-purpose financial intermediaries have been established. Third, and quite important, was the fact that sufficient statistical data were available for Mexico during the 1945–1959 period to permit the construction of flow-of-funds tables which include both banks and nonbank financial intermediaries.

Chapter II is a description of the Mexican financial sector; particular emphasis in this description is on the control techniques available in Mexico during the past two decades for planning the uses of intermediary funds. In Chapter III the funds flows between the financial and the nonfinancial sectors during the 1945–1959 period are described, with particular emphasis on the flows between the financial sector and the business and individual sector. For this purpose the financial sector is not only studied as a unit but also is disaggregated into the following subsectors: (1) monetary intermediaries, (2) nonmonetary intermediaries, (3) government intermediaries, (4) private intermediaries, (5) the central bank, (6) government nonmonetary intermediaries, (7) deposit and savings banks, and (8) private nonmonetary intermediaries.

The flow-of-funds tables of the financial sector are compared with those of the nonfinancial sectors in Chapter IV. In order to render these flows readily comparable, they are presented as percentages of gross national product. In Chapter V the theoretical analysis of Chapter I is applied to the empirical observations of the 1945–1959 period in an interpretation of the relation of financial intermediary activities and control to Mexican economic development during this period. In a final chapter the conclusions of the study are presented.

CHAPTER I

Financial Intermediary Activities and Economic Development

SOCIAL ACCOUNTING FRAMEWORK OF ANALYSIS

THE DEVELOPMENT in the recent writings of John G. Gurley and Edward S. Shaw[1] of a theory of finance which includes analysis of the activities of all financial intermediaries has provided an indispensable analytical framework for the student of the effect of financial intermediary activities on economic development. Unless specifically stated otherwise, Gurley and Shaw's terminology and social accounting framework are utilized in this section.

Economic decision-making units are divided into two sectors—spending units and financial intermediaries—on the basis of the type of transactions in which they engage. Spending units engage primarily in goods and services transactions; financial intermediaries give virtually their entire attention to financial transactions. This relative specialization is reflected in the balance sheets of the decision-making units by the fact that goods predominate in the assets of spending units, while financial claims predominate in the assets of financial intermediaries.

Spending units are further classified as deficit spending units, balanced budget spending units, and surplus spending units. In a time period the

[1] John G. Gurley and Edward S. Shaw, "Financial Aspects of Economic Development," *American Economic Review*, XLV (September, 1955), 515–538; "Financial Intermediaries in the Saving-Investment Process," *Journal of Finance*, XI (May, 1956), 257–276; and *Money in a Theory of Finance*.

net purchases of goods and services are greater than disposable income for a deficit spending unit. Net purchases of goods and services are equal to disposable income of the time period for a balanced budget spending unit. Net purchases of goods and services of the time period are less than disposable income for a surplus spending unit.[2]

The financial intermediary sector is divided into a monetary intermediary subsector and a nonmonetary intermediary subsector. Some liability of monetary intermediaries is a portion of the medium of exchange; no liability of nonmonetary intermediaries is a portion of the medium of exchange.

In addition to these Gurley-Shaw classifications it will be useful to refer to government decision-making units and private decision-making units. The government spending unit subsector is divided into government nonfinancial enterprises and government. Government nonfinancial enterprises are government dependencies which regard their sales of goods and services as of more than incidental importance. Government is considered one spending unit which includes all spending units having power to tax and dependencies of these taxing units not classified as government nonfinancial enterprises or government financial intermediaries.

Financial assets are either primary securities or indirect securities; indirect securities are further classified as money and nonmonetary indirect securities. Primary securities are the liabilities and equities of spending units; indirect securities are the liabilities and equities of financial intermediaries. Money is the liabilities of monetary intermediaries that are used as the medium of exchange; nonmentary indirect securities are all other liabilities and equities of financial intermediaries.

A deficit spending unit finances its deficit—the amount by which its net purchases of goods and services exceeds its disposable income—through financial transactions. Measuring the transactions as net for a time period, the deficit may be financed through net issues of primary securities—sales of new primary securities less repayments of outstanding securities. The deficit may also be financed through net sales of primary securities owned by the deficit unit or net sales of nonmonetary indirect securities owned by the deficit unit. Assuming that no transactions in goods occur other than those included in the current period's

---

[2] Gurley and Shaw use the term current income rather than disposable income. The former probably excludes depreciation allowances; the latter includes them.

gross national product, the remaining source of financing for the deficit is a net reduction in the unit's money holdings.

A surplus spending unit may retain its surplus—the amount by which its disposable income exceeds its net purchases of goods and services—as an increase in its money holdings or may use it in financial transactions. These financial transactions, measured net for the time period, could be net purchases of primary securities, net purchases of nonmonetary indirect securities, or negative net issues of primary securities—repayments of its outstanding primary securities in greater amounts than new issues of those securities.

All goods and services purchases by financial intermediaries during a time period are assumed to be costs of the goods and services sales of financial intermediaries for the same time period. Net income carried to the surplus accounts of financial intermediaries is assumed to be an issue of equities by the financial intermediaries. A financial intermediary obtains its funds through net issues of its own indirect securities, net sales of primary securities, net sales of nonmonetary indirect securities, or net reductions in its money holdings. A financial intermediary uses its funds for net purchases of primary securities, net purchases of indirect securities, or net increases in its money holdings.

The following important relationships are implied in this social accounting framework:

(1) Aggregate net purchases of goods and services equal aggregate disposable income
(2) Aggregate deficits equal aggregate surpluses
(3) Aggregate net issues of primary securities equal aggregate net purchases of primary securities
(4) Aggregate net issues of nonmonetary indirect securities equal aggregate net purchases of nonmonetary indirect securities
(5) Aggregate net issues of money equal aggregate net increases in money holdings

The following sectors and subsectors are used in applying this social accounting framework to the Mexican economy; sources and uses of funds are shown for each sector.

I. Business and Individual Sector (including government nonfinancial enterprises)
   A. Sources of Funds
      1. Disposable income
      2. Net issues of primary securities

    B. Uses of Funds
       1. Net purchases of goods and services
       2. Net purchases of primary securities
       3. Net purchases of government securities
       4. Net purchases of nonmonetary indirect securities
       5. Net increases in money holdings
  II. Government Sector
    A. Sources of Funds
       1. Net tax receipts (total tax and miscellaneous receipts less refunds)
       2. Net issues of government securities
    B. Uses of Funds
       1. Net purchases of goods and services
       2. Government transfer payments
       3. Net purchases of primary securities
       4. Net purchases of nonmonetary indirect securities
       5. Net increases in money holdings
 III. Financial Sector (monetary and nonmonetary subsectors)
    A. Sources of Funds
       1. Net issues of money (nonmonetary intermediaries do not have this source of funds)
       2. Net issues of nonmonetary indirect securities
    B. Uses of Funds
       1. Net purchases of primary securities
       2. Net purchases of government securities
       3. Net purchases of nonmonetary indirect securities
       4. Net increases in money holdings
 IV. Rest-of-World Sector
    A. Sources of Funds
       1. Mexican imports
       2. Net Mexican purchases of foreign securities
       3. Net increases in Mexican holdings of foreign exchange
    B. Uses of Funds
       1. Mexican exports
       2. Net foreign purchases of Mexican primary securities
       3. Net foreign purchases of Mexican government securities
       4. Net foreign purchases of Mexican nonmonetary indirect securities
       5. Net increases in foreign holdings of Mexican money

If new issues of primary securities or government securities are purchased by a sector other than the financial intermediary sector, these activities are called direct finance. If issues of primary securities or government securities are purchased by financial intermediaries, the activities are called indirect finance. The basic relationships of this social accounting framework require that the amount of primary security issues purchased by the financial sector be equal to net purchases by other sectors of nonmonetary indirect securities plus net increases in money holdings of other sectors.

FINANCIAL INTERMEDIARIES, PRICES, AND OUTPUT

In order to relate the approach of this study (which emphasizes the qualitative aspects of financial intermediary activities) to the Gurley-Shaw approach (which gives primary attention to the quantitative aspects of financial intermediary behavior and control), two aggregative static models are presented in which full employment and an absence of distribution effects are assumed. The first does not include nonmonetary intermediaries; the second includes both monetary and nonmonetary intermediaries. The assumption of absence of distribution effects is then dropped in a third, less aggregative model in order to discuss some of the qualitative effects on the economy of the quantitative activities of financial intermediaries. In the following section a less formal model is presented with a view towards stating the hypotheses and assumptions guiding the present study of Mexican financial intermediaries and relating these hypotheses and assumptions to the quantitative approach used more generally. This rather detailed procedure is required in order to demonstrate that the primarily qualitative approach in no way conflicts with conclusions from the quantitative approaches. It supplements them in a manner which indicates that financial intermediaries may have an important permissive role in economic development.

The Gurley-Shaw social accounting framework presented above is simplified here to include only a household sector, a business sector, and a financial sector. The government is considered as one among many spending units in the business sector[3] whose output, input, price, and financing decisions contribute to the output, price relationships, and financial asset relationships prevailing in the economy. The government is assumed to be unable to use fiat money in financing its purchases, and government decisions with respect to output, input, price policy, and

---

[3] Hence, government securities are primary securities.

financing are assumed to be based on the same criteria as private spending unit decisions. Of course, a government might actually be expected, in addition to or in connection with the ordinary tax policy implicit in the above decisions, to use tax and subsidy policy as a method of influencing private decisions or as a method of controlling the price level. However, since primary emphasis in this study is on financial intermediary activities, it is assumed that fiscal policy is not used for control purposes. Monetary or financial policy is formulated exclusively by a governmental monetary or financial authority and is effectuated exclusively through the financial sector.

The financial sector includes all government financial intermediaries, such as the central bank. The financial authority is considered to be a separate entity from the central bank, in that the financial authority does not participate directly in purchases or sales of goods and services or in purchases or sales of financial claims. The financial authority is engaged exclusively in making *decisions* with respect to the aggregate quantity of indirect securities and with a view towards influencing either the price level or the rate of interest or both. The monetary or financial policy decisions are effected through some such devices as specification of intrafinancial-sector asset and liability distributions (possibly reserve requirements) which, while determining the nominal stock of indirect securities, do not require the financial authority to buy or sell. It is further assumed that the financial authority is restricted in its policy decisions by the requirement of what was called in the Introduction, above, a "technically efficient medium of exchange"—that is, full convertibility at fixed rates among the various forms of the medium of exchange. All indirect securities are assumed to be the liabilities of the financial sector; that is, all money is what Gurley and Shaw call "inside" money.

This particular set of assumptions concerning the type of financial sector and its type of control is chosen for three primary reasons. First, recent theoretical developments, primarily the works of Gurley and Shaw, emphasize the theoretical significance of particular assumptions concerning both the type of indirect securities and the type of regulations under which the financial sector operates. Second, the above assumptions, both as to the type of indirect securities and as to the extent of the control of the financial sector by the monetary or financial authority, appear more appropriate to the Mexican environment than various alternative assumptions also developed in this literature. Though Mexico, of course, uses some types of money which would not qualify as "inside" money, it is also true that fixing the proportion between "inside" and "outside" money[4] would receive little consideration as a policy tool. Also, a somewhat unified financial policy for the entire financial sector is formulated in Mexico, so that it appears appropriate to consider the sector as a single regulated unit rather that as a regulated monetary subsector and an unregulated nonmonetary subsector. Finally, since primary emphasis in this study is on the financial sector as a tool of development policy, it is appropriate to emphasize alternative policy prescriptions for a regulated financial sector rather than to emphasize the implications of varying degrees of absence of policy prescriptions.

In a review of Gurley and Shaw's *Money in a Theory of Finance,* Don Patinkin uses a basic model which, with only insignificant modifications, serves here as a point of departure.[5] This model is quite useful in that it demonstrates some basic theoretical developments by Gurley and Shaw in a more familiar manner than does the Gurley-Shaw approach. What Professor Patinkin calls the "government" is called the "financial sector" here, and the portions of his demand functions relevant to a discussion of "outside" money are not included here.

Assume a three-sector economy consisting of a household sector of surplus spending units, a business sector of deficit spending units, and a financial sector. The only indirect securities are "inside" money, while the only primary securities are homogeneous bonds. These bonds are perpetuities paying $1 interest annually, so that the reciprocal of the rate of interest is the price of bonds. In addition to a market for labor services, which is assumed to be continuously in full-employment equilibrium,[6] there are markets for commodities, bonds, and money. In the discussion which follows, the superscripts h, b, and f are used to refer to the particular sectors, while the superscripts d and s are used to refer

---

[4] Outside money is money which is not created through purchases of primary securities by monetary intermediaries.

[5] Don Patinkin, "Financial Intermediaries and the Logical Structure of Monetary Theory," *American Economic Review,* LI (March, 1961), 95–116.

[6] This Gurley-Shaw and Patinkin assumption can be related to an underdeveloped economy with disguised unemployment by assuming that savings are a constant fraction of income, that investment is financed solely with savings, and that the capital-output ratio is constant (substitution of capital for labor or labor for capital is not possible and relative prices of factors do not change). Increases in the capital stock are then necessary for increases in output, and the capital stock will be changing proportionally to changes in output.

to demand and supply, respectively. The subscript $_o$ is used to refer to initial quantities, and real national income, Y, is assumed to be constant at Y_o.[7]

The social accounting framework used by Gurley and Shaw and, hence, by Patinkin in connection with this model implies the following identities:

(1) $M_o = M_o^h + M_o^b$

(the initial quantity of money equals the initial money stock of households plus the initial money stock of businesses),

(2) $B_o = B_o^h + B_o^f$

(the initial number of bonds equals the initial bond holdings of households plus the initial bond holdings of the financial sector, and

(3) $M_o = \dfrac{B_o^f}{i}$

(the initial nominal quantity of money equals the initial nominal bond holdings of the financial sector—all money is "inside" money).

Household and business demands are assumed to depend on individual wealth and the rate of interest. Wealth is the sum of the discounted value of the noninterest income stream (which is constant in this stationary state and hence is disregarded) and net real financial asset holdings. The crucial assumption is made that there are no distribution effects —among other things, that the distribution of financial assets between the household sector and the business sector does not affect aggregate demand. In view of this, in the aggregate demand functions the individual sectors' net real financial assets are added together, giving a sum of zero,

[7] To relate this discussion to a growth context it may be helpful for the reader to consider income and the stocks of bonds, money, and nonmonetary indirect securities in the models of this section as per capita quantities rather than aggregate quantities and to assume that the labor supply and number of firms increase at the same rate as population. Such a manner of consideration would leave the conclusions obtained from the models unchanged. To relate these models to a development context in which per capita income is increasing, we would need to specify the (per capita) income supply and demand elasticities of bonds, nonmonetary indirect securities, and money. The assumption in this respect which would preserve the conclusions of the models in the text is that the elasticities are all unity. The discussion of effects of monetary policy would then have to be in terms of the effects of proportional changes in the per capita money stock relative to proportional changes in per capita income, rather than in terms of absolute changes in the money stock as in the text.

since all money is inside money owned by the nonfinancial sectors. Thus from (1), (2), and (3),

$$(4) \quad \frac{\dfrac{B_o^h}{i} + M_o^h}{p} + \frac{-\dfrac{B_o}{i} + M_o^b}{p} = 0$$

(initial household real bond and money stocks plus initial business real bond and money stocks are equal to zero by definition, where p is the price level and i is the rate of interest).

Since aggregate net financial assets of the nonfinancial sectors equals zero, in this model household and business aggregate demand functions depend on the rate of interest and the given level of real noninterest income (or discounted value of the real income stream). The assumption of full-employment equilibrium in the labor market permits us to ignore the supply function of commodities, and by assumption the monetary authority sets the nominal supply of money. In the bond demand and supply functions below, r is used to indicate that in the individual's view no specific rate of interest is required but rather a combination of a number of dollars of interest income per year and an interest rate which, together, give the demanded nominal quantity. The remaining supply and demand functions may be written as follows:

(5) $E = F(Y_o, i)$
(aggregate demand for commodities);

$$(6) \quad \frac{B^{dh}}{rp} = H\left(Y_o, i, \frac{\dfrac{B_o^h}{i} + M_o^h}{p}\right)$$
(household's demand for real bond holdings as a stock);

$$(7) \quad \frac{B^s}{rp} = J\left(Y_o, i, \frac{-\dfrac{B_o}{i} + M_o^b}{p}\right)$$
(businesses' supply of real bond holdings as a stock); and

$$(8) \quad \frac{M^d}{p} = L(Y_o, i)$$
(aggregate demand for real money holdings as a stock).

The demands are assumed to be positively dependent on income and net real financial assets; the bond supply is assumed to be negatively dependent on these variables.

The assumption of absence of distribution effects permits combination of the nonfinancial *excess* demand function for bonds—which is the households' demand minus the firms' supply—as follows:

(9) $B(Y_o, i) = H(\quad) - J(\quad)$.

The general equilibrium conditions for this model may be written:

(10) $F(Y_o, i) - Y_o = 0$ (commodities market),

(11) $B(Y_o, i) + \dfrac{M_o}{p} = 0$ (bond market), and

(12) $L(Y_o, i) - \dfrac{M_o}{p} = 0$ (money market).

It will be recalled that [from (3)] M_o/p may represent the financial sector's real bond holdings as in (11) or its real monetary liabilities as in (12).

The major conclusions as to the efficacy of monetary policy (changes in M_o) in this model may now be stated briefly. First, the monetary authority cannot affect the equilibrium rate of interest by changing M_o since (10) indicates that only one equilibrium rate of interest exists with income fixed at Y_o. Since the monetary authority cannot affect the equilibrium rate of interest it cannot affect the equilibrium real demand for commodities or, for that matter, any equilibrium real demand or supply in system (10)-(12). Second, the monetary authority, by (say) raising M_o, can effect an increase in the price level as a result of the excess supply of money (from 12) and the excess demand for bonds (from 11) which would accompany an increase in M_o/p. Third, though a change in the price level is effected, this would matter only to the monetary authority, since in system (10-12) no nonfinancial sector aggregate supply or demand function includes p. These conclusions follow largely from the assumption that real income is constant, the assumption that only the monetary authority suffers from money illusion, and the assumption of absence of distribution effects.

Let us now introduce regulated nonmonetary intermediaries and non-monetary indirect securities into this basic model. Since this study concentrates on Mexico and since financial intermediaries are all subject to rather detailed control by Mexico's financial authorities, it is appropriate to consider nonmonetary indirect securities as more similar to money than to bonds in this model. With respect to the supply function of indirect securities, the Mexican financial authority could determine both the supply of money and the supply of nonmonetary indirect securities. And as a matter of policy in Mexico, a high degree of liquidity is maintained for nonmonetary indirect securities. In view of these facts the present method of treating nonmonetary indirect securities is more similar to that of Gurley and Shaw than to that of Patinkin.[8]

Assume that financial policy decisions are based on the total real quantity of indirect securities rather than the real quantity of money. Specifically, assume nonmonetary indirect securities, M', to be obligations to pay \$1 two years from the date of issue. Assume that at any particular time the quantity of these securities outstanding is composed of 730 equal parts, one of which matures daily and is replaced with a similar number of two-year obligations. Hence, the average nonmonetary indirect security outstanding at any particular time has a maturity of one year, and its price is given by the reciprocal of *1* plus the rate of discount for nonmonetary indirect securities, i'. The value of the nominal stock of nonmonetary indirect securities is given by $M'/1 + i'$ (the number of nonmonetary indirect securities, divided by one plus the interest rate on nonmonetary indirect securities). The financial authority fixes the interest rate on nonmonetary indirect securities through open market purchases and sales of these securities, with such purchases or sales spread evenly over the maturities outstanding. With these modifications the model would be written as follows:

(13) $M_o = M_o^h + M_o^b,$

(14) $M_o' = M_o'^h + M_o'^b$

    (the initial number of nonmonetary indirect securities equals the initial household stock plus the initial business stock),

(15) $B_o = B_o^h + B_o^f,$

(16) $M_o + \dfrac{M_o'}{1 + i'} = \dfrac{B_o^f}{i}$

---

[8] Patinkin suggests that a parameter be introduced into the bond demand functions for the degree of liquidity of bonds. This parameter would be changed by the introduction of nonmonetary intermediaries and nonmonetary indirect securities. It seems more appropriate to treat an increase in their supply as more closely resembling an increase in the quantity of money than an increase in the liquidity of bonds if, as in the Mexican case, a high degree of liquidity is maintained for nonmonetary indirect securities.

(the initial nominal quantity of indirect securities equals the initial nominal primary security holdings of the financial sector—all indirect securities are "inside" securities),

(17) $E = F(Y_o, i, i')$

(aggregate demand for commodities),

(18) $\dfrac{B^{dh}}{rp} = H\left(Y_o, i, i', \dfrac{\dfrac{B_o^h}{i} + M_o^h + \dfrac{M_o'^h}{1 + i'}}{p}\right)$

(household demand function for real bond holdings as a stock),

(19) $\dfrac{B^s}{rp} = J\left(Y_o, i, i', \dfrac{-\dfrac{B_o}{i} + M_o^b + \dfrac{M_o'^b}{1 + i'}}{p}\right)$

(business supply function of real bond holdings as a stock),

(20) $\dfrac{M^d}{p} = L(Y_o, i, i')$

(aggregate money demand function),

(21) $\dfrac{M'^d}{(1 + r')p} = L'(Y_o, i, i')$

(aggregate nonmonetary indirect security demand function),

(22) $B(Y_o, i, i') = H(\quad\quad) - J(\quad\quad)$

(nonfinancial excess demand function for bonds),

(23) $F(Y_o, i, i') - Y_o = 0$

(equilibrium condition for the commodities market),

(24) $B(Y_o, i, i') + \dfrac{M_o + \dfrac{M_o'}{1 + i'}}{p} = 0$

(equilibrium condition for the bond market), and

(25) $L(Y_o, i, i') + L'(Y_o, i, i') - \dfrac{M_o + \dfrac{M_o'}{1 + i'}}{p} = 0$

(equilibrium condition for the indirect securities market).

Assume the demand for commodities, as well as the demand for bonds and the demand for money, to be negatively dependent on the rate of interest on nonmonetary indirect securities. It is apparent from (23) that, given Y_o as constant, so long as i' is unchanged the equilibrium condition of the commodities market uniquely determines the bond rate of interest. From this it follows that a policy decision to increase the money supply while holding i' constant will affect no real demand or supply of system (23)-(25).[9] An increase in M_o alone will increase the price level, however, by creating an excess supply of indirect securities and an excess demand for bonds. As in the model which did not include nonmonetary indirect securities, this increase in the price level effects no change in a real variable since the price level is of significance as a decision-making variable only to the financial authority.

Suppose now that the financial authority (with a view to raising the price level) chooses to lower the interest rate on nonmonetary indirect securities while holding the money supply constant.[10] This lower i' not only increases the real supply of indirect securities and the real demand for bonds by increasing $\dfrac{M_o + \dfrac{M_o'}{1+i'}}{p}$ it also affects F, B, and L positively and L' negatively. The equilibrium condition for the commodities market, (23), together with the assumption that the aggregate demand for commodities is negatively dependent on both i and i', uniquely determines the new bond rate of interest at a higher level. One might expect this effect on the bond rate of interest to be quite small if nonmonetary indirect securities are significantly better substitutes for bonds and for money than for commodities and if bonds are significantly better substitutes for commodities than are nonmonetary indirect securities. In any event, the real demand for commodities, F, is unaffected by the changes in interest rates.

The real demand for nonmonetary indirect securities is permanently lower owing to the permanently higher bond rate of interest and the permanently lower i'; for the same reasons the real demand for bonds of the nonfinancial sector, B, is permanently higher. The fact that the new equilibrium real nonfinancial demand for bonds, B, is higher, to-

---

[9] In order to hold i' constant the financial authority would have to increase somewhat the nominal supply of nonmonetary indirect securities (M_o'), but in the process the nominal quantity of money would be correspondingly reduced. The process through which the adjustments would take place would be: (1) the financial sector purchases bonds with money (thus temporarily lowering the bond rate of interest), and (2) the initial bond sellers purchase goods (bidding up their price)—indirect securities supplied by the financial sector in sufficient quantity to hold i' constant—and hold the remainder of the proceeds of the bond sale as money. In the final equilibrium the price level, the nominal stock of money, the nominal stock of nonmonetary indirect securities, and the nominal stock of bonds would all be greater than initially.

[10] To accomplish this the financial sector would have to make open-market purchases of nonmonetary indirect securities (thus bidding up their price to the desired level) and, concomitantly, would have to sell a similar number of primary securities in order to prevent M_o from rising.

gether with the initial increase in $M_o + \dfrac{M'_o}{+i'}$, means that (from 24) the
new equilibrium price level is higher. Whether the real demand for money
in the new equilibrium is higher or lower depends on the negative effect
of the higher bond rate of interest and the positive effect of the lower
rate of interest on nonmonetary indirect securities. The assumptions
made so far do not permit determination of these effects. Equations
(23)-(25) require that $\Delta B + \Delta L + \Delta L' \equiv 0$. Hence, if $\Delta B + \Delta L'$
$> 0, 0, < 0$ then ΔL is, respectively, $< 0, 0, > 0$. If the demand for
money is in fact, say, increased, then the necessary increase in the price
level is lower than if the demand for money is decreased.

It may be concluded, then, that in a comparative statics analysis (and
the quasi-dynamic interpretations of a comparative statics analysis
suggested in Note 7) at the level of aggregation of this model and the
first one, which assumes absence of money illusion on the part of spending units, which assumes absence of distribution effects, and which
assumes output to depend on no variable which the monetary authority
can manipulate, the following observations are permitted with respect to
the effects of financial intermediary activities as tools of development
policy: (1) financial intermediary activities do not affect output; (2)
financial intermediary activities affect the price level; and (3) the price
level does not affect output. Both of these models, however, were developed originally for the specific purpose of discussing the relationships
between financial intermediaries and the price level. The conclusions of
these models with respect to both the price level and the level of output
do not follow for other models developed for different purposes. When
one reduces the level of abstraction one step by disaggregating the nonfinancial sector into a household sector and a business sector, then the
importance of financial intermediaries is apparently increased.

Let us construct a disaggregated model using money to represent all
indirect securities, as in the first model, since our method of considering
nonmonetary indirect securities makes them analytically similar to
money. The equilibrium conditions of such a disaggregated model are
as follows:

(26) $F\left(Y_o, i, \dfrac{\dfrac{B^h_o}{i} + M^h_o}{p}\right) + F'\left(Y_o, i, \dfrac{-\dfrac{B_o}{i} + M^b_o}{p}\right) - Y_o = 0$

(equilibrium condition for the commodities market where F is the household sector's demand for commodities and F' is that of the business sector),

$$(27) \quad \frac{M_o}{p} + H\left(Y_o, i, \frac{\frac{B_o^h}{i} + M_o^h}{p}\right) - J\left(Y_o, i, \frac{-\frac{B_o}{i} + M_o^b}{p}\right) = 0$$

(equilibrium condition for the bond market),

$$(28) \quad L\left(Y_o, i, \frac{\frac{B_o^h}{i} + M_o^h}{p}\right) + L'\left(Y_o, i, \frac{-\frac{B_o}{i} + M_o^b}{p}\right) - \frac{M_o}{p} = 0$$

(equilibrium condition for the indirect securities market where L' is the business sector's demand for indirect securities and L is that of the household sector).

In system (26)-(28) the financial authority can still change the quantity of money and thus create an excess demand for bonds and an excess supply of money. Since both the rate of interest and the price level appear in the demand functions for commodities, the real demands for commodities can be affected by the activities of the financial sector. A model of this type is always used to point to differences between spending units—to the possibility that they base decisions on different variables or differently on the same variables. In this model, for instance, the fact that one of the spending units is indebted while the other holds financial assets makes their behavior with respect to the price level different. Thus distribution effects become the main point at issue.

When distribution effects of financial intermediary activities are recognized and studied, the activities of these intermediaries are seen to affect the pattern of demand on the commodities markets. Even though aggregate income is given in this model, the sectoral distribution of that income can be changed through changes in the quantity of indirect securities. The financial authority is still assumed to base its decisions solely on the *quantity* of indirect securities and the price level. But distribution effects are unavoidable consequences of the resulting activities of financial intermediaries. When a time dimension is introduced into this model and when the level of income is made a function of the sectoral distribution of commodities, the quantitative activities of intermediaries are made to appear even more important to economic activities. When, in addition, the entire general equilibrium system of supply and demand functions for individual commodities and financial claims is visualized as lying behind the three equilibrium conditions of this elementary model, several observations on the effect of financial intermediary quantitative activities are permitted.

First, the activities of financial intermediaries that, say, increase the quantity of indirect securities are a force in the direction of an increased demand for complements of increased indebtedness. The preferences of particular financial intermediaries for borrowers and the preferences of those borrowers for commodities determine the particular commodity demands which are affected. The extent of the effect on output of this increase in the quantity of indirect securities through lending depends on the extent of the effect of the lending on the demand for particular goods and services and on the extent of the effect of this demand on output.

Second, the activities of financial intermediaries that, say, increase the demand for indirect securities are a force in the direction of a decreased demand for relatively good substitutes for indirect securities. The commodity preferences of the particular households which refrain from purchasing commodities determine the particular commodity demands affected. The extent of the effect on output of this increased indirect security demand depends on the extent of the effect of the force on particular commodity demands, and the extent to which the changes in these demands affect output.

Third, the activities of financial intermediaries that, say, raise the general price level contribute to the wealth of spending units which sell at prices rising more rapidly than the prices at which they buy. A portion of this increased wealth may be taxed away, and a portion may be used to add to the spending unit's financial asset holdings. The remainder of this increased wealth resulting from inflation adds to the demand for commodities which have relatively high income elasticities of demand in the view of this more wealthy group. The spending units which sell at prices advancing more slowly than the prices at which they buy experience a decline in wealth. This may be accompanied by a decline in their financial asset holdings and a decline in the demand for commodities which, in the view of this group, have relatively high income elasticities of demand. The extent of the effect on output of financial intermediary activities which are an inflationary force depends on the extent of the effect of the force on inflation, the extent to which inflation redistributes wealth, the extent to which the wealth redistribution affects the allocation of commodities, and the extent to which the reallocation of commodities affects output.[11]

FINANCIAL INTERMEDIARIES AND ECONOMIC DEVELOPMENT

The Nonfinancial Sectors and Innovation Financing

The first two models used in the last section emphasize the quantitative aspects of financial intermediary activities, while the quality of those activities is assumed to be the most beneficial possible with respect to output. Let us now emphasize the qualitative aspects of financial intermediary activities suggested by the third model. It will be helpful in this discussion to make a distinction between a "traditional economy" (one in which per capita output is relatively low and constant over a long time period) and a "transitional economy" (a recently traditional economy in which long-run per capita output is rising relatively rapidly). We wish the assumed institutional and behavioral characteristics in our model of the traditional economy to be consistent with observed traditional economies.

The firms of the traditional economy are closely held by owner-managers, and investment is financed from depreciation allowances, retained earnings, issues of equities to the owner-manager or a small group of his close associates, and short-term borrowing from the financial sector.[12] The owner-manager and his close associates who participate in financing the firm are also households; it is assumed that these "interested households" devote, and have devoted, their savings to financing the enterprises in which they are interested or to accumulating money and other liabilities of commercial banks. These owner-managers are

---

[11] Perhaps it was this large number of (possibly quite small) elasticities connecting the quantitative activities of financial intermediaries and output that prompted John Kenneth Galbraith to refer to monetary policy as having been "graced by effects not only mysterious but magical." John Kenneth Galbraith, *The Affluent Society* (Boston: Houghton Mifflin Company, 1958), p. 228.

[12] The first three sources of investment financing are hereafter called self-finance; self-finance and short-term loans from the financial sector together are called traditional finance.

quite reluctant to divulge information concerning their firms to outsiders, but they have developed strong traditional connections with particular financial intermediaries. Thus only one financial intermediary has, or could obtain, sufficient information on which to base a decision to lend to any one traditional firm.

The household sector includes an interested subsector and a non-interested subsector. The interested households own firms and have property incomes; the noninterested households do not own firms and do not have property incomes. Middle income groups, which do a substantial quantity of saving in developed economies, are absent in the traditional economy, so that saving is exclusively from the property incomes of interested households and firms.[13]

The government sector of the traditional economy we assume to have a balanced budget in the long run so that government debt is zero in the average year. Thus, both the government sector and the noninterested household subsector are balanced-budget spending units. Interested households are surplus spending units and firms are deficit spending units accounting for all investment spending.

The financial sector in the traditional economy includes only commercial banks and a central bank. The liabilities of the commercial banks are demand deposits and debt to the central bank; the liabilities of the central bank are currency and commercial bank reserve deposits. The assets of the commercial banks are short-term loans to firms and reserve deposits at the central bank; the assets of the central bank are short-term loans to firms, loans to commercial banks, and foreign exchange reserves. Firms and interested households own all of the demand deposits of commercial banks; noninterested households own some portion of the currency issued by the central bank.[14]

By definition the traditional economy over a long period has had a low and almost constant real per capita income; we discuss only the case in which per capita income is constant in real terms. Let us assume

[13] While the noninterested households own some currency, we assume that they are indebted by a similar amount to firms so that their net financial assets are zero.

[14] It will be convenient to assume that the currency owned by the noninterested households is equal to the foreign exchange reserves owned by the central bank. The firms, in turn, can be assumed to receive an equal quantity of trade credit from foreign suppliers and to lend this amount to noninterested households. Then the liabilities of the financial sector to interested households and firms would just equal the loans of the financial sector to firms.

that technological change is just sufficient to offset the effect on output of diminishing returns to nature with a growing population and labor force. With the population and labor force growing at the same rate, the capital stock would have to grow at the same rate in order to maintain per capita output constant. In a traditional economy, under the above assumptions, the sources of investment financing would have to be growing in real terms by precisely the rate of increase in the population. The sources of investment financing are depreciation allowances, retained earnings, sales of equities to owner-managers, and short-term loans from the financial sector. If property, labor, and government incomes were all constant fractions of aggregate income, and if savings were a constant fraction of property income, then the conditions necessary for a constant per capita income would be met. With both the real demand for financial sector liabilities and the real demand for loans functions of real per capita income, the price level would be constant if the nominal liabilities and nominal assets of the financial sector increase at the same rate as population.

It is important to note two characteristics of the traditional economy which follow from the assumed institutional and behavioral characteristics. First, the existing real financial flows of the economy are necessary for maintaining the constant level of real per capita income. Second, the productive activities of the traditional economy result largely in doing more of the same things in approximately the same ways as population grows, rather than in doing new things. Innovations, the introduction of discontinuous changes in production functions,[15] are virtually absent in traditional economies. However, significant increases in per capita output require innovations, and these are a characteristic of the transitional economy. How can the initial innovations in the transitional economy be financed?

The financial markets in the traditional economy are highly personalized, so that changes in interest rates on borrowed funds would be ineffective as stimulants to increased savings or redirection of the uses of past savings. Each interested household has a particular firm or group of firms and a particular financial institution to which its savings are made available. Each firm has particular interested households and a

---

[15] This definition of innovation and many other characteristics of this model are taken from Schumpeter's *The Theory of Economic Development* (Cambridge: Harvard University Press, 1934).

particular financial institution from which it can obtain funds. Even if property income as a fraction of aggregate income were to increase, in the absence of substantial changes in relative consumer preferences (and without innovation having occurred previously) the increased property income would be spread rather evenly over the existing firms and interested households and would result in marginal increments in investment in existing types of activities. But an increased property share of income means a reduced labor and/or government share of income. If the wage were near the subsistence level, a reduction in labor's income share might result in reduced efficiency of the labor force. If government services were provided at the optimum rate initially, a reduction in government's income share reduces economic efficiency. If the positive effect on output of the increased net investment were offset by the negative effects of reduced real wages or government services, then an increase in per capita output would not result from increasing the property share of income.

Self-finance of government innovations could result from increases in taxes as a fraction of aggregate income. Many of the innovations of strategic importance in economic development result either in inappropriable products or in risks considered unduly great by the private sector. If the increased government income share were at the expense of noninterested household income, then the previously mentioned possibility of reduced efficiency of the labor force might offset the positive effect of the increased net investment. If the increased government income share were at the expense of interested household and firm income shares, then investment as a fraction of income is raised or the efficiency of the allocation of a given investment quantity is improved.

Innovation could be financed by direct finance—issues of open-market securities (including government securities) to nonfinancial sectors. Through direct finance, increases in the property share of income could be directed toward innovation financing as a result of pooling increments in many individual incomes. Also through direct finance, increases in per capita tax collections could be made available for government-financed private innovation. Since issues of bonds and government securities are absent in the traditional economy, direct finance presumes changes in financial techniques and changes in the preference functions of spending units. It presumes the invention of the security contracts, the introduction of institutions for distributing these securities, and the custom on the part of households and firms of purchasing these securities—all of which Gurley and Shaw call financial innovations. The discontinuous increase in the real demand functions for bonds or government securities required for their introduction results in decreases in the real demand functions for consumer goods and for other forms of holding savings—investment goods and liabilities of financial intermediaries. To the extent that bonds and government securities are substituted for consumer goods, an increase in the rate of capital accumulation above the rate of population increase occurs. To the extent that bonds and government securities are substituted for other forms of holding savings, innovation spending is substituted for traditional investment spending if constant prices are maintained. The price level is maintained constant by reducing the nominal quantity of indirect securities in an amount equal to the decline in the real demanded quantity and, hence, a similar reduction in the real quantity of loans is required. This forces firms to finance a greater portion of their investment through self-finance and therefore reduces the aggregate quantity of traditional investment spending.

In an open economy innovation can be financed by issues of securities to the rest-of-world sector. These issues include bonds, government securities, and equities represented by new direct foreign investment; however, they would not include self-finance, such as reinvested profits and transfers of funds between parent and subsidiary firms.

Finally, initial innovations can be financed by indirect finance, in which firms or governments issue bonds or government securities to the financial sector which, in turn, issues nonmonetary indirect securities or money to the nonfinancial sectors. As in the case of direct finance, an increased property income share can become a source of innovation financing through indirect finance. Important financial innovations are required as the traditional economy becomes a transitional economy through indirect financing of innovations. Financial intermediaries, which in the traditional economy invested only in short-term loans and reserves, must develop a demand for bonds and government securities. In order for this indirect innovation financing to be noninflationary, financial sector purchases of loans must be reduced as financial sector purchases of bonds and government securities are increased, or innovations in indirect finance must increase the real demand for nonmonetary indirect securities and money.

We designate as "innovation financing" the above sources of financing the initial innovations which permit the traditional economy to become a transitional economy in which per capita real income is increasing significantly. Thus innovation financing includes increases in per capita real taxes of firms and interested households, direct finance, issues of securities to the rest-of-world sector, and indirect finance. These sources of financing are unnecessary and unavailable in the traditional economy; they are necessary for the traditional economy to become a transitional economy.

Innovation financing is also needed to maintain the continued per capita output growth of the transitional economy. The initial innovations, which raise the level of per capita output, result in plants and firms which soon have their own sources of self-finance. Some of this newly generated self-finance is necessary to replace the plant and equipment as it depreciates; some is necessary for sufficient net investment to maintain per capita output of the firm constant. Let us call "excess traditional financing" any traditional financing generated by the benefiting firms that is more than sufficient to maintain the firm's per capita output constant. With rather liberal assumptions concerning various uses of the firm's funds, it is seen that little, if any, excess traditional financing would be available. Assume that labor costs are 48 per cent of output and that capital gross returns are the remaining 52 per cent of output. With a capital-output ratio of two, gross returns to capital are 26 per cent of initial innovation financing or capital. If taxes are 8 per cent of output, they are 4 per cent of capital; interest costs are 5 per cent of capital if half of the initial investment was financed by borrowing at a 10 per cent interest rate. Assume that replacement costs are 5 per cent of capital and that reinvestment of 6 per cent of capital is necessary to increase output proportionately with population (a capital-output ratio of 2 and population growing at 3 per cent annually). The capital share would then be exhausted and no excess traditional financing available if consumer spending from property income were only 6 per cent of capital—an amount equal to the retained and reinvested profits assumed.[16] It is thus seen that under these assumptions, even under

---

[16] We do not consider retirement of outstanding innovation financing as one of the uses of funds in determining the excess traditional financing, since such funds would be available for further innovation financing.

somewhat more relaxed assumptions, only minor increases in per capita output could be sustained from excess traditional financing in the transitional economy.

The Financial Sector and Innovation Financing

The financial sector in the transitional economy is composed of traditional intermediaries and innovating intermediaries.[17] Traditional intermediaries specialize in receiving funds from the traditional business sector and households and in supplying funds to these sectors. The innovating intermediaries specialize in supplying funds for financing innovations.[18] Commercial banks are the major portion of the traditional intermediary subsector. If the economy is characterized by an absence of middle-income groups and by the provision of virtually all the income of the upper-income group from property, then virtually all commercial bank liabilities would be owned by interested households and traditional firms. The liquid savings of the noninterested households might be represented almost exclusively by holdings of currency—a liability of the central bank.

Under the assumptions of the model described above, attention is focused on innovation as the primary source of increases in per capita output. The process of industrialization through innovation is accompanied by substantial effects on the initial institutional characteristics described in the model. Though new firms are presumed to begin ordinarily as innovating firms, they pass rather quickly to the traditional sector as financing from retained earnings becomes possible. This does

[17] For convenience let us adopt the following definitions for the discussion which follows:
(1) "traditional intermediaries" are those present in the traditional economy that supply only short-term loans to firms,
(2) "innovating intermediaries" are those that engage in innovation financing,
(3) "traditional firms" are those whose investment spending is financed only with "traditional financing,"
(4) "innovating firms" are those whose investment spending is financed only with "innovation financing" (thus an actual firm for our purposes might be both a traditional and an innovating firm), and
(5) "innovation" is the investment spending financed with "innovation financing."
[18] Both financial subsectors would, of course, supply funds in the quantities and to the sectors or spending units required by the financial authority. The relative specialization of these intermediaries postulated in the text is assumed to result from differences between intermediaries in institutional characteristics, such as customary lending terms, customary motivation in lending decisions, and other "market imperfections," rather than from financial authority controls.

not mean, however, that the recently innovating firms transfer their financial connections from the innovating to the traditional financial subsector. These relatively new traditional firms, just like the initial traditional firms, are assumed to maintain strong ties to particular financial intermediaries. The particular intermediaries with which recently innovating firms deal are the innovating intermediaries. Thus the innovating intermediaries provide financing to both traditional and innovating firms and receive savings from recently innovating firms and households or receive credit from the central bank. The lending required of the innovating financial sector for support of a given growth rate of income increases faster than the lending required of the traditional financial sector. However, since the firms which borrow from the innovating financial sector are assumed to be net debtors with respect to these intermediaries, since interested households are assumed to purchase liabilities of traditional intermediaries primarily, and since noninterested households might purchase liabilities of both financial subsectors, a deficiency of funds available to the innovating financial sector and a surplus of funds available to the traditional financial sector may develop. The investment spending plans of firms borrowing from the traditional financial sector become chronically overfinanced while the investment spending plans of firms borrowing from the innovating financial sector become chronically underfinanced in the absence of a flow of funds between the two financial sectors.

The major point of this model from the perspective of development policy is that an inefficient allocation of resources is implicit under institutional conditions which prevent marginal adjustments in supplies and demands for loanable funds as responses to changes in relative interest rates. Flows of funds between financial intermediaries are a more realistic possibility for improving this allocation than are changes in other conditions of the market for loanable funds. Substantial changes in the direction of the allocation of loanable funds can, under certain conditions, be made much more rapidly through inter-intermediary funds flows than through changes in other institutional characteristics of the loanable-funds market.

The financial authority can improve the allocation of loanable funds by breaking the connection between the quantity of funds flowing to a particular intermediary from the nonfinancial sectors and the quantity of funds flowing from the intermediary to the nonfinancial sectors. Requiring intermediary deposits at the central bank and specifying the quantity of central bank credit available to particular intermediaries is one technique which could be used for this purpose. A system of inter-intermediary claims bearing incentive interest rates could also be used. These qualitative controls of financial sector lending are somewhat different from the controls usually suggested by that term. The controls described here leave the individual intermediary relatively free to allocate the funds made available to it by the financial authority; however, the quantity of these funds is dependent for its value on a variable other than the quantity of that institution's liabilities held by the nonfinancial sectors.

Inter-intermediary funds transfers, together with more specific types of qualitative credit controls, are an outstanding characteristic of Mexican developmental financial planning. This control device has an almost infinite number of possible variations in a setting in which a large number of relatively specialized types of financial institution exist or are created. In such a setting the granting of central-bank credit to a particular financial intermediary for financing a particular development project need result in no increase in the quantity of indirect securities, much less in a multiple increase in the money supply, provided offsetting restraints are imposed on some other intermediary. The effect of these qualitative controls through inter-intermediary funds flows is much the same as would be the effect of a change in the quality of the allocation decisions of each financial intermediary. However, imperfections in the market for loanable funds imply that the inter-intermediary funds flows are likely to be the more effective.[19]

Having described a model that explicitly recognizes many institutional patterns characteristic of economies lacking highly developed money and capital markets, let us now focus attention on the net flow of funds to and from the financial sector. The analysis of these flows is directed primarily toward indicating possible relationships between the growth rate of income, the financing of innovations, and forced saving. In the first two highly aggregated, static models of the last section, all increases

---

[19] Even in countries with highly developed money and capital markets this might be the case. See, for instance, Lester V. Chandler, "Monopolistic Elements in Commercial Banking," *Journal of Political Economy* (February, 1938), pp. 1–22; and Gurley and Shaw, "Financial Aspects of Economic Development," pp. 532 and 537.

in the nominal quantity of indirect securities were inflationary. In this disaggregated growth model such is not necessarily the case. Let us begin by assuming that no innovation is occurring, that no innovating financial subsector exists, that the net investment of the traditional sector is of such quality and quantity as to maintain a constant level of per capita real income, that population is increasing at an annual rate of 3 per cent,[20] and that the initial stock of indirect securities is one-third of initial aggregate income.[21] Beginning with these assumed conditions we inquire into the possibilities for raising the growth rate of output through providing financing by innovating intermediaries for technically feasible innovations by an innovating sector or the government sector. Under what conditions would this financing require only voluntary saving?

Increases in the growth rate of output may result from either a decline in the incremental capital-output ratio or from an increase in the number of units of investment with a given incremental capital-output ratio. The output in question refers to the entire economy rather than the particular investing firm; hence, when speaking of the incremental capital-output ratio of a particular investment project, social cost and social benefits are at issue rather than private cost and privately anticipated income.

Increases in the growth rate of output that result from increases in the fraction of net output devoted to investment require increases in the fraction of net income saved. This is a definitional rather than a substantive matter. These increases in the fraction of income saved are forced if ex-ante saving is less than ex-ante investment. If, however, one investment project is substituted for another investment project requiring the same quantity of resources, no change is required in the average propensity to save, but changes in the growth rate of output may result from differences in the incremental capital-output ratios of the two projects.

If we assume full employment, initially the financial sector's financing of innovations under conditions which do not require forced saving must rely largely, but not entirely, on differences between incremental capital-output ratios of particular investment spending projects.[22] Let us assume

[20] Mexico's population approached this annual growth rate during the period studied here.

[21] Mexico's stock of indirect securities owned by businesses and individuals approached one-third of national income in the early 1940's.

[22] This is not intended to suggest that the capital-output ratio is the most appropriate criterion to use in allocating investment funds, but in view of the assumptions in Note 6 above, it is a reasonably adequate criterion.

that the demanded quantity of indirect securities increases at the same rate as real income if real per capita income is constant and that it increases at a faster rate than real income if real per capita income increases. Under the assumptions of this model in which population increases at 3 per cent per annum and per capita income is initially constant, the demanded real quantity of indirect securities increases at the same rate as population. This 3 per cent per annum increase in the real quantity of indirect securities is reflected before industrialization begins in the assets of traditional intermediaries as an increase in the indebtedness of the traditional business sector.[23] An increase of 3 per cent per annum in the quantity of indirect securities is equal to 1 per cent of annual income, assuming indirect securities are initially equal to one-third of initial income. Let us analyze some possible effects of diverting the entire annual increment in the stock of indirect securities from financing the investment of the traditional sector to financing that of the innovating sector through innovating intermediaries.

If, initially, net investment is 6 per cent of aggregate income then one-sixth of traditional-sector investment is foregone for a similar quantity of investment in innovation. This implies an initial average incremental capital-output ratio of two. If the innovating intermediaries allocate these funds to innovations that promise the highest increments in output per unit of investment, while the traditional firms sacrifice those investments that are expected to provide the smallest increments in output per unit of investment, then the average incremental capital-output ratio will be significantly lowered. However, in this model there are strong reasons to expect this large a reduction in the funds available for investment spending by the traditional sector to result not only in a decline in the average incremental capital-output ratio but also in an increase in the average propensity to save. This is because of the intimate connection between the interested household subsector and the traditional business sector. Assuming that these sectors are unable to change their aggregate profits as a fraction of aggregate income, they are still able to retain or reinvest a larger fraction of the available profits as an alternative to financing by financial intermediaries. This increased saving of the interested households raises the average propensity to save for the economy as a whole, since the noninterested households' saving is

[23] Recognition of the possibility of consumer debt would not change the argument of the text significantly.

unaffected by these activities. Though this increased saving could not be assumed to replace entirely the funds formerly provided by financial intermediaries, it could be assumed to replace a portion of those funds. Thus, the decision to permit innovation is accompanied in this model by both a decline in the incremental capital-output ratio and an increase in the planned fraction of aggregate income saved and invested. Both of these act to raise the growth rate of output without forced saving when the quantity of innovation financing is limited to increases in the real demanded quantity of indirect securities and when a similar increase in traditional intermediary lending is foregone.

The above assumptions permit 1 per cent of income to be devoted to innovation without forced saving. This percentage can be increased through improvements in the quality of indirect securities that result in the use of a larger fraction of money income for purchases of indirect securities. Such financial innovations as introducing deposit insurance, including miscellaneous services with indirect security purchases, and diversifying indirect securities in other ways are among the possibilities suggested by Gurley and Shaw for accomplishing an increase in the fraction of income used to purchase indirect securities. As a supplement to (or a partial substitute for) the initial financing of innovation by diverting funds from the traditional financial sector to the innovating financial sector, we could assume that the latter began financing innovation as it created liabilities especially attractive to households (and, possibly, to traditional intermediaries). To the extent that innovating-intermediary liabilities are substituted for traditional-intermediary liabilities in spending-unit portfolios and to the extent that innovating-intermediary liabilities are substituted for primary securities in traditional-intermediary portfolios, the effects on the growth rate of output are the same as those described in the last paragraph—increases in traditional investment spending are sacrificed in an amount similar to the amount of financing of innovation. But if, in addition, the saved fraction of noninterested-household income is raised owing to the increased attractiveness of intermediary liabilities (recall that interested households are assumed to devote their savings to purchases of indirect securities or primary securities of traditional firms), then there is provided an additional source of faster growth that does not result from forced saving.

Unless the rate of population increase is assumed to rise above 3 per cent, the higher output growth rate resulting from the initial permission of innovation implies an increase in per capita output or income. If indirect securities are assumed to be a luxury good, the annual flow of funds to the entire financial sector increases at a faster rate than the growth rate of output. If all, or a constant fraction, of this flow of funds to intermediaries is directed toward financing innovation, then the growth rate of output per capita would rise secularly, planned saving as a fraction of income would rise secularly, and the incremental capital-output ratio might decline secularly.[24]

Of course, the financial authority in this model could permit an even faster increase in the growth rate of output through permitting forced saving. Possibly it is excessively unrealistic to assume that the financial authority freezes the value of traditional intermediaries' holdings of primary securities at their initial level, as we assume above.[25] More realistic would be the assumption that, particularly in the early stages of the development effort, a significant portion of innovation is financed through forced saving with a concomitant increase in the price level. Then later, as the financial authority perfects techniques of control and as alternative sources of innovation financing such as direct finance become available, a smaller and smaller fraction of innovation would be financed with forced saving and, as a result, the secular rate of inflation would decline.

SUMMARY

The general premise underlying this study is that planning for economic development in today's industrializing country is necessary for attaining the socially desired and technically attainable rate of economic development. As a part of a country's planned development effort, its financial sector can provide a flow of funds to finance development

---

[24] The secular decline in the incremental capital-output ratio would not follow, necessarily, unless during this economic development process either the ratios for old but untried projects decline or new projects with relatively low ratios replace the projects that become innovations.

[25] An alternative assumption, which would substantially modify the form but not the substance of the model and which would make the model conform more closely to Mexican financial practices, would be the assumption that the financial authority permits traditional intermediaries to choose between financing innovation (or other financing which requires pressure on the intermediaries greater than that provided by market forces) or frozen primary security holdings.

projects which, under certain conditions, does not require forced saving. The flow of funds from financial intermediaries may permit significant increases in the growth rate of output if the funds are allocated to uses which are strategic in the process of resource creation; if they are allocated to approximately the same uses as other funds in the economy, their contribution to economic development is less. Since these funds are not initially associated with a specific use, it may prove more feasible politically to use them, rather than other sources of funds, for development financing. The concomitant relative decline in the importance of other uses of financial intermediary funds might force a greater efficiency in the nonplanned uses of intermediary funds.

The above theory, which focuses attention on the uses of intermediary funds, does not conflict with theories which emphasize the sources of intermediary funds. Those theories make the uses of intermediary funds as developmental as possible by assumption; the theory used here assumes a less-than-optimum developmental allocation of intermediary funds and inquires into techniques for improving this allocation. Differences between intermediaries with respect to their uses of funds are studied here, while similarities in their sources of funds are emphasized. The Gurley-Shaw theory is particularly useful for this purpose, since it emphasizes the similarities between indirect securities while recognizing some effects of imperfections in the primary security markets.

Applying the Gurley-Shaw theory of the relation of finance to economic development is difficult in a country that lacks highly developed money and capital markets, since that theory relies heavily on marginal adjustments of demands, supplies, prices, and interest rates. However, the Gurley-Shaw theory, together with an emphasis on the strategic importance of innovation in economic development, does provide a useful theory of the relation of financial intermediaries to economic development. In the Schumpeterian theory, innovations—discontinuous changes in the production function—are required for economic development. Marginal adjustments of supplies and demands, and marginal changes in the production function are insufficient to begin the cumulative process of development from the circular flow economy. But once the process of development gains momentum, discontinuous changes in the production function become more or less built into the system.

Financing discontinuous changes in the production function requires quantities of funds that are discontinuous from the point of view of the innovator and that are required for a relatively long time period. In the Schumpeterian theory this long-term financing is provided by the capitalist, who exercises a veto power over the development plans proffered by entrepreneurs.[26] The role of the capitalist is not creative but permissive in the Schumpeterian theory. Financial intermediaries in the present study have this same permissive role with respect to economic development. However, this role may be particularly important in institutional settings in which alternative sources of long-term financing for large-scale spending projects do not exist. If alternative flows of funds are traditionally directed toward nondevelopmental spending, then a significant time interval may be required to redirect these flows. It is also true that flows of funds from private sectors may continuously avoid some development projects as a result of extraordinary risks or inappropriable products.

Thus, for a variety of reasons, the flow of funds from financial intermediaries to innovations is particularly important during the early years of a development effort. As economic development progresses, the strategic importance of this source of funds is likely to diminish as a result of the increasing availability of alternative sources of development financing. This does not mean that the strategic permissive role of financing diminishes as development progresses; it is always important that technically feasible productive activities be permitted by financial practices. But the development of industrial activities in an economy is likely to be accompanied by the development of a greater variety of sources of financing for those industrial activities.

The permissive nature of the role of financial intermediaries in economic development means, of course, that financial intermediaries as such cannot initiate a cumulative process of economic development. But if the technological capabilities of an economy have progressed sufficiently for financial institutions to act as an obvious bottleneck to the attainment of that economy's production capabilities, then improvements in financial, institutional practices can permit the economy to operate nearer to its technical capacity. Financial intermediaries can also participate in the more active functional roles in economic development,

---

[26] In the Gurley-Shaw theory this veto power is not explicitly discussed, but implicitly the monetary authority is performing this function through managing the rate of interest and, hence, determining whether or not marginal investment spending projects will be undertaken.

such as preparing plans for establishing plants, supervising the activities of new going concerns, or any other function different from that of providing money funds. In Mexico the government intermediaries and private *financieras* participate in many of these activities which would not be included in a narrow definition of financial intermediary. These "other" activities may be more significant as an explanation of Mexican economic development in recent years than the funds which these intermediaries have provided; however, the present study inquires only into the relationships between the funds flows of financial intermediaries and economic development.

In the following chapter the institutional background of the Mexican economy is described briefly for the period from the Mexican Revolution of 1910–1917 to the substantial changes in Mexican financial laws of the early 1940's. This description shows that Mexico had developed sufficiently by the early 1940's for finance to play its permissive role at that time. The Mexican financial intermediaries are then described with particular emphasis placed on the control system under which they operate. This control system is seen to be such that the entire Mexican financial sector can be considered as a unit, rather than as a group of distinct intermediaries, when the actual flows of funds to and from intermediaries are at issue. However, Chapter III, in which the funds flows of the various subsectors are analyzed, shows each financial subsector to be quite specialized in either its sources or uses of funds or both. The control system which welds these diverse institutions into a unified whole is seen in Chapter V to be significantly explanatory of Mexican production and price experience during the past two decades.

CHAPTER II

The Mexican Financial Sector
and Its Control

AN understanding of Mexico's present financial, institutional practices requires a knowledge of the profound changes in Mexico's economic, social, and political institutions that resulted from the Mexican Revolution of 1910–1917. Though the Revolution proper culminated in the 1917 Constitution, in a real sense the Mexican Revolution continues to the present time as an orderly process of improvement in the social and economic conditions of the masses of Mexican agricultural, industrial, and government workers.[1]

The Revolution began with the relatively bloodless forcing of an election which in 1910 ended the three-decade dictatorship of Porfirio Díaz and made Francisco I. Madero the elected president of Mexico. This "revolution" in political procedures might eventually have resulted

---

[1] In this study primary attention is focused on the Mexican Revolution as it affected financial intermediaries. The Agrarian Reform aspect of this Revolution has received careful treatment by Jesus Silva Herzog in *El agrarismo mexicano y la reforma agraria: Exposición y crítica* (México: Fondo de Cultura Económica, 1959), which includes a wealth of quotations from important documents of relevance to this subject. A comprehensive treatment of the Mexican Revolution as a fifty-year process of cultural change is the four-volume collection of essays by distinguished Mexican authors entitled *México: Cinquenta años de revolución* (México: Fondo de Cultura Económica, 1960–1962). Volume I of this work deals with economic aspects, Volume II deals with social aspects, Volume III deals with political aspects, and Volume IV deals with cultural aspects of the Mexican Revolution.

in substantial changes in Mexican social and economic institutions had a full-scale, bloody revolution not begun in 1913.[2]

Whereas Madero's revolution emphasized political reform primarily, the Constitutional Revolution, which was supported primarily by Mexico's propertyless groups, emphasized social and economic as well as political reform. The major source of support for the revolutionary armies[3] was the landless rural population, since Mexico City, at that time almost the only residence of an urban proletariat, was initially under the control of the counterrevolutionary forces. Although the rallying cries of the Revolution were largely for land reform, the constitution that emerged from this Revolution established constitutional rights for urban workers, along with rights of agricultural workers to land. Workers' rights and land reform were only two of the principles laid down in the Constitution that evidenced its primary economic and social revolutionary character. That Constitution made a revolutionary break with semifeudal institutional patterns through establishing the concept that all property rights are created by society and can be changed by society through orderly legal processes.

Mexico's modern financial history begins with the Mexican Revolution since one, and perhaps a minor, change in the social, economic, and political institutions ushered in by the Revolution was a change in financial institutions. The major change in the financial institutions was an increased government participation in the financial sector, both in a controlling and in a proprietary capacity. In 1913 Venustiano Carranza indicated in these words the attitude of what was to become the new revolutionary government:

> We will change all the present banking system, preventing monopoly by private businesses which for many years have absorbed the wealth of Mexico; and we will abolish the right of privately owned banks to issue notes or paper money. The right to issue notes should be the exclusive privilege of the nation. When the revolution is won a Single

[2] Madero was murdered in 1913, and Huerta, who engineered the assassination, took over the presidency. The unconstitutional manner in which he took office, together with his close association with reactionary groups, touched off the bloody Constitutional Revolution in 1913 which resulted in the Constitution of 1917.

[3] The plural is used advisedly since, after Venustiano Carranza's army took Mexico City and conquered the forces of the *status quo ante*, several years of fighting between Carranza, Villa, and Zapata were required to finally establish the claim of Carranza to the presidency. Carranza is considered to have been a somewhat less vocal advocate of social reform than Villa and Zapata.

Bank of Issue, a Government Bank, will be established, protecting its existence necessarily by the disappearance of any banking institution which is not controlled by the government.[4] Despite Carranza's attitude, the General Law of Credit Institutions, passed in 1887 under the dictator Díaz, continued to be the legal foundation of the financial sector until the end of 1924, when the revolutionary approach to financial institutions was codified in the General Law of Credit Institutions and Banking Establishments. The Mexican Minister of Finance in his report to congress for the year 1924 explained the essential difference between the Díaz regime's approach to finance and that of the revolutionary government:

> Consequently, under the previous law [of 1897], the guarantee of [bank] liabilities was the essential thing and, once this was accomplished, within the limits which these liabilities permitted, the banks could use their funds in the manner in which they wished. On the other hand, the new law indicates a new orientation in that its article five states that the credit institutions have in common the function of facilitating the use of credit and are distinguished one from the other by the nature of the liabilities which they issue or by the services which they render the public. This last concept marks a completely new tendency, since it follows the intent of the State to channel the capital invested in the credit industry toward accomplishing specific objectives. Under the new system it is not enough that the liabilities issued by credit institutions are well secured; it is necessary that the capital obtained through issues of such liabilities goes to enrich sources of public wealth and this capital may not be used as an instrument in creating monopolies for certain industries or individuals.[5]

Though it was some time before this objective of government determination of the uses of financial intermediary funds was an accomplished fact, as distinct from a legal principle, it is still significant that from the earliest years of the Revolution this objective was stated explicitly.

While the period from 1910 through the mid-1920's was one of consolidation of the military and political changes of the Revolution, in the late 1920's and in the 1930's the basic economic and social in-

---

[4] This was part of a speech by Carranza in Hermosillo, Sonora, on September 24, 1913, as quoted in Antonio Manero, *La reforma bancaria en la Revolución Constitucionalista* (México: Biblioteca del Instituto Nacional de Estudios Históricos de la Revolución, 1958), p. 67.

[5] Secretaría de Hacienda y Crédito Público, Dirección General de Crédito, *Legislación Bancaria* (México: 1957), I, pp. 27–28.

stitutional bases of Mexico's recent rapid progress were laid. Banco de México, S. A., the first central bank and the sole bank of issue in Mexico, was established in September of 1925. Originally the institution functioned as an ordinary commercial bank with branches throughout the Republic and, in addition, acted as fiscal agent for the government and as the bank of issue. The bank was a government institution in that the Mexican government owned a majority of the bank's voting stock, but the powers of Banco de Mexico to control the privately owned banks were quite restricted during this period. The bank appears to have functioned as a supplement to the existing credit institutions of the country rather than as a coordinator of their activities during its formative period.[6]

In March of 1926 the National Agricultural Credit Bank (Banco Nacional de Crédito Agrícola y Ganadero) began operations as an attempt on the part of the Mexican government to fill a large gap in the existing credit facilities of the country. Article 27 of the 1917 Constitution, in addition to reaffirming the provision of the 1857 Constitution that prohibited ownership of real estate by religious organizations, made provision for land redistribution on a vast scale. One estimate of the distribution of property ownership toward the end of the Díaz regime is that 1 per cent of the population owned 97 per cent of the land, individuals with small holdings owned 2 per cent of the land area, and villages and communities owned 1 per cent of the land area.[7] Naturally the prerevolutionary agricultural credit facilities of the country were oriented toward providing credit under such conditions of land ownership, but they were not adequate to meet the needs of the beneficiaries of the new program of land redistribution. Some of the land was redistributed to groups of individuals (*ejidos*) rather than to individual members of the groups (*ejidatarios*), and mortgaging redistributed land was prohibited. Since the new landowners in most cases owned little

---

[6] The most complete history and analysis of the Mexican financial sector is O. Ernest Moore's *Evolución de las instituciones financieras en México* (México: Centro de Estudios Monetarios Latino-americanos, 1963). Much of the discussion in this chapter relies also on the excellent study of Mexican government enterprises by William Patton Glade, Jr., "Las empresas gubernamentales descentralizadas," *Problemas Agrícolas e Industriales de México* (México: 1959), XI, Núm. 1.

[7] Herzog, *El agrarismo mexicano*, p. 502.

else, it was virtually impossible for their credit needs to be served through the traditional credit facilities of the country. In order to provide credit facilities for *ejidos, ejidatarios*, and other owners of small plots or farms, the National Agricultural Credit Bank was established.

The Agricultural Credit Law of 1926, which provided for the National Agricultural Credit Bank, also provided for the organization of regional and local credit societies through which the National Bank's funds would be channeled to agriculture. In 1926 four Ejido Agriculture Banks were established in various parts of the Republic, largely with capital provided by the national government.[8] Each of these *ejido* banks discontinued operations rather quickly; this, together with the National Bank's initial reluctance to use its funds to aid small-holders and *ejidos*, indicates that Mexico's deficiency of agricultural credit was not overcome quickly.

The next step in the development of agricultural credit institutions in Mexico was the founding of the National Ejido Credit Bank (Banco Nacional de Crédito Ejidal) by the government in 1935. As the name suggests, this institution was set up to specialize in providing credit to *ejidos* and *ejidatarios*; the National Agricultural Credit Bank retained the function of supplying credit to privately owned agriculture. The *ejido* was becoming an increasingly important feature of Mexican culture in 1935 as a result of the distribution of an annual average of 504,293 hectares of land from 1915 to 1935.[9] Though this fact might establish that the Ejido Bank was needed in Mexico in 1935, the overriding necessity for the bank was the sharply increased rate of land redistribution planned for the late 1930's. From 1935–1940 an annual average of 2,934,856 hectares were distributed to *ejidos*.[10]

[8] *Ibid.*, p. 340.
[9] *Ibid.*, p. 405.
[10] From 1915 to 1961 there were 46,500,000 hectares (23 per cent of the land area of the nation) redistributed in Mexico. The 1950 census showed 39,000,000 hectares owned by 17,579 *ejidos* which included 1,378,326 *ejidatarios*. Slightly under half of the total cultivated land in 1950 was in *ejidos*. The distribution of Mexico's cultivated land in 1950 by type of ownership, size of individual unit, number of units, and total area was as follows:

Type of Ownership	Hectares	Number of Units	Total Hectares
Private	0–5	1,020,747	1,504,397
Private	6–50	190,672	3,026,371
Private	51–100	15,930	1,192,641
Private	101–400	7,826	1,391,123
Private	over 400	1,546	4,022,863
Ejidos (farmed collectively)		35,364 persons	294,286
Ejidos (farmed individually)		1,342,962 persons	8,451,931

Ibid., pp. 513–514, and *México: Cinquenta años de revolución*, II, 231–232.

In 1936 the government inaugurated a program of providing government-owned agricultural product warehouses (Almacenes Nacionales de Depósito). Though warehouses for agricultural products are not financial intermediaries, this program was an important step in encouraging agricultural loans, since warehouse receipts issued by these institutions provided reasonably adequate security.[11]

The National Foreign Commerce Bank (Banco Nacional de Comercio Exterior) was established in 1937 as a government-owned credit institution specializing in financing foreign commerce. Though many of this bank's activities are not directly related to agriculture, a major function of the National Foreign Commerce Bank was financing a program of development of agricultural products for export.

Through newly created government-owned credit institutions (the National Agricultural Credit Bank, the National Ejido Credit Bank, the National Deposit Warehouses, and the National Foreign Commerce Bank), the Mexican government during the late 1920's and during the 1930's directed loanable funds toward agricultural development. In this manner Mexican financial, institutional patterns were changed as the patterns of land ownership changed.

By the early 1930's the Mexican government was planning a large-scale program of public works. A law dating from 1897 prohibited the use of mortgages on government property as a means of securing financing for these public works, and in the early 1930's the market for direct government debt was quite narrow. As a result of these circumstances the National Urban Mortgage and Public Works Bank (Banco Nacional Hipotecario Urbano y de Obras Públicas)[12] was established in 1933; it was to finance public works by selling its own liabilities to the public. The following year Nacional Financiera was established, with the objective of creating a wider market for direct government debt. After passing the remainder of the 1930's in relative obscurity, this institution became the most important Mexican financial intermediary that engages directly in the financing of industrialization. During the 1930's Banco de Mexico, the National Mortgage Bank, and Nacional Financiera were the three Mexican financial institutions that specialized either in financing public works directly (as in the case of the National Mortgage Bank) or in

---

[11] Of course the major significance of these warehouses and the loans to agricultural producers was (and is) the elimination of middlemen.

[12] This name is hereafter shortened to National Mortgage Bank.

financing public spending in general through creating a market for government securities.

One small government-owned financial intermediary was created during the 1930's to specialize in providing funds to industry. This was the National Workers Bank for Industrial Promotion (Banco Nacional Obrero de Fomento Industrial), whose functions were later transferred to the National Cooperative Development Bank. Though the previously mentioned government-owned credit institutions established between 1925 and 1940 have since become the "big six" government intermediaries, the Workers Bank and its successor remained relatively small. It should be noted that this bank was established more as an aid to producer cooperatives—a special type of enterprise under an unusual form of ownership—than as an aid to industry in general.[13]

When the Mexican government began the process of formulating a new banking code in 1923, thirty-five private intermediaries were operating under concessions from the government. Twenty-five of these institutions were commercial banks which had previously been banks of issue, three were mortgage loan banks, and seven were equipment loan banks.[14] The mortgage loan banks (*hipotecarios*) were specialized in making loans secured by improved rural or urban real estate; the equipment loan banks (*refaccionarios*) were specialized in making medium-term loans to mining, industrial, and agricultural enterprises.

The new banking law of 1924 governing private financial inter-

---

[13] One should not infer from the fact that only one government bank for industry was established prior to 1940 that the Mexican government did not actively participate in the allocation of funds to industry. Until 1932 Banco de Mexico conducted the full range of commercial bank activities through its main office in Mexico City and its branches throughout the country. Some of the activities of the Foreign Commerce Bank were directed toward private industry. These facts, together with the fact that the industrial sector in Mexico at that time was quite small relative to the agricultural sector, indicate that industrial financing was not neglected by the government prior to 1940.

[14] *Legislación Bancaria*, II, 11. The status of many of the commercial banks was in doubt during the period from 1915 through most of the 1920's. These banks had provided most of the financing of counterrevolutionary forces during the Revolution by issuing bank notes. The revolutionary generals financed their campaigns with government paper money. Carranza announced his intention of canceling the concessions of banks which could not meet the legal specie reserve requirements in 1915. Only seven banks could meet these requirements, though subsequent modifications in the decrees permitted nineteen banks to continue operations. For a detailed history of commercial banks during the period from roughly 1910–1925, see Manero, *La reforma bancaria,* in which many important documents of the period are reproduced.

mediaries provided for a high degree of specialization for the various groups of intermediaries, both in their sources and uses of funds. However, in 1932 a new General Law of Credit Institutions was passed; this law made possible significant reductions in the degree of specialization and apparently was an attempt to increase the availability of long-term and medium-term credit to industry and agriculture.[15] A most significant feature of this 1932 law was the provision for establishing *financieras* which, in addition to providing medium and long-term funds to industry and agriculture, were permitted to participate actively in the promotion and ownership of businesses. Recently (since 1955) these *financieras* have become a very progressive and important portion of the Mexican financial sector.

Thus during the period from 1910 to 1940 the institutional bases of Mexico's present financial sector were laid. From 1925 to 1940 the government-owned portion of this financial sector was added to the private portion, and by 1945 government intermediaries accounted for 40 per cent of the financial sector's loans to and investments in the securities of businesses and individuals. The period of primary importance in this study begins with three laws passed in 1940–1941 which gave the Mexican financial sector substantially the form that obtains today. First, Nacional Financiera's charter law was changed at the end of 1940, making Nacional Financiera the most important single institution in the Mexican capital market.[16] Second, in mid-1941 Banco de Mexico's charter law was changed so that this institution was better able to coordinate the money market. And third, in 1941 the General Law of Credit Institutions was substantially rewritten to provide for a greater degree of specialization for the groups of private intermediaries.[17] Although many changes in Mexico's laws relating to financial intermediaries have occurred since 1941, these changes have almost all been refinements of the structure provided for in the laws mentioned above. In view of this, the following description of the Mexican financial sector and its control omits discussion of most changes during the 1942–1960 period and concentrates on a description of conditions in 1960.

---

[15] For the texts of laws and decrees pertaining to private intermediaries during the period from 1897–1940 see *Legislación Bancaria*, I, II, and III.
[16] For the text of this law see *Diario Oficial*, December 31, 1940.
[17] For the text of this law see *Legislación Bancaria*, IV, 9–127.

THE PRIVATE INTERMEDIARIES

Mexico's private financial intermediaries are divided into the following functional categories: (1) deposit banks (*bancos de depósito*), (2) savings banks (*operaciones de depósito de ahorro*), (3) *financieras*, (4) mortgage loan banks (*hipotecarias*), (5) capitalizers (*capitalizadoras*), (6) home savings and loan banks (*bancos de ahorro y préstamo para la vivienda familiar*), and (7) trust operations (*fiduciarias*).[18] With the approval of the Minister of Finance and Public Credit, an institution may establish branches; one institution is permitted to perform savings operations, trust operations, and one other function listed above. In case one firm performs more than one of the seven functions, separate departments with separate records and separate assets must be established for each function.

Both the government and private subsectors of Mexico's financial sector operate under the jurisdiction of the Ministry of Finance and Public Credit. Within this Ministry are the National Banking Commission and the National Securities Commission, which administer some of the detailed regulation and supervision of the private subsector. However, Banco de Mexico is responsible for most of the detailed regulation of the private subsector with respect to the allocation of funds. In a later section the control of private intermediaries is discussed; the discussion which immediately follows is limited to the functions which the various types of private intermediaries perform and does not include restrictions placed on private intermediary activities.

At the end of 1959 Mexico had 103 deposit banks operating 942 offices.[19] Deposit banks are permitted to engage in the following activities of significance to this study. First, they may receive sight and time deposits from the general public. Deposits which may be withdrawn after less than thirty-days notice bear no interest. Time deposits may have

---

[18] The following description of the functions and control of private intermediaries is based on the 1941 General Law of Credit Institutions as amended through 1959. This amended law is found in *Leyes y Códigos de México: Legislación Bancaria* (Second edition; México: Editorial Porrua, S. A., 1960).

[19] The figures on the number of private institutions and offices presented in this section are taken from Secretaría de Industria y Comercio, Dirección General de Estadística, *Anuario Estadístico de los Estados Unidos Mexicanos 1958–1959* (México: 1960), p. 728.

maturities no greater than five years and may take the form of savings certificates with maturities from ninety days to five years. Deposits may be stated in Mexican pesos or in foreign currencies. Second, deposit banks may make loans with maturities of five years or less.[20] Third, these banks may accept drafts and issue letters of credit. Finally, deposit banks may buy and sell stocks and bonds for their own accounts (within limits) and for the accounts of third parties.

Savings banks and savings departments are authorized to receive savings deposits on which interest is paid; the deposit of one person is limited to a maximum of $100,000 (pesos).[21] A savings institution may agree to pay up to 30 per cent of each deposit or $1,000 (pesos), whichever is greater, on demand. If a withdrawal is $1,000 (pesos) or less, a depositor must wait seven days before the next withdrawal; if a withdrawal is more than $1,000 (pesos), the waiting period is fifteen days. With an additional authorization from the Minister of Finance and Public Credit, a savings bank or department may evidence savings deposits with transferable savings bonds of maturities no less than six months and no more than twenty years. Funds received from savings deposits—including savings bonds—may be invested in money, loans, stocks, or bonds, much the same as in the case of deposit banks. However, the restrictions placed on deposit banks are largely restrictions on the amount of long-term obligations, while the restrictions placed on savings banks or departments are largely on short-term obligations. At the end of 1959 one hundred and seven savings banks or departments were operating 924 offices.

At this same time 97 *financieras* were operating 122 offices in Mexico. A *financiera* is permitted to act as a promoter of new firms, as an investment bank in new issues of securities, as a broker and dealer in securities, as indenture trustee for securities issues, and as fiscal agent for firms. A *financiera* may issue bonds (*bonos financieros*) secured by specific financial assets owned by the institution. Funds may also be obtained by a *financiera* through loans with minimum maturities of 90

[20] In Mexico loans of greater than one-year maturity are usually divided into working-capital or crop loans (*de habilitación* or *de avío*) and equipment or term loans (*refaccionarios*). The number of such loans that deposit banks may make is controlled carefully.

[21] The symbol "$" refers to either pesos or dollars, depending on which word follows in parentheses. At 1954–1964 exchange rates, twelve and one-half pesos equal one dollar.

days and through loans callable in no less than 30 days. *Financieras* may receive time deposits which have minimum maturities of 180 days or which require a minimum of 30 days notice for withdrawal. As a final source of funds, a *financiera* may receive demand deposits that result from its own lending activities or that result from its acting as fiscal agent for firms. The *financieras* have greater freedom in lending and investing than do the other types of private financial institutions in Mexico. Although many particular types of lending and investing operations of *financieras* are limited by law or regulation, *financieras* are specifically authorized to:

(1) grant loans secured by warehouse or trust receipts;

(2) grant working-capital and equipment loans;

(3) grant loans with or without mortgage collateral to industry, agriculture, and ranching;

(4) issue letters of credit for purchases of equipment, machinery, or raw materials;

(5) accept drafts and endorse or guarantee notes;

(6) make loans or extend lines of credit;

(7) make loans to governments and make loans for construction or improvement of public works; and

(8) purchase and hold any class of securities.

Of much less significance (both in numbers and in value of assets) than the three aforementioned groups of private intermediaries are the mortgage loan banks. At the end of 1959 twenty-six of these institutions operated forty-one offices in Mexico. Mortgage loan banks are authorized to issue mortgage bonds and to guarantee mortgage notes issued by businesses. They may also act as broker and dealer in these mortgage securities. The proceeds of the sale of mortgage bonds may be invested only in mortgage bonds or notes which are liabilities of other mortgage loan banks, in loans secured by mortgages on real estate or improvements, and in loans for public works (which may not be mortgaged) guaranteed by a trust fund into which the income from the public works is paid.

The capitalizers in Mexico—of which there were thirteen operating thirty-five offices in 1959—carry on a type of operation which, in some respects, is unfamiliar in the United States. They issue policies or contracts with maximum maturities of twenty-five years and with a fixed sum payable at maturity. The sum payable at maturity, the terms of the contract, and the contractual rate of interest determine the regular premiums paid to the issuing institution. The novel feature of these savings policies is that a maximum of thirteen drawings may be held annually to determine "winners" whose policies are declared to have matured immediately. The investment of funds received as premiums on these policies is regulated closely; though capitalizers may make most types of loans and may purchase many types of securities, they are required to invest heavily in government securities and in low-cost housing projects. Capitalizers lend to policy holders in amounts up to the current value of the policy and for a maximum term of the maturity of the policy.

The home savings and loan banks in Mexico numbered three in 1959. This type of institution was added to the Mexican financial sector in a 1946 amendment to the General Law of Credit Institutions. These institutions have four sources of funds. First, they may enter into contracts with savers that provide for regular deposits by the saver and for a loan for home purchase when the total deposit reaches a specified amount. Second, these banks may issue housing bonds that may provide for participation in the income realized from investing the proceeds of the bonds. Third, the home savings and loan banks may issue real estate bonds. Finally, these banks may receive credit from the National Mortgage Bank through using their financial assets as collateral for loans. Most of the funds received by this class of credit institution must be invested in low-cost one or multi-family dwellings or in liabilities of the National Mortgage Bank.

There were 112 trust departments or banks operating 612 offices in 1959. These banks or departments may engage in any financial operation that is necessary for their acting as trustee.

CONTROL OF THE PRIVATE INTERMEDIARIES

Responsibility for controlling the activities of private financial intermediaries lies with the following government dependencies: (1) the Ministry of Finance and Public Credit, (2) the National Banking Commission, (3) the National Securities Commission, (4) Banco de Mexico, and (5) the National Mortgage Bank. The present General Law of Credit Institutions usually specifies a range of possibilities within which one of these control agencies may make specific requirements to meet the changing circumstances of the rapidly developing Mexican economy. The frequent revisions of the 1941 General Law of Credit Institutions tended toward (1) extending controls over more and more private intermediary activities and (2) making more and more controls subject to agency discretion.

Policy tools affecting the allocation of funds by Mexican private intermediaries include tools which specifically limit an institution's liabilities, since the institutions are specialized in their uses of funds and since particular uses of funds are often by law directly dependent on the quantity of a particular type of liability. Without attempting to list every control which government agencies exercise over the activities of private intermediaries, let us list the ones more directly available as tools for coordinating financial intermediary lending activities.

The Minister of Finance—in some cases with the advice of other control agencies—exercises discretion with respect to the following:

(1) granting charters to new institutions;

(2) permitting the opening of branches and departments;

(3) setting the minimum capital required of each institution;

(4) passing on the charter and amendments to the charter of each institution;

(5) setting the capital-liabilities ratio of deposit banks;

(6) setting the ratio to capital of nonfinancial assets and stocks of building-owning companies for all institutions except trust banks and departments;

(7) specifying the particular securities (among those approved for this purpose by the National Securities Commission) that deposit and savings banks may purchase;

(8) specifying the types of economic activities for which deposit and savings banks may make equipment loans;

(9) setting the proportion for deposit and savings banks of total securities with maturities greater than one year that may be working-capital loans, equipment loans, and investments in securities;

(10) setting the total permissible amount of long-term loans and investments in securities for deposit banks;

(11) approving the terms and conditions of savings deposits for each savings institution;

(12) setting the legal reserve requirements for contingent liabilities of *financieras*;

(13) setting the government-security reserves required of capitalizers and specifying, in some cases, investments that may be substituted for government securities to satisfy these reserve requirements;

(14) approving the maximum amount, the schedule of amortization, and other characteristics of loans by capitalizers to finance low- and medium-priced dwellings;[22]

(15) specifying conditions under which home savings and loan banks may defer meeting their loan obligations to savers;

(16) approving the terms and conditions of issues of real estate bonds by home savings and loan banks;

(17) approving all characteristics and the amount of an issue of real estate bonds that is not guaranteed by the National Mortgage Bank;

(18) approving the localities in which the real estate used as security for loans by home savings and loan banks may be constructed;

(19) specifying the source of funds and the rate of interest for loans by the National Mortgage Bank to home savings and loan banks for meeting loan contracts of savers whose loans are greater than their savings;

(20) specifying the conditions under which the assets of deposit banks may be used as collateral for loans from institutions other than Banco de Mexico;

(21) establishing rules for the valuation and holding of securities by credit institutions in circumstances of a general character that affect the securities markets; and

(22) establishing all regulations for persons and businesses dealing in foreign exchange.

The National Banking Commission is a dependency of the Ministry of Finance and Public Credit. Six of its nine members (including its president) are appointed by the Minister of Finance and Public Credit; one member is a representative of deposit banks; and two members are representatives of the other credit institutions. In addition to exercising supervision over private intermediaries, this Commission has the discretionary control powers of:

(1) making recommendations to the Minister of Finance on matters pertaining to money and credit;

(2) making recommendations to Banco de Mexico on some matters for which that bank is primarily responsible;

(3) permitting *financieras* to sell bonds before the specific collateral for those bonds is obtained by the *financieras*;

(4) specifying the securities, other than government and financial

---

[22] It should be noted that the President of the Republic, through the Minister of Finance and Public Credit, may by decree alter provisions of the General Law of Credit Institutions dealing with capitalizers and home savings and loan banks (Article 41, Paragraph XX).

intermediary obligations, that may serve as collateral for *financiera* bond issues;

(5) determining in particular cases whether specialized improvements may serve as collateral for a loan by mortgage loan banks in an amount equal to 30 per cent or 50 per cent of the value of the improvement;

(6) passing on all loans made by mortgage loan banks;

(7) fixing for each mortgage loan bank the evaluation of its overdue loans and its loans of maturities greater than twenty years and thirty days (which, in turn, affects the quantity of stocks of credit institutions which these banks may own);

(8) passing on all loans by capitalizers for financing low- and medium-cost dwellings;

(9) passing on capitalizers' loans on urban real estate and investments in real estate;

(10) passing on the particular financing techniques used and the proportions in which possible techniques are used as sources of funds for home savings and loan banks;

(11) verifying that funds lent by home savings and loan banks to their savers for purchases of real estate were used for the intended purposes;

(12) establishing rules for evaluations of assets and liabilities of financial intermediaries;

(13) approving all issues of securities by *financieras*, capitalizers, and mortgage loan banks; and

(14) fixing the conditions of various reserves which financial intermediaries may deduct from gross income in calculating their income tax base (which, in turn, affects the net yield to the intermediary from particular types of earning assets).

The National Securities Commission, which is a unit of the Ministry of Finance and Public Credit, lists the securities from which each type of financial institution must choose its investments in securities. *Financieras* may invest in any security approved by the Commission for issue; other credit institutions have more restricted lists of approved securities.

In effectuating its monetary and credit policies Banco de Mexico may choose among the following control techniques:

(1) recommending to the Minister of Finance and Public Credit that the capital-liabilities ratios of deposit banks be permitted to fall below the legal minimum of 1:10 to a minimum of 1:15;

(2) permitting deposit banks to accept deposits that would violate the legal capital-liabilities ratio, provided that these deposits are matched by 100 per cent reserves of liabilities of Banco de Mexico;

(3) fixing the legal minimum ratio of capital to contingent liabilities for deposit banks;

(4) fixing rules for securities transactions of deposit banks (a power shared with the National Securities Commission);

(5) specifying reserves in the form of deposits at Banco de Mexico required of all credit institutions within the limits of 5 per cent and 50 per cent of savings deposits and within the limits of 15 per cent and 50 per cent of demand and time deposits;

(6) fixing without limit the required reserves for increments in demand, time, or savings deposits;

(7) fixing different required reserve percentages for different areas of the country, different cities, and different classes of deposits;

(8) fixing, within the limits of (5) and (6) above, the required reserve percentages for all liabilities of all credit institutions (in the case of *financieras* only demand and time deposits are liabilities subject to this provision of the law);

(9) setting the maximum rate of interest payable on time deposits, savings deposits, and certificates of deposit;

(10) fixing discount rates on loans by Banco de Mexico to other financial intermediaries;

(11) setting the required reserve percentage of liabilities of *financieras* (other than demand and time deposits and bonds) between the limits of 5 per cent and 30 per cent, and setting without limit the required reserve percentage of increments in these liabilities;

(12) fixing the percentage of required reserves of the special guaranty fund for issues of *financiera* bonds; and

(13) authorizing *financieras* to substitute specific investments for the required reserves indicated in (11) and (12) above.

The National Mortgage Bank acts as a central bank for the home savings and loan banks. Its control activities take a somewhat different form from the control activities which Banco de Mexico performs with respect to the money market. Whereas Banco de Mexico's activities are directed more toward allocating funds among various types of credit institutions through reserve requirements and the provision of central-bank credit, the National Mortgage Bank's controls are directed more toward affecting the allocation of funds by the individual bank. The National Mortgage Bank's controls are its discretion with respect to the liabilities of home savings and loan banks that it will guarantee and with respect to the mortgages for which it will provide a secondary market. The National Mortgage Bank has wide discretion in entering into agreements with home savings and loan banks for financing low- and medium-cost housing projects.

THE GOVERNMENT INTERMEDIARIES[23]

Nacional Financiera's 1940 charter law gave that institution a prominent position in the Mexican capital market. Since Nacional Financiera was authorized to operate both as a *financiera* and as a savings bank, a wide variety of sources and uses of funds was available to the institution. It was to regulate the national securities markets and the market for long-term credit and, in addition, was to act as fiscal agent for the government in matters pertaining to government debt. This institution was to act in some respects as a central bank for *financieras* since it could grant credit to them and purchase securities held by them. Nacional Financiera, in general, was to promote investment for creating or expanding enterprises. In 1947 Nacional Financiera was made the institution through which foreign loans requiring the Mexican government's guarantee were channeled; at the same time it was directed to use its resources to develop basic industries.

Perhaps some idea of the importance of Nacional Financiera's activities can be obtained from the following information taken from the institution's 1960 annual report.[24] The value of outstanding loans at the end of 1959 that had been allocated by Nacional Financiera was approximately 8 per cent of Mexican gross national product in 1959. Nacional Financiera managed two revolving funds for the government: (1) the Medium and Small Industry Guaranty and Development Fund, for which 600 loans were made in 1959 aggregating approximately $100,000,000 (pesos); and (2) the Tourist Guaranty and Development Fund. In round numbers in 1959 Nacional Financiera (1) endorsed for businesses issues of $168,000,000 (pesos) of mortgage bonds, (2) allocated $1,700,000,000 (pesos) of funds from foreign sources, (3) had $1,800,000,000 (pesos) of its own securities outstanding, and (4) made a profit of $143,000,000 (pesos) on its operations. That the institution is considered a sound credit risk is witnessed by the Prudential Insurance Company of America's investment in 1960 of $100,000,000 (dollars) in

---

[23] In order to avoid repetition, Banco de Mexico is not discussed separately in this section. Banco de Mexico was discussed in other sections of this chapter and is discussed separately in the following chapters.

[24] Nacional Financiera, S. A., *Informe Anual 1960* (México: 1960). Nacional Financiera's annual reports are hereafter referred to as *NFIA*.

Nacional Financiera bonds.[25] In mid-1961 Nacional Financiera owned stock in sixty industrial enterprises; in thirteen of these it was the majority stockholder.[26] Transactions occurred in stocks of only twenty-five companies during the week to which this statement applies; three of these companies were ones in which Nacional Financiera was majority stockholder. The above miscellaneous facts concerning Nacional Financiera are offered to substantiate the statement that this institution is and has been the most important Mexican financial intermediary specializing in financing the development of Mexico's basic industries and infrastructure.

In addition to Nacional Financiera, which might be considered *the* industrial development bank in Mexico, the government financial intermediaries include the following more specialized and smaller industrial development banks:

(1) The National Cooperative Development Bank (Banco Nacional de Fomento Cooperativo) was established in 1944 and replaced the smaller National Workers Bank established in 1937. Both banks functioned primarily to develop and finance production by small businesses organized as producer cooperatives. In 1959 the credit granted by this institution was $115,000,000 (pesos).[27]

(2) The National Motion Picture Bank (Banco Nacional Cinematográfico) was established in 1947 as a government institution financing the development of a Mexican motion picture industry. Credit equal to $173,000,000 (pesos) was granted by this bank in 1959.

(3) The National Sugar Industry Financiera (Financiera Nacional Azucarera) was organized as a national credit institution (formerly a private *financiera*) in 1953. This institution works closely with the National Sugar Producers' Union established through government efforts in 1938 to coordinate the activities of cooperatives in the sugar industry. The credit authorized by the National Sugar Industry Financiera in 1959 was $600,000,000 (pesos).

(4) The National Transportation Bank (Banco Nacional de Transportes) was originally a private deposit institution but was converted into a government institution in 1953. The bank now acts as a *financiera* for the urban transportation industry. In 1959 the institution authorized $295,000,000 (pesos) of credit.

(5) The Sinaloa Regional Bank (Banco Provincial de Sinaloa) was es-

[25] "Los créditos del exterior en 1960," *El Mercado de Valores*, January 16, 1961, p. 2.
[26] "Evaluación de Nacional Financiera y su impacto en el desarrollo económico de México," *El Mercado de Valores*, August 7, 1961.
[27] The figures for credit granted by this and the other government credit institutions are from *México: Cinquenta años de Revolución*, I, 413–444.

tablished in 1943 as a mixed enterprise—partly government owned and partly privately owned. This bank, located in Culiacan, Sinaloa, should possibly be treated as an agricultural credit institution; however, a large portion of its activities, though directly connected with agriculture, are directed toward financing such industrial establishments as sugar mills. This bank is the major institution through which the National Foreign Commerce Bank channels funds to the Sinaloa area.

The National Urban Mortgage and Public Works Bank, like Nacional Financiera, has played a growing role in Mexican economic development since 1940. It specializes primarily in urban development through planning and financing such activities as public utilities, low-cost multifamily dwellings, and sanitation projects. Foreign loans requiring government guarantee for such projects as the above are now channeled through the National Mortgage Bank, and a large portion of the institution's funds are obtained through issues of its own mortgage bonds. In the last section several of the National Mortgage Bank's activities with respect to the home savings and loan banks were noted. The credit granted by this institution in 1959 totaled $1,826,000,000 (pesos).

Since its establishment in 1937, the National Foreign Commerce Bank has increased its scale of operations rapidly. During the 1941–1960 period the major sources of the bank's funds were increases in its capital, additions to its reserves, and loans from other banks. One use of these funds is to facilitate Mexican importing and exporting. A second use of the bank's funds is financing production primarily for export. In this financing of export production the Foreign Commerce Bank attempts to work through regional banks such as the Sinaloa bank discussed above, through the Agriculture or Ejido bank, or through its own two branches in the little-developed isthmus region of southern Mexico. Where such banking facilities are unavailable but the prospects of increasing agricultural production or exportable production are good, either the bank organizes cooperatives through which it lends or it grants credit directly to individuals.[28] A third use of the National Foreign Commerce Bank's funds is maintaining low retail prices on basic food items while maintaining higher prices for producers of these products. In this activity the National Foreign Commerce Bank lends price-support funds to the National Mass Consumption Goods Company (Companía

[28] Banco Nacional de Comercio Exterior, S. A., *Informe del consejo de administración a la XXIV asamblea general ordinaria de accionistas* (México: Editorial Cultura, T. G., S. A., 1961), p. 47.

Nacional de Subsistencias Populares)—formerly the Mexican Export-Import Company (CEIMSA).[29] The National Foreign Commerce Bank's total earning assets at the end of 1960 were slightly under $800,000,000 (pesos).[30]

In the field of agricultural credit the two government institutions established before 1940—the National Agricultural Credit Bank and the National Ejido Credit Bank—continue to predominate. In 1959 the credit authorized by the agriculture bank was $902,000,000 (pesos) while that by the *ejido* bank totaled $1,304,000,000 (pesos). Substantial changes in the agricultural credit system resulted from the Agricultural Credit Law of December 31, 1955, as amended.[31] This law envisions the two original banks as central banks for a system of regional banks which, in turn, lend to local credit societies. Two of these regional banks had been established in 1961 and two more were planned. This law established improved organization and control techniques in an attempt to enhance the probability that funds made available to the system would be used more for the benefit of a large number of agricultural producers than for the benefit of a few who might or might not be agricultural producers.[32]

The remaining institutions of the government financial intermediary subsector include the following:

(1) The Federal District Small Commerce Bank (Banco de Pequeño Comercio del Distrito Federal) was established in 1943 to provide credit at reasonable prices to those who sell in the public markets. The credit authorized by this bank in 1959 totaled $8,500,000 (pesos).

(2) The National Pawn Shop and Savings Institution (Nacional Monte de Piedad, Institución de Ahorro) was made a government in-

[29] Glade's work gives an exceptionally good account of how CEIMSA aided in the economic development of Mexico. Glade, *"Las empresas,"* pp. 149–159.

[30] Banco Nacional de Comercio Exterior, S. A., *Informe del consejo,* p. 93. This figure is not strictly comparable with the figures given for credit authorized by other government institutions, both because the date is different and because the source of the data for other institutions does not make explicit whether the data are flows or stocks (probably most are end-of-year stocks).

[31] For the text of this law as amended through 1960, see *Leyes y Códigos de México: Codigo Agrario y leyes complementarias* (Seventh edition; México: Editorial Porrua, S. A., 1961), pp. 329–368.

[32] For one opinion of the agricultural credit system in Mexico see Hector Fernández Moreno, "Intervención estatal en el crédito agrícola y ejidal," *Revista de Economia,* November, 1960, pp. 323–335. For a slightly more optimistic view of the present Mexican situation, see Victor Manzanilla Schaffer, "La Reforma Agraria," *México: Cinquenta años de Revolución,* III, 253–259. Both of these authors imply that in a country such as Mexico, in which some two-thirds of the population are dependent on agricultural income, even greater efforts should be made to improve conditions in agriculture.

stitution in 1949. This institution is Mexico's oldest financial intermediary and has operated continuously since 1775.[33] In 1959 the
National Pawn Shop authorized $41,000,000 (pesos) of credit.

(3) The National Army-Navy Bank (Banco Nacional del Ejército y la
Armada) was established in 1946 as a deposit and savings bank
for the armed forces. With respect to both sources and uses of
funds, members of the armed forces are the bank's most important
clients. Credit authorized by the National Army-Navy Bank in
1959 was $45,000,000 (pesos).

(4) The National Savings Association (Patronato del Ahorro Nacional)
was founded in 1949 to sell savings bonds to the public. At the
end of 1959 the quantity of these savings bonds outstanding was
$526,000,000 (pesos).

CONTROL OF THE GOVERNMENT INTERMEDIARIES

The government financial intermediaries in Mexico are directly under
the supervision of the Minister of Finance and Public Credit. The
General Law of Credit Institutions states, with respect to government
intermediaries, "The Ministry of Finance and Public Credit has exclu-
sive authority in all matters relative both to the creation and the functioning of the national credit institutions."[34]

In 1959 the Coordinating Committee for Government Credit Institutions was established. The president of this committee is the Minister
of Finance; the other four members are the chief executive officers of
Banco de Mexico, Nacional Financiera, the National Foreign Commerce
Bank, and the National Mortgage Bank.[35] This committee advises the
President of the Republic in matters pertaining to relations among government intermediaries, relations between government intermediaries
and private intermediaries, and relations of all intermediary activities to
economic development.

Government credit institutions are required to submit to the Coordinating Committee detailed yearly budgets of their proposed operations, together with a defense of these budget proposals. Three times

[33] For a brief discussion of the early history of the Monte de Piedad, see Diego
López Rosado, *Ensayos sobre historia económica de México* (México: Imprenta
Universitaria, 1957), pp. 39–50. Actually Mexico's mint (Casa de Moneda) was
established before the Monte de Piedad and is still operating. A history of the
mint is also found in López Rosado's book.
[34] *Leyes y Códigos de México: Legislación Bancaria*, p. 8.
[35] For the text of the regulation establishing this Committee, see *ibid.*, pp.
199–207.

per year these institutions report on their progress toward attaining the budgeted goals. The Minister of Finance may veto specific items in these budgets. The Minister of Finance has complete control of all borrowing and lending activities of each government institution, and he issues regulations that provide general rules for specific types of borrowing and lending activities. The board of directors of each government credit institution meets once per month to receive a report from the chief executive officer on the activities of the institution during the previous month. Though the administrative organization and procedure established by this 1959 regulation is of recent origin, one should recall that during the entire period studied here the Minister of Finance had the power to regulate all activities of the government intermediaries.

Through this control system for government intermediaries and the control system for private intermediaries described earlier, the entire Mexican financial sector can be made responsive to the financial needs of Mexico's economic development program. Most of the detailed day-to-day supervision of the money market is done by Banco de Mexico; most of such supervision of the capital market is done by Nacional Financiera. As a matter of policy these two institutions have maintained a high degree of liquidity for nonmonetary indirect securities and for fixed-interest primary securities during the past two decades. This fact is an important reason for considering the availability of funds rather than the cost of funds as more important during this period and for considering money and nonmonetary indirect securities as very similar analytically.

Several characteristics peculiar to the Mexican market for loanable funds tend to minimize the inflationary impact of this policy of maintaining a high degree of liquidity for nonmonetary indirect securities and bonds. First, the aggregate quantity of fixed-interest securities has been small relative to the aggregate quantity of money; the distribution of fixed-interest securities has been such that if the public had exchanged all its holdings for money, the quantity of money would have increased less than 30 per cent and the quantity of money plus time deposits would have increased only approximately 18 per cent.[36] Second, the control system for the Mexican financial sector makes it possible to "lock-in" much of the two-thirds of the fixed-interest securities outstanding that are owned by financial intermediaries or government dependencies. Third, the power of Banco de Mexico to require 100 per cent reserves

---

[36] At the end of 1960 the quantity in millions of pesos of the indicated financial assets was the following: (See bottom of page 60.)

for increments in deposit liabilities (both demand and time deposits of all private intermediaries) and to specify the financial claims which qualify as reserves makes it possible for Banco de Mexico to prevent multiple expansion of the money supply resulting from the open-market operations necessary for maintaining the liquidity of bonds. Finally, the National Banking Commission's control over the terms and timing of new issues of securities (both stocks and bonds) can be used to affect the supply of securities at any particular time.

This description of the Mexican financial sector and its control shows that a wide variety of financial claims is available to Mexican surplus spending units as alternative forms in which their surpluses can be held. These surplus spending units are free to choose among these financial claims. In the absence of flows of funds among financial intermediaries, surplus spending units in allocating their surpluses among intermediaries would be determining to an important extent the funds available for allocation by particular intermediaries. However, the control system of the Mexican financial sector described in this chapter makes possible a reallocation of funds within the financial sector, so that the final allocation of funds to deficit spending units more nearly approaches that desired by Mexican financial authorities. These institutional conditions should be kept constantly in mind while reading the following chapters which deal with various flows of funds in Mexico during the period from 1945 through 1959.

	Total Outstanding	Owned by Businesses and Individuals
Government Securities	$ 6,996	$ 18
Government Financial Intermediary Securities	5,001	1,240
Private Financial Intermediary Securities	841	682
Business and Individual Fixed-Interest Securities	5,042	3,682
Total Fixed-Interest Securities	$17,880	$ 5,622
Currency and Demand Deposits		18,771
Time Deposits, etc.		12,023
Total Money and Time Deposits		$30,794

(See Appendix Table 1 and Banco de México, S. A., _Informe Anual 1960_, [México: 1961], pp. 122–123.)

Banco de Mexico's annual report (in recent years _Informe Anual_ and in earlier years _Asamblea general ordinaria de accionistas_) is hereafter referred to as _BMIA_.

CHAPTER III

Financial Intermediary Sources and Uses of Funds 1945-1959

STATISTICAL DATA AND PROCEDURES

Banco de Mexico has published end-of-year balance sheets since 1945 for the financial intermediary sector and for three subsectors—private credit institutions, Banco de Mexico, and other government credit institutions. In this series the private subsector is further divided into six groups of institutions—deposit and savings banks, *financieras*, home savings and loan banks, capitalizers, mortgage loan banks, and trust institutions.[1]

The financial intermediary sector is defined in the present study to include only the credit institutions included in this series published by Banco de Mexico. The activities of these institutions were described in the preceding chapter.

The financial subsectors used in this study are defined as follows:

(1) "Total monetary intermediaries" includes only Banco de Mexico and deposit and savings banks.
(2) "Total nonmonetary intermediaries" includes only other government credit institutions, *financieras*, home savings and loan banks, capitalizers, mortgage loan banks, and trust institutions.
(3) "Total government intermediaries" includes only Banco de Mexico and other government credit institutions.

[1] *BMIA*, 1947–1960.

(4) "Total private intermediaries" includes only deposit and savings banks, *financieras*, home savings and loan banks, capitalizers, mortgage loan banks, and trust institutions.

(5) "Banco de Mexico" includes only that institution.

(6) "Government nonmonetary intermediaries" includes only those institutions included in the Banco de Mexico series called "other government credit institutions (*otros nacionales*)."

(7) "Deposit and savings banks" includes only deposit banks, savings banks, and savings departments of private credit institutions.

(8) "Total private nonmonetary intermediaries" includes all private credit institutions not classified as deposit and savings banks.

Banco de Mexico has also published a monthly series of selected assets and liabilities of financial intermediaries which begins in 1944. This series is less detailed than the annual series, and deposit and savings banks are the only private subsector shown separately in this monthly series. Both the annual series and the monthly series classify most intermediary assets and liabilities for a three-sector economy—a business and individual sector, a government sector, and a financial sector. Government nonfinancial enterprises are classified in the business and individual sector.

All levels of government are included in most series of data for the government sector. Private and government pension funds, insurance and guaranty companies, credit unions, and open-end investment funds are all classified in the nonfinancial sector, unfortunately.

The same sector definitions are used here; however, a rest-of-world sector is also included in this study. The gold, silver, and foreign-exchange assets of each financial intermediary are treated as liabilities of the rest-of-world sector; the time and sight liabilities of government nonmonetary intermediaries, which are not deposits (either demand or time) but which are stated in foreign currencies, are treated as assets of the rest-of-world sector. A substantial portion of the assets and liabilities of Nacional Financiera were not included as such by Banco de Mexico in data on the financial sector for the 1945–1952 period. In the present study these assets and liabilities are included with the financial sector for the entire 1945–1960 period.[2]

[2] The liabilities of Nacional Financiera referred to in the text were its participation certificates which were unconditionally guaranteed by the Mexican government and which evidenced part ownership of a common fund invested in various

One characteristic of these series published by Banco de Mexico is unsatisfactory from the point of view of this study. When an intermediary rediscounts a customer note at Banco de Mexico, the latter is considered to have made the original loan in these series. If attention is focused on the ultimate source of funds for the lending activities of financial intermediaries, then this method of treating rediscounts is appropriate. In this study attention is focused on the uses of intermediary funds; hence, for our purposes, rediscounts would more appropriately be considered as intrafinancial-sector loans, and the original loan would more appropriately appear as an asset of the institution making the initial allocation of funds. Since a correction for this factor was not made in the present study, Banco de Mexico appears to have allocated a larger amount of funds to businesses and individuals than was, in fact, the case.

In the Banco de Mexico series which form the basis of our statistical summary of Mexican intermediary activities for the 1945–1959 period, fixed-interest securities (including the obligations of capitalizers which have a lottery feature) as intermediary liabilities are not classified by owning sector. In this study the portion of these securities owned by businesses and individuals other than insurance and guaranty companies is considered to be held by businesses and individuals; the remaining portion of these securities is treated as though it were owned by financial intermediaries.

Capital and surplus reserves of the financial intermediaries are treated here as a portion of the equity of stockholders; these reserves are apportioned among the stockholder sectors in proportion to their holdings of common stock.

In most cases, between 5 and 10 per cent of the assets and liabilities of financial intermediaries remain unclassified by sector. Most unclassified assets are buildings and equipment and most unclassified liabilities are deferred charges. Since the difference between unclassified assets and unclassified liabilities is small in relation to the individual classified assets

---

financial claims. The assets of Nacional Financiera referred to in the text were the financial claims which formed the common fund for these participation certificates. During the 1945–1952 period Banco de Mexico, in effect, treated these participation certificates as liabilities of the government sector; during the 1953–1960 period they were treated as liabilities of Nacional Financiera. They were included for the entire period in the present study; see Note 1 at the beginning of the Appendix.

and liabilities used in this study, total classified assets are used here as a reference base in discussion of both asset and liability distributions.[3]

The balance sheets of the financial sector and its various subsectors are presented for the period 1945–1960 in Appendix Tables 1–9. Assets and liabilities are classified in these balance sheets by the sector owing or owning the financial claim. Only loans of maturities greater than one year are considered long-term loans. These long-term loans, together with securities, are considered long-term primary securities held by intermediaries. In the intermediary liabilities money is defined as coins and bank notes in circulation (both are Banco de Mexico liabilities), checking accounts (cuentas de cheques), and sight deposits (depósitos a la vista). The classification "securities" includes only open-market fixed-interest obligations and the obligations of capitalizers which have a lottery feature (títulos de capitalización). The remaining intermediary liabilities which are classified by sector are called "other deposits, etc." and include time deposits, savings accounts, and other sight and time obligations.

Tables of real sources and uses of funds were computed from the financial sector balance sheets. These are presented in Appendix Tables 10–18. Flows, sources, and uses are here defined as annual changes in the corresponding stock series from the balance sheets. In view of the fact that the various flows used here are somewhat less detailed than the balance sheet data, it was possible to use the Banco de Mexico monthly series of selected intermediary assets and liabilities to obtain sufficient data for the flows of 1944 and 1945.[4]

Following the Gurley-Shaw terminology introduced in Chapter I, non-monetary indirect securities are defined in the flow-of-funds tables to include all liabilities and equities of financial intermediaries which are classified by sector but which are not classified as money. Similarly, primary securities are defined to include all liabilities and equities of the nonfinancial sectors (both the loans and the investments of inter-mediaries).

For the years 1948, 1949, and 1954 it was necessary to adjust some flows with a view of eliminating the effects of the Mexican currency

[3] In effect, the present study treats unclassified intermediary assets and liabilities as a portion of the wealth of the business and individual sector.
[4] The procedure used in this respect is described in Note 2 at the beginning of the Appendix.

devaluations of those years. The procedure used for this adjustment was as follows: first, the balance sheet figures for assets or liabilities in foreign currencies, and for gold and silver, for the years 1947, 1948, and 1953 were stated in terms of the new exchange rates prevailing in 1948, 1949, and 1954; second, the restated quantities were subtracted from the original quantities; and third, the differences were added algebraically to the appropriate 1948, 1949, and 1954 flows.

In 1960 the government nonmonetary intermediaries were instrumental in financing the purchase by the Mexican government of various foreign-owned electric companies operating in Mexico. This disinvestment by the foreign companies was for the sum of approximately $1,456,000,000 (pesos). During this same year these intermediaries received extraordinarily large amounts of funds from the rest-of-world sector. This transaction is excluded from the financial intermediary flows of funds presented in this study since it was almost equal to the total uses of funds by these intermediaries for each of the two preceding years and since, even after deducting this transaction, 1960 government nonmonetary intermediary total uses of funds remained almost double those of 1959.[5]

The sources and uses of funds for the financial sector were deflated with the Mexico City General Wholesale Price Index series published by Banco de Mexico.[6]

The data in the Appendix provide the reader sufficiently detailed information for analysis of Mexican financial intermediaries on a year-by-year basis. However, the most important objectives of this study are (1) to provide a summary of the more lasting effects of economic development and Mexican financial policy on financial intermediaries during the 1945–1959 period and (2) to provide an interpretation of these data which points to possible effects of Mexican intermediaries on economic development. Hence, most of the information from Appendix Tables 1–18 was reduced to the summary tables of this chapter in the manner described below.

The 1945–1959 period was broken into three short cycles—1945–

---

[5] See Appendix Table 7. This was the only transfer of its type for which an adjustment was made in the financial sector funds flows.

[6] This series published in *BMIA* is based on 210 commodities and is considered the most adequate available for the purposes of this study. The annual financial sector series were deflated with the annual averages of monthly figures of the price series.

1949, 1950–1954, and 1955–1959—identified by the rate of change in gross national product and the rate of change in industrial production. Each of the years 1945, 1950, 1955, and 1960 had a higher percentage increase in industrial production than the preceding or following two years, and each except 1960 had a higher percentage increase in real gross national product than the following four years. The annual real financial intermediary flows were summed for each of the short cycles, and the resulting total flows for the cycles were expressed as percentages of the total classified uses of funds of the appropriate subsector for the appropriate cycle and as percentages of the corresponding flows of the total financial sector for the appropriate cycle.

The percentages of total classified uses of funds are used in the remainder of this chapter to answer the following two questions. First, what was the relative importance of various real sources and uses of funds to each financial subsector? Second, what significant trends were present during the 1945–1959 period in the relative importance to each financial subsector of its various sources and uses of funds? Subsector funds flows as percentages of total financial sector flows are used in the remainder of this chapter to answer the following two questions. First, what was the relative importance of the flows of each subsector to the flows of the financial sector as a unit? Second, what significant trends were present in the relative importance of particular flows of particular subsectors to the aggregate financial sector's flows?

BANCO DE MEXICO

Banco de Mexico's activities for the 1945–1959 period are summarized in Table 1. The most significant change during this period was the reduction in the importance of Banco de Mexico relative to the other financial subsectors. Total financial assets of Banco de Mexico were 46 per cent of those of the total financial sector in 1944, but real increases in these assets were only some 20 per cent of those of the financial sector during each of the three cycles, so that by the end of 1959 Banco de Mexico accounted for only 24 per cent of the financial sector's total financial assets.

Like the Federal Reserve System in the United States, Banco de

TABLE 1

BANCO DE MEXICO: ANALYSIS OF SELECTED REAL SOURCES AND USES OF FUNDS

End-of-1944 and 1945–1959

	Millions of 1950 Pesos				Per Cent of Total Uses of Funds					Per Cent of Total Financial Sector				
	End 1944	1945–49	1950–54	1955–59	End 1944	1945–49	1950–54	1955–59	End 1959	End 1944	1945–49	1950–54	1955–59	End 1959
Real Sources of Funds														
Businesses and Individuals														
Nonmonetary	94	250	−189	33	2	15	−10	1	1	4	13	−7	1	1
Money	3029	677	1874	1623	71	42	95	48	67	54	45	43	38	43
Total	3123	927	1685	1656	73	57	85	49	68	40	27	23	21	25
Government														
Capital and Deposits	150	107	65	201	4	7	3	6	5	27	12	15	19	17
Sales of Government Securities								14						
Total								20						
Financial Intermediaries (percentage figures net of similar uses)	1794	54	979	404	19	29	25	16	26	60	7	36	17	40
Statistical Discrepancy	191	104	−270	497	4	7	−13	15	1					
Total Classified Sources of Funds	5258	1192	2459	2758	100	100	100	100	100	46	19	22	19	24
Real Uses of Funds														
Businesses and Individuals														
Long-Term Loans and Securities	38	331	−33	108	1	21	−2	3	4	3	11	−1	3	3
Short-Term Loans	795	−321	494	883	19	−20	25	26	22	30	−21	16	19	16
Total	833	10	461	991	20	1	23	29	26	22	0.2	7	10	9
Government Securities	1003	1602	239	−478	24	99	12		14	61	101	50	−60	37
Financial Intermediaries	988	−409	480	−141						26	*	19	−7	12
Rest-of-World	2434	−11	1279	2386	56	0	65	71	60					
Total Classified Uses of Funds	5258	1192	2459	2758	100	100	100	100	100	46	19	22	19	24

Source: Appendix Tables 1, 6, 10, 15, and 26. All gold, silver, and foreign exchange evaluated with current exchange rates and assumed held by Banco de Mexico.
* Aggregate financial sector quantity near zero.

Mexico's liabilities were virtually all currency issues and reserve deposits of financial institutions and its assets were virtually all precious metals (the Federal Reserve System owns gold certificates rather than the gold) or foreign exchange, government securities, and discounts and advances. Unlike the Federal Reserve System, Banco de Mexico's stock was partially owned by the federal government, Banco de Mexico invested in small quantities of stocks and bonds issued by businesses and individuals (primarily government nonfinancial enterprises),[7] discounts and advances to financial intermediaries were a much larger fraction of total assets than were holdings of government securities,[8] and Banco de Mexico purchased stocks and bonds issued by other financial institutions—primarily government nonmonetary intermediaries.

In its direct relations with the business and individual sector during this period, Banco de Mexico was specialized as a recipient of funds through issues of currency, and it invested in securities issued by businesses and individuals only to a nominal extent. At the end of 1944 and 1959, 73 per cent and 68 per cent, respectively, of total classified liabilities were monetary liabilities to businesses and individuals. On these same dates only 1 and 4 per cent, respectively, of total classified assets were investments in business and individual securities. The decline in the importance of currency relative to the total Mexican money supply is reflected by the fact that in 1944 Banco de Mexico's monetary liabilities to businesses and individuals were 54 per cent of the money supply; by 1959 they had declined to only 43 per cent. This declining relative importance of currency occurred during each of the three cycles and, together with the declining importance of money relative to nonmonetary liabilities of financial institutions held by the public, this trend resulted in Banco de Mexico's share of the financial sector's liabilities to businesses and individuals declining from 40 per cent in 1944 to 25 per cent in 1959. Although during the 1945–49 cycle Banco de Mexico provided 11 per cent of the financial sector's long-term funds to businesses and individuals, at the end of both 1944 and 1959 its holdings

---

[7] In Table 1 the category "Businesses and Individuals: Long-Term Loans and Securities" is entirely securities, since Banco de Mexico was prohibited from making loans of greater than one year maturities.

[8] In Table 1 the category "Businesses and Individuals: Short-Term Loans" is entirely rediscounts of customer paper for other financial institutions—primarily the National Foreign Commerce Bank and, prior to 1955, the National Agricultural Credit and Ejido Credit Banks.

of business and individual securities were only 3 per cent of those of the financial sector.

Banco de Mexico's government securities holdings as a percentage of total classified assets declined between 1944 and 1960 from 24 per cent to 14 per cent, while government ownership of Banco de Mexico's liabilities and capital remained a relatively constant 4 or 5 per cent. This downward trend in Banco de Mexico financing of the government sector is even more apparent when the real flows of funds of the individual subperiods are analyzed. During the 1945–49 cycle Banco de Mexico's real additions to government securities holdings were 99 per cent of its net classified uses of funds.[9] During the 1954–59 cycle, however, reductions in Banco de Mexico's holdings of government securities were equal to 14 per cent of its net classified uses of funds. At the end of 1944 Banco de Mexico's government securities holdings were 61 per cent of those of the entire financial sector, but at the end of 1959 they were only 37 per cent. Thus, during this period Banco de Mexico allocated an ever smaller fraction of its funds to purchases of government securities, and in addition the total funds allocated by Banco de Mexico were a sharply declining fraction of those allocated by the entire financial sector. We return to this significant trend when the government securities market is discussed in Chapter IV.

Approximately three-fifths of Banco de Mexico's funds were allocated to holdings of gold, silver, and foreign exchange at the end of both 1944 and 1959. During the 1945–49 cycle there was virtually no change in these holdings if the changes due to the 1948–49 devaluation of the peso are included in the calculations. Similar treatment of the effects of the 1954 devaluation gives figures indicating that somewhat more than three-fifths of the real net classified uses of funds in the 1950–54 and the 1955–59 cycles were additions to these claims on the rest-of-world sector. In these calculations the relatively minor holdings of gold,

[9] This would be 70 per cent if the effects of the following transactions were removed. In 1949 the federal government exchanged a new issue of Agricultural Development Bonds for $490,000,000 (1950 pesos) of notes which the Agricultural and Ejido banks had rediscounted at Banco de Mexico. This decreased Banco de Mexico's short-term loans to businesses and individuals by the same amount as its government securities holdings were increased. The government, in effect, used these notes as payment for a subscription to the capital of the Agricultural and Ejido banks. This last transaction increased the funds provided by the government to government nonmonetary intermediaries by the same amount as the loans of these intermediaries to businesses and individuals were increased. These transactions are described in *BMIA* 1950, p. 19.

silver, and foreign exchange by other financial intermediaries are included in the Banco de Mexico figures.

At the end of 1944 Banco de Mexico's claims on financial intermediaries (including rediscounts) were roughly equal to the claims of other intermediaries on Banco de Mexico. By the end of 1959 these latter were some 15 per cent greater than the former. During the 1945–49 cycle liabilities of Banco de Mexico to other intermediaries remained almost constant while its holdings of other intermediary liabilities declined substantially (owing, in part, to the transactions described in Note 9). The two flows grew by approximately the same amount during the 1950–54 cycle, and during the 1955–59 cycle Banco de Mexico provided more funds to financial intermediaries than it received from them. The liabilities and capital of Banco de Mexico were approximately three-fifths of total financial sector holdings of financial intermediary liabilities at the end of 1944, but by the end of 1959 this was reduced to two-fifths—reflecting the increased availability and attractiveness of the liabilities of other intermediaries relative to those of Banco de Mexico. These statistics on inter-intermediary funds flows indicate that as an average for the entire period—and particularly during the 1945–49 cycle—Banco de Mexico was providing less lending ability to other financial intermediaries through discounts and advances than was being absorbed through increased reserves in the form of liabilities and capital of Banco de Mexico. But the gross amount of the inter-intermediary funds flows is more important in Mexico than the net relationship, since the intermediaries providing funds to Banco de Mexico were primarily monetary intermediaries, while those receiving funds from Banco de Mexico were primarily the government nonmonetary intermediaries.

THE GOVERNMENT NONMONETARY INTERMEDIARIES

The specialized government-owned nonmonetary intermediaries became during the 1945–1959 period the largest financial subsector in terms of holdings of financial assets and in terms of holdings of claims on the business and individual sector. The individual institutions were described briefly in Chapter II, and the subsector's real sources and uses of funds are analyzed in Table 2. The end-of-1944 and 1959

TABLE 2

GOVERNMENT NONMONETARY INTERMEDIARIES: ANALYSIS OF SELECTED REAL SOURCES AND USES OF FUNDS

End-of-1944 and 1945–1959

	Millions of 1950 Pesos				Per Cent of Total Uses of Funds					Per Cent of Total Financial Sector				
	End 1944	1945–49	1950–54	1955–59	End 1944	1945–49	1950–54	1955–59	End 1959	End 1944	1945–49	1950–54	1955–59	End 1959
Real Sources of Funds														
Businesses and Individuals														
Nonmonetary	528	405	1575	278	46	16	39	6	21	25	21	55	7	25
Money	21	140	222	68	2	5	5	1	3	0.5	9	5	2	3
Total	549	545	1797	346	48	21	44	7	24	7	16	25	4	12
Rest-of-World														
Intermediary Liabilities	64	607	438	923	6	24	11	20	22	100	100	100	100	100
Int. Contingent Liabilities	0	43	420	1865	0	2	10	40	24	100	100	100	100	100
Government														
Capital and Deposits	399	750	360	874	35	29	9	19	18	73	88	85	81	83
Sales of Government Securities		162				6								
Financial Intermediaries (per cent net)	526	173	1304	472	9	10	24	13	15	17	21	48	20	30
Statistical Discrepancy	51	187	90	79	3	8	2	1	-3					
Total Classified Sources of Funds	1589	2467	4409	4559	100	100	100	100	100	14	38	40	31	33
Real Uses of Funds														
Businesses and Individuals														
Long-Term Loans and Securities	452	1851	2946	3124	39	73	73	67	69	42	61	79	67	69
Short-Term Loans	191	692	1008	1467	17	27	25	31	29	7	45	32	31	31
Total	643	2543	3954	4591	56	100	97	98	98	17	55	57	49	50
Government Securities	508		103	104	44		3	2	2	31	-10	21	13	8
Financial Intermediaries	438	-76	352	-136						12	*	14	-6	8
Total Classified Uses of Funds	1589	2467	4409	4559	100	100	100	100	100	14	38	40	31	33

Source: Appendix Tables 1, 7, 10, 16, and 26. All gold, silver, and foreign exchange evaluated with current exchange rates and assumed held by Banco de México. Foreign official loans with intermediary guar-antee are contingent liabilities.

* Aggregate financial sector quantity near zero.

balance sheets indicate that the government nonmonetary intermediaries' total financial assets went from 14 per cent to 33 per cent of those of the financial sector during this period and that their claims on businesses and individuals went from 17 per cent to 50 per cent of those of the financial sector. This rapid growth relative to that of the other financial subsectors occurred entirely during the 1945–49 and 1950–54 cycles; during the 1955–59 cycle private nonmonetary intermediaries became the fastest growing subsector, and the government nonmonetary intermediaries grew somewhat less rapidly than the total financial sector in terms of total financial assets and total claims on businesses and individuals.

Throughout the 1945–1959 period the government nonmonetary intermediaries used 97 per cent or more of their net classified funds to purchase claims on the business and individual sector. At the end of 1944 their government securities holdings were 44 per cent of their net classified financial assets, but during the 1945–49 cycle these holdings were reduced and only small quantities were purchased from 1950–1959. By the end of 1959 government securities were only 2 per cent of net classified assets, and they made up only 8 per cent of the government securities holdings of the entire financial sector. Of the funds allocated to the business and individual sector by the government nonmonetary intermediaries, a relatively constant 70 per cent were in the form of long-term loans and investments in securities—the highest percentage for any of the financial subsectors. Thus, in allocating funds the government nonmonetary intermediaries assigned virtually all their funds to the business and individual sector, and they allocated between two-thirds and three-fourths of these funds to long-term loans and investments. The long-term loans and investments of government nonmonetary intermediaries were only 42 per cent of those of the total financial sector at the end of 1944, but by the end of 1959 they were 69 per cent. During the 1950–54 cycle the flow of long-term funds from government nonmonetary intermediaries to businesses and individuals reached a phenomenal 79 per cent of that of the entire financial sector.

While the government nonmonetary intermediaries were quite specialized in their uses of funds, they drew on a wide variety of sources of funds. Between December 31, 1944, and December 31, 1959, the percentage of government nonmonetary intermediary net classified sources of funds provided by the various sectors changed as follows: businesses and individuals declined from 48 per cent to 24 per cent, the rest-of-world increased from 6 per cent to 46 per cent, the government declined from 35 per cent to 18 per cent, and other financial intermediaries increased from 9 to 15 per cent.

Analysis of government nonmonetary intermediary sources of funds for each of the cycles indicates the great flexibility of these institutions. During the 1945–49 cycle the government sector was the most important source of funds, with the rest-of-world sector second in importance. The business and individual sector was the most important source of funds in the 1950–54 cycle, with other financial intermediaries second in importance. During the 1955–59 cycle the rest-of-world provided 60 per cent of government nonmonetary intermediary funds, and the government sector was the next most important source of funds. Three major factors explain these changes in the relative importance of various sectors as sources of these intermediaries funds. First, during the 1945–49 and the 1955–59 cycles transactions described in Footnote 9 substantially increased the apparent relative importance of the government sector as a source of funds. Second, the private nonmonetary intermediaries, whose liabilities are relatively good substitutes for those of government nonmonetary intermediaries in business and individual portfolios, had a period of rapid growth during the 1945–49 cycle and a period of very rapid growth during the 1955–59 cycle, but during the 1950–54 cycle they grew very little. Finally, during the 1955–59 cycle the Mexican government nonmonetary intermediaries became extraordinarily adept at obtaining funds from the rest-of-world sector, primarily in the form of loans to Mexican businesses and individuals guaranteed by the government intermediaries.

THE DEPOSIT AND SAVINGS BANKS

Whereas the government nonmonetary intermediaries specialized in providing funds to the business and individual sector, the deposit and savings banks were highly specialized in receiving funds from that sector. Table 3 indicates that almost all of the deposit and savings banks' net classified sources of funds were from the business and individual sector, with monetary liabilities accounting for approximately three-fourths and nonmonetary liabilities and capital accounting for approximately one-fourth of the total. Monetary liabilities of deposit and savings banks

TABLE 3

DEPOSIT AND SAVINGS BANKS: ANALYSIS OF SELECTED REAL SOURCES AND USES OF FUNDS

End-of-1944 and 1945–1959

	Millions of 1950 Pesos				Per Cent of Total Uses of Funds					Per Cent of Total Financial Sector				
	End 1944	1945–49	1950–54	1955–59	End 1944	1945–49	1950–54	1955–59	End 1959	End 1944	1945–49	1950–54	1955–59	End 1959
Real Sources of Funds														
Businesses and Individuals														
Nonmonetary	848	443	913	892	25	35	28	27	28	40	24	32	23	27
Money	2554	695	2212	2617	76	55	68	80	73	45	46	51	61	54
Total	3402	1138	3125	3509	101	90	96	107	101	44	34	44	43	42
Financial Intermediaries (Per cent net)	360	379	258	602						12	46	10	26	15
Statistical Discrepancy	−35	117	125	−234	−1	10	4	−7	−1					
Total Classified Sources of Funds	3727	1634	3508	3877	100	100	100	100	100	32	27	31	26	28
Real Uses of Funds														
Businesses and Individuals														
Long-Term Loans and Securities	63	257	457	342	2	21	14	10	11	6	8	12	7	9
Short-Term Loans	1391	884	1378	1046	41	70	42	32	38	53	57	43	22	33
Total	1454	1141	1835	1388	43	91	56	42	49	39	25	27	15	21
Government Securities	96	118	148	801	3	9	5	25	13	6	7	31	101	39
Financial Intermediaries	2177	375	1525	1688	54	0	39	33	38	58	*	62	79	68
Total Classified Uses of Funds	3727	1634	3508	3877	100	100	100	100	100	32	27	31	26	28

Source: Appendix Tables 1, 8, 10, 17, and 26. All gold, silver, and foreign exchange evaluated with current exchange rates and assumed held by Banco de Mexico.
* Aggregate financial sector quantity near zero.

were a gradually increasing fraction of the Mexican money supply during this 1945–1959 period, but the nonmonetary liabilities of deposit and savings banks declined from 40 to 27 per cent of those of the financial sector during this period. These two divergent trends approximately offset each other, so that of the total liabilities and capital of financial institutions held by businesses and individuals, those of deposit and savings banks accounted for 44 per cent at the end of 1944 and 42 per cent at the end of 1959.

Deposit and savings bank balance sheets for the end of 1944 and 1959 indicate that between 40 and 50 per cent of the liabilities to businesses and individuals were matched by holdings of business and individual liabilities. But during the 1945–49 cycle deposit and savings banks provided to businesses and individuals approximately the same quantity of funds as was received from them, and during the 1950–54 cycle 56 per cent of net deposit and savings bank funds went to businesses and individuals. The importance of deposit and savings banks in relation to the financial sector in providing funds to businesses and individuals declined from 39 per cent to 21 per cent during the 1945–1959 period, with most of the decline occurring in the 1955–59 cycle. This decline in relative importance resulted from a decline in the relative importance of short-term lending by deposit and savings banks from 53 to 33 per cent of the financial sector, since deposit and savings bank long-term loans and securities increased from 6 to 9 per cent of those of the financial sector. The deposit and savings banks specialized in short-term lending to the business and individual sector—devoting only 2 per cent of their classified assets to long-term holdings in 1944 and 11 per cent in 1959—but compared to the pre-1945 period they became less specialized in this respect during the 1945–1959 period.

Government securities were purchased by Mexican deposit and savings banks in only minor quantities prior to 1955, but during the 1955–59 cycle 25 per cent of their funds were used to purchase government securities, and at the end of 1959 these securities were 13 per cent of net classified assets. During this cycle Banco de Mexico was disinvesting in government securities while deposit and savings banks were investing heavily in them. Whereas at the end of 1944 deposit and savings banks held only 6 per cent of the government securities held by the financial sector, at the end of 1959 they held 39 per cent. This major change in the portfolio distribution of deposit and savings banks resulted from very high reserve requirements on increments in deposit liabilities—requirements which could be satisfied by government securities as well as some other types of assets.

Deposit and savings banks were the only Mexican financial subsector that during the 1945–1959 period supplied more funds to other financial intermediaries than were received from other intermediaries. At the end of 1944 more than half of deposit and savings bank net classified assets were liabilities of the other financial intermediaries, but by the end of 1959 this figure was only 38 per cent. Most of the decline in the importance of other intermediary liabilities as uses of deposit and savings bank funds was registered during the 1945–49 cycle when these banks received approximately the same quantity of funds from other intermediaries as they supplied to other intermediaries. Although this use of funds declined in importance relative to total uses of deposit and savings bank funds, it increased from 58 to 68 per cent of the total financial sector's similar uses of funds between 1945 and 1959.

This analysis of the sources and uses of deposit and savings bank funds in Mexico from 1945–1959 indicates that businesses and individuals in Mexico chose to allocate to deposit and savings banks more than 40 per cent of the funds which they allocated to the total financial sector. But it also indicates that Mexican institutions effectively prevented the deposit and savings banks from allocating a similar quantity of funds to businesses and individuals, since more than half of these funds were diverted either to other financial intermediaries or to the government sector.[10] It is interesting to note that the rate of inflation in Mexico from cycle to cycle declined as the fraction of these funds so diverted increased (see Appendix Table 33).

THE PRIVATE NONMONETARY INTERMEDIARIES

Mexican private nonmonetary intermediaries included private financieras (by far the most important part of this subsector), mortgage loan banks, home savings and loan banks, capitalizers, and trust departments. These institutions specialized in dealing with businesses and individuals primarily; Table 4 indicates that regularly more than four-fifths of both

---

[10] Since interest earnings on government securities and on liabilities of other financial institutions were substantially lower than earnings on the same quantity of business and individual securities during this period in Mexico, it was necessary to use reserve requirements to force much of this diversion of funds.

TABLE 4

PRIVATE NONMONETARY INTERMEDIARIES: ANALYSIS OF SELECTED REAL SOURCES AND USES OF FUNDS

End-of-1944 and 1945–1959

	Millions of 1950 Pesos				Per Cent of Total Uses of Funds					Per Cent of Total Financial Sector				
	End 1944	1945–49	1950–54	1955–59	End 1944	1945–49	1950–54	1955–59	End 1959	End 1944	1945–49	1950–54	1955–59	End 1959
Real Sources of Funds														
Businesses and Individuals														
Nonmonetary	665	784	557	2630	81	85	90	95	93	31	42	20	69	47
Money	20	0	30	−27	2	0	4	−1	0	0.5	0	1	−1	0
Total	685	784	587	2603	83	85	94	94	93	9	23	8	32	21
Financial Intermediaries (per cent net)	326	212	164	871	22	19	8	5	6	11	26	6	37	15
Statistical Discrepancy	−47	−39	−14	18	−5	−4	−2	1	1					
Total Classified Sources of Funds	964	957	737	3492	100	100	100	100	100	8	16	7	24	15
Real Uses of Funds														
Businesses and Individuals														
Long-Term Loans and Securities	522	596	355	1070	63	65	57	39	45	49	20	10	23	19
Short-Term Loans	268	299	278	1329	33	32	45	48	45	10	19	9	28	20
Total	790	895	633	2399	96	97	102	87	90	21	20	9	26	20
Government Securities	33	25	−11	369	4	3	−2	13	10	2	2	−2	46	16
Financial Intermediaries	141	37	115	724						4	*	5	34	12
Total Classified Uses of Funds	964	957	737	3492	100	100	100	100	100	8	16	7	24	15

Source: Appendix Tables 1, 9, 10, 18, and 26. All gold, silver, and foreign exchange evaluated with current exchange rates and assumed held by Banco de Mexico.
* Aggregate financial sector quantity near zero.

their sources and uses of funds were accounted for by the business and individual sector. At the end of 1944 and during the 1945–49 cycle, other financial intermediaries supplied approximately one-fifth of the funds of these intermediaries, but during the remainder of the period the net funds from this source were negligible. However, this tends to obscure the fact that during the 1955–59 cycle, when the private financieras were growing at such phenomenal rates, deposit and savings banks were supplying substantial quantities of funds which were largely offset by financiera purchases of liabilities of government intermediaries to hold as reserves. Also during the 1955–59 cycle the financieras were required to invest in substantial quantities of government securities which accounted for 13 per cent of net classified uses of funds during this cycle whereas before their government securities purchases had been negligible. There was a progressive decline in the long-term funds in comparison to short-term funds provided by these intermediaries to businesses and individuals. At the end of 1944 and during the 1945–49 cycle approximately two-thirds were long-term funds, but during the 1955–59 rapid-growth cycle more than half were short-term, and at the end of 1959 short-term loans were approximately equal to long-term loans and investments in securities.

Perhaps the most significant statistics in Table 4 are those indicating the changes during the 1945–1959 period in the importance of the private nonmonetary intermediaries in relation to the total financial sector flows to and from businesses and individuals. Liabilities and capital of private nonmonetary intermediaries held by businesses and individuals went from less than one-tenth of those of the financial sector at the end of 1944 to more than one-fifth at the end of 1959. Of the nonmonetary indirect securities held by businesses and individuals, those of private nonmonetary intermediaries accounted for less than one-third at the end of 1944, for almost one-half at the end of 1959, and for an amazing 69 per cent during the 1955–59 cycle. As percentages of the total financial sector claims on businesses and individuals, those held by private nonmonetary intermediaries were approximately 20 per cent at both the beginning and the end of the 1945–1959 period, but short-term claims rose from 10 per cent to 20 per cent, while long-term claims declined from 49 per cent to 19 per cent.

Although during the later years of the period covered in this study the private nonmonetary intermediaries became the second most important financial subsector in capturing the savings of the Mexican public, Mexican financial authorities were successful in diverting a portion of these funds to purchases of government securities and liabilities of other financial subsectors.

TOTAL MONETARY INTERMEDIARIES

Banco de Mexico and the deposit and savings banks are combined in this section into a monetary intermediary subsector. In the following section the government and private nonmonetary intermediaries are combined into a nonmonetary intermediary subsector. Statistics on the funds flows of the monetary intermediary subsector are presented in Table 5, from which it is seen that almost all of the funds available to monetary intermediaries came from the business and individual sector. The major uses of these funds were short-term loans to businesses and individuals and holdings of gold, silver, and foreign exchange—together they accounted for approximately two-thirds of net classified uses of funds, with short-term loans being slightly the more important at the end of the period and rest-of-world liabilities being slightly the more important at the beginning of the period. Long-term claims on businesses and individuals rose from 1 per cent of net classified uses of funds at the end of 1944 to 9 per cent at the end of 1959 (with most of the increased importance occurring in the 1945–49 cycle) and net claims on other financial intermediaries declined from 15 per cent to 9 per cent. Although government securities holdings declined from 16 per cent of net classified uses of funds at the beginning of the period to 15 per cent at the end of the period, during the 1945–49 cycle this use accounted for 60 per cent of net classified uses of funds.

Thus the monetary intermediaries were specialists in receiving funds from the public primarily in the form of monetary liabilities—nonmonetary liabilities to businesses and individuals were slightly less than one-sixth at the end of 1944 and slightly more than one-sixth at the end of 1959 of total liabilities to the business and individual sector. But in importance relative to the total financial sector's liabilities held by businesses and individuals, the monetary intermediaries declined from 84 per cent to 67 per cent between the end of 1944 and 1959. This

TABLE 5

TOTAL MONETARY INTERMEDIARIES: ANALYSIS OF SELECTED REAL SOURCES AND USES OF FUNDS

End-of-1944 and 1945–1959

	Millions of 1950 Pesos				Per Cent of Total Uses of Funds					Per Cent of Total Financial Sector				
	End 1944	1945–49	1950–54	1955–59	End 1944	1945–49	1950–54	1955–59	End 1959	End 1944	1945–49	1950–54	1955–59	End 1959
Real Sources of Funds														
Businesses and Individuals														
Nonmonetary	942	693	724	925	14	24	15	16	17	44	37	25	24	28
Money	5583	1372	4086	4240	82	48	86	75	80	99	91	94	99	97
Total	6525	2065	4810	5165	96	72	102	91	97	84	61	67	64	67
Government Capital and Deposits	150	107	65	201	2	4	1	4	3	27	12	15	19	17
Financial Intermediaries (Per Cent of Total Net of Similar Uses)	2154	433	1237	1006		16		5		72	53	46	43	55
Statistical Discrepancy	156	221	−145	263	2	8	−3		0					
Total Classified Sources of Funds	8985	2826	5967	6635	100	100	100	100	100	78	46	53	45	52
Real Uses of Funds														
Businesses and Individuals														
Long-Term Loans and Securities	101	588	424	450	1	20	9	8	9	9	19	11	10	12
Short-Term Loans	2186	563	1872	1929	32	20	40	34	35	83	36	59	41	49
Total	2287	1151	2296	2379	33	40	49	42	44	61	25	34	25	30
Government Securities	1099	1720	387	323	16	60	8	6	15	67	108	81	41	76
Financial Intermediaries	3165	−34	2005	1547	15		16	10	9	84	*	81	72	80
Rest-of-World	2434	−11	1279	2386	36	0	27	42	32	100	100	100	100	100
Total Classified Uses of Funds	8985	2826	5967	6635	100	100	100	100	100	78	46	53	45	52

*Aggregate financial sector quantity near zero.

Source: Tables 1 and 3.

change resulted from the decline in the monetary intermediaries' relative share of nonmonetary liabilities from 44 per cent to 28 per cent during this period.

While they owed 87 per cent of the financial sector's liabilities to businesses and individuals at the end of 1944, the monetary intermediaries held only 61 per cent of the financial sector's claims on that sector. At the end of 1959 these percentages were 67 and 30, respectively. The monetary subsector's share of the long-term claims actually increased from 9 to 12 per cent during this period, but its share of short-term loans declined drastically from 83 per cent to 49 per cent. Thus, in the strategic matter of allocating funds to businesses and individuals, the decisions of monetary intermediaries declined significantly in relative importance during the period under study. Given the imperfections in the money and capital markets during this period in Mexico, which would be expected to preclude borrowers from having many alternative sources of loans, this decline in the relative importance of monetary intermediary allocation decisions may have reflected a declining relative importance of such inflationary and/or nondevelopmental uses of financial sector funds as for speculative inventory accumulation, consumer purchases, and purchases of foreign assets.

During the 1944–1959 period the monetary intermediaries increased their share of the financial sector's government securities holdings from two-thirds to three-fourths. However, during the 1955–59 cycle their real acquisitions of government securities were only 41 per cent of those of the financial sector.

TOTAL NONMONETARY INTERMEDIARIES

Whereas the monetary intermediaries regularly received more funds from the business and individual sector than they provided, the nonmonetary intermediaries regularly were net suppliers of funds to that sector. Table 6 shows that, although at the end of 1944 government securities holdings accounted for more than one-fourth of net classified assets, during the entire 1945–1959 period virtually all the nonmonetary subsector's funds were allocated to businesses and individuals. At the beginning of the period slightly more than two-thirds of these funds were

TABLE 6

TOTAL NONMONETARY INTERMEDIARIES: ANALYSIS OF SELECTED REAL SOURCES AND USES OF FUNDS

End-of-1944 and 1945–1959

	Millions of 1950 Pesos				Per Cent of Total Uses of Funds					Per Cent of Total Financial Sector				
	End 1944	1945–49	1950–54	1955–59	End 1944	1945–49	1950–54	1955–59	End 1959	End 1944	1945–49	1950–54	1955–59	End 1959
Real Sources of Funds														
Businesses and Individuals														
Nonmonetary	1193	1189	2132	2908	61	36	46	39	42	56	63	75	76	72
Money	41	140	252	41	2	4	5	1	2	1	9	6	1	3
Total	1234	1329	2384	2949	63	40	51	40	44	16	39	33	36	33
Rest-of-World														
Intermediary Liabilities	64	607	438	923	3	19	9	12	16	100	100	100	100	100
Int. Contingent Liabilities	0	43	420	1865	0	1	9	25	17	100	100	100	100	100
Government Capital and Deposits	399	750	360	874	20	23	8	12	13	73	88	85	81	83
Financial Intermediaries (Per Cent of Total Net of Similar Uses)	852	385	1468	1343	12	13	21	10	12	28	47	54	57	45
Statistical Discrepancy	4	148	76	97	2	4	2	1	-2					
Total Classified Sources of Funds	2553	3262	5146	8051	100	100	100	100	100	22	54	47	55	48
Real Uses of Funds														
Businesses and Individuals														
Long-Term Loans and Securities	974	2447	3301	4194	50	74	71	57	61	91	81	89	90	88
Short-Term Loans	459	991	1286	2796	23	30	27	37	34	17	64	41	59	51
Total	1433	3438	4587	6990	73	104	98	94	95	38	75	66	75	70
Government Securities	541	-137	92	473	27	-4	2	6	5	33	-8	19	59	24
Financial Intermediaries	579	-39	467	588						16	*	19	28	20
Total Classified Uses of Funds	2553	3262	5146	8051	100	100	100	100	100	22	54	47	55	48

Source: Tables 2 and 4.

* Aggregate financial sector quantity near zero.

long-term loans and investments; at the end of the period slightly less than two-thirds were long-term loans and investments, with the 1955–59 cycle showing the lowest relative long-term flow. At the end of 1944 businesses and individuals held 63 per cent of the nonmonetary intermediaries liabilities and capital; by the end of 1959 this figure had declined to 44 per cent as a result of the increased relative importance of the rest-of-world sector as a supplier of nonmonetary intermediary funds.

A relatively constant one-eighth of nonmonetary intermediary funds were supplied by other financial intermediaries; the government sector supplied one-fifth at the end of 1944 and only one-eighth at the end of 1959. As a supplier of nonmonetary intermediary funds the rest-of-world sector rose in relative importance from 3 per cent at the beginning to 33 per cent at the end of the 1945–1959 period. During the 1955–59 cycle the rest-of-world sector supplied almost as large a fraction of nonmonetary intermediary funds as did the business and individual sector.

As a percentage of the total financial sector the nonmonetary intermediary liabilities to businesses and individuals increased from 16 per cent at the beginning to 33 per cent at the end of the 1945–1959 period. But their nonmonetary liabilities were 56 per cent and 72 per cent, respectively, of those of the financial sector. Although nonmonetary intermediary liabilities to businesses and individuals were only 13 per cent of the financial sector's at the end of 1944, their claims on businesses and individuals were 38 per cent of the financial sector's. These percentages had risen to 33 and a phenomenal 70, respectively, by the end of 1959. And during both the 1945–49 and the 1955–59 cycles, nonmonetary intermediaries allocated three-fourths of the funds allocated to businesses and individuals by the financial sector. Regularly approximately nine-tenths of the long-term loans and investments of the financial sector were made by the nonmonetary intermediaries. Their short-term loans rose from 17 per cent of the financial sector's to 51 per cent by the end of the period.

Government securities holdings of nonmonetary intermediaries declined during the period from one-third to one-fourth of those of the financial sector. During the 1955–59 cycle, however, the nonmonetary intermediaries acquired 59 per cent of the government securities acquired by the financial sector.

It is not surprising that the Mexican nonmonetary intermediaries grew at a faster rate during this period than did the monetary intermediaries. But considering their relative importance at the end of 1944, it is surprising that the nonmonetary intermediaries so rapidly attained their dominant position with respect to the allocation of funds to the business and individual sector.

TOTAL PRIVATE INTERMEDIARIES

The deposit and savings banks and the private nonmonetary intermediaries are aggregated in this section to form a private financial subsector whose funds flows are presented in Table 7. Except for the 1945–49 cycle, when financial intermediaries provided 8 per cent of private intermediary net classified funds, the private intermediaries received virtually all of their funds from the business and individual sector. Nonmonetary liabilities and capital were only 60 per cent of monetary liabilities at the end of 1944, but by the end of 1959 they were slightly more important than monetary liabilities as a source of private intermediary funds. During both the 1945–49 cycle and the 1955–59 cycle, nonmonetary liabilities and capital issues were greater than new money issues of private intermediaries. During the entire 1945–1959 period the private intermediaries accounted for more than half of the public's purchases of indirect securities; the actual percentage rose from 53 per cent at the end of 1944 to 63 per cent at the end of 1959, with the 1955–59 cycle witnessing the private intermediaries capturing 75 per cent of the funds flowing from businesses and individuals to the financial sector. Private intermediaries accounted for an increasing share of both nonmonetary and monetary liabilities during this period, but the level of their dominance was much more pronounced in the nonmonetary market, where by 1960 they accounted for three-fourths of the liabilities and capital, versus only 54 per cent for monetary liabilities.

Whereas nearly all of private intermediary funds came from the business and individual sector during this period, at the end of 1944 only 56 per cent and at the end of 1959 only 65 per cent of private intermediary net classified assets were claims on businesses and individuals.

TABLE 7

TOTAL PRIVATE INTERMEDIARIES: ANALYSIS OF SELECTED REAL SOURCES AND USES OF FUNDS

End-of-1944 and 1945–1959

	Millions of 1950 Pesos				Per Cent of Total Uses of Funds					Per Cent of Total Financial Sector				
	End 1944	1945–49	1950–54	1955–59	End 1944	1945–49	1950–54	1955–59	End 1959	End 1944	1945–49	1950–54	1955–59	End 1959
Real Sources of Funds														
Businesses and Individuals														
Nonmonetary	1513	1227	1470	3522	38	56	38	60	51	71	66	52	92	74
Money	2574	695	2242	2590	64	32	59	44	49	45	46	52	60	54
Total	4087	1922	3712	6112	102	88	97	104	100	53	57	52	75	63
Financial Intermediaries (Per Cent net)	686	591	422	1473	−2	8	3	−4	0					
Statistical Discrepancy	−82	78	111	−216						23	72	16	63	30
Total Classified Sources of Funds	4691	2591	4245	7369	100	100	100	100	100	40	43	38	50	43
Real Uses of Funds														
Businesses and Individuals														
Long-Term Loans and Securities	585	853	812	1412	15	39	21	24	23	55	28	22	30	38
Short-Term Loans	1659	1183	1656	2375	41	54	43	40	42	63	76	52	50	53
Total	2244	2036	2468	3787	56	93	64	64	65	60	45	36	41	41
Government Securities	129	143	137	1170	3	7	4	20	12	8	9	29	147	55
Financial Intermediaries (Per Cent of Total Net)	2318	412	1640	2412	41		32	16	23	62	*	67	113	80
Total Classified Uses of Funds	4691	2591	4245	7369	100	100	100	100	100	40	43	38	50	43

* Aggregate financial sector quantity near zero.

Source: Tables 3 and 4.

The relative importance of this use of funds was much higher during the 1945–49 cycle (93 per cent) than during the two later cycles (64 per cent). Short-term loans were more important than long-term loans and investments in the portfolios of private intermediaries, but this tendency was less pronounced at the end than at the beginning of the period, since short-term loans declined from 74 to 65 per cent of the portfolio. This change, however, occurred largely during the 1945–49 cycle, when short-term loans were only 58 per cent of private intermediary real acquisitions of claims on businesses and individuals.

Although private intermediaries received an increasing share of the financial sector's funds from businesses and individuals during this period, their share in allocations of funds to them declined from 60 per cent to 41 per cent—during the 1950–54 cycle their share was only 36 per cent. This trend of declining relative importance of private intermediary to financial sector claims on businesses and individuals was present both for the long-term and the short-term portions of the flow. Private intermediaries, however, continuously allocated more than half of the short-term portion of the flow, while their share of the long-term flow (which was 55 per cent for the pre-1945 period) varied between 22 and 30 per cent during the three cycles of this study.

The substantial increases in private intermediary liabilities to businesses and individuals not matched by increases in their claims on this sector were devoted to purchases of government securities and liabilities of other intermediaries. Government securities purchases accounted for approximately 5 per cent of net classified uses of funds prior to 1955, but were 20 per cent during the 1955–59 cycle and by the end of the period were 12 per cent of net classified assets. This shift to government securities by the private intermediaries was largely at the expense of their holdings of liabilities of other intermediaries, since the total of these two types of assets remained almost constant at a little more than one-third of net classified uses of funds. While the private intermediaries were traditionally net suppliers of substantial amounts of funds to government intermediaries, their participation in the government securities market was unimportant relative to that of the government intermediaries prior to the 1955–59 cycle. But during that cycle the private intermediaries not only acquired almost all of the new issues of government securities, but also acquired a substantial quantity of government securities from Banco de Mexico's portfolio. Thus, by the end of 1959 the private intermediaries owned 55 per cent of the government securities held by the financial sector—having owned only 8 per cent at the end of 1944.

TOTAL GOVERNMENT INTERMEDIARIES

Banco de Mexico and the government nonmonetary intermediaries are grouped here into a government intermediary subsector whose activities during the 1945–1959 period are presented in Table 8. With respect to sources of funds, the most pronounced trends during this period were an increasing reliance on the rest-of-world sector and a decreasing reliance on the business and individual sector. From providing 68 per cent of government intermediary funds at the end of 1944, the business and individual sector declined to 42 per cent at the end of 1959 (and provided only 25 per cent during the 1955–59 cycle), while the rest-of-world share of government intermediary financing rose from 1 per cent to 27 per cent. Monetary liabilities to businesses and individuals declined from 56 per cent to 30 per cent of government intermediary sources of funds during this period, but nonmonetary securities remained constant at 12 per cent. Funds provided by the government sector rose slightly from 10 per cent to 13 per cent of the total during this period, and net funds provided by other intermediaries increased from 17 to 20 per cent of the total.

But the most important changes in the balance sheets of the government intermediaries during this 1945–1959 period were changes in the distribution of their assets. Between the end of 1944 and the end of 1959, government intermediary holdings of gold, silver, and foreign exchange declined from 45 per cent to 25 per cent of net classified assets; government securities holdings declined from 28 per cent to 7 per cent; and holdings of claims on businesses and individuals rose from 27 per cent to 68 per cent. Between these same dates holdings of short-term claims on businesses and individuals rose from 18 to 26 per cent of net classified assets, and holdings of long-term claims rose phenomenally from 9 to 42 per cent. With the exception of behavior with respect to government securities purchases, all these changes in the behavior patterns of government intermediaries were already obvious in the behavior of the flows of funds during the 1945–49 cycle.

TABLE 8

TOTAL GOVERNMENT INTERMEDIARIES: ANALYSIS OF SELECTED REAL SOURCES AND USES OF FUNDS

End-of-1944 and 1945-1959

	Millions of 1950 Pesos				Per Cent of Total Uses of Funds					Per Cent of Total Financial Sector				
	End 1944	1945–49	1950–54	1955–59	End 1944	1945–49	1950–54	1955–59	End 1959	End 1944	1945–49	1950–54	1955–59	End 1959
Real Sources of Funds														
Businesses and Individuals														
Nonmonetary	622	655	1386	311	12	16	23	4	12	29	34	48	8	26
Money	3050	817	2096	1691	56	21	35	21	30	55	54	48	40	46
Total	3672	1472	3482	2002	68	37	58	25	42	47	43	48	25	37
Rest-of-World														
Intermediary Liabilities	64	607	438	923	1	15	7	12	13	100	100	100	100	100
Int. Contingent Liabilities	0	43	420	1865	0	1	7	23	14	100	100	100	100	100
Government Capital and Deposits	549	857	425	1075	10	22	7	13	13	100	100	100	100	100
Sales of Government Securities														
Financial Intermediaries (Per Cent of Total Net)	2320	227	2283	876	17	18	24	20	20	77	28	84	37	70
Statistical Discrepancy	242	291	−180	576	4	7	−3	7	−2					
Total Classified Sources of Funds	6847	3497	6868	7317	100	100	100	100	100	60	57	62	50	57
Real Uses of Funds														
Businesses and Individuals														
Long-Term Loans and Securities	490	2182	2913	3232	9	55	48	41	42	45	72	78	70	72
Short-Term Loans	986	371	1502	2350	18	9	25	29	26	37	24	48	50	47
Total	1476	2553	4415	5582	27	64	73	70	68	39	55	64	59	59
Government Securities	1511	1440	342	−374	28	36	6		7	92	91	71	−47	45
Financial Intermediaries	1426	−485	832	−277						38	*	33	−13	20
Rest-of-World	2434	−11	1279	2386	45	0	21	30	25	100	100	100	100	100
Total Classified Uses of Funds	6847	3497	6868	7317	100	100	100	100	100	60	57	62	50	57

Source: Tables 1 and 2.

* Aggregate financial sector quantity near zero.

The most pronounced trends in the importance of government intermediaries relative to the financial sector as a whole from 1945 through 1959 were the increase from 45 per cent to 72 per cent in the share of long-term claims on businesses and individuals and the decline from 92 to 45 per cent in the share of government securities holdings. The government intermediaries at the end of 1944 received 47 per cent of the funds received by the financial sector from businesses and individuals and provided only 39 per cent of the financial sector's funds going to businesses and individuals; by the end of 1959 they received only 37 per cent and provided 59 per cent. Thus the government intermediaries became less specialized in capturing the savings of the public but became much more important in the decisions with respect to allocating funds to the public—particularly long-term funds.

THE FINANCIAL INTERMEDIARY SECTOR

Data on the total financial sector's real sources and uses of funds during the 1945–1959 period and balance sheet data for the end of 1944 and 1959 are presented in Table 9. Comparison of Columns 5 and 9 of Table 9 indicates the changes which occurred between 1944 and 1959 in the distribution of the financial sector's assets and liabilities. In 1944 for every two pesos of liabilities to businesses and individuals the financial sector had claims on them of only one peso, approximately. By the end of 1959 this relationship was approximately one peso for one peso, indicating that by that date the financial sector's holdings of claims on the government and rest-of-world sectors were matched by liabilities to those sectors rather than by liabilities to businesses and individuals as in 1944. Comparison of Columns 6, 7, and 8 indicates that this shift in asset and liability distribution was concentrated in the 1945–49 and the 1954–59 cycles, since the flows from and to the business and individual sector in the 1950–54 cycle were approximately equal.

At the end of 1944, of the total liabilities of the financial sector to businesses and individuals, only 27 per cent were nonmonetary liabilities, but by the end of 1959 nonmonetary liabilities were 42 per cent of this total. In each of the cycles the flow of nonmonetary liabilities was 40 per

TABLE 9

FINANCIAL INTERMEDIARY SECTOR: ANALYSIS OF SELECTED REAL SOURCES AND USES OF FUNDS

End-of-1944 and 1945–1959

	Millions of 1950 Pesos				Per Cent of Total Uses of Funds				
	End 1944	1945– 49	1950– 54	1955– 59	End 1944	1945– 49	1950– 54	1955– 59	End 1959
Real Sources of Funds									
Businesses and Individuals									
Nonmonetary	2135	1882	2856	3833	27	31	33	31	31
Money	5624	1512	4338	4281	72	24	50	34	42
Total	7759	3394	7194	8114	99	55	83	65	73
Rest-of-World									
Intermediary Liabilities	64	607	438	923	1	10	5	7	9
Int. Contingent Liabilities	0	43	420	1865	0	1	5	15	9
Government	549	857	425	1075	7	14	5	9	8
Statistical Discrepancy	−578	1260	164	574	−7	20	2	4	1
Total Classified Sources of Funds	7794	6161	8641	12551	100	100	100	100	100
Real Uses of Funds									
Businesses and Individuals									
Long-Term Loans and Securities	1075	3035	3725	4644	14	49	43	37	38
Short-Term Loans	2645	1554	3158	4725	34	25	37	38	36
Total	3720	4589	6883	9369	48	74	80	75	74
Government Securities	1640	1583	479	796	21	26	6	6	10
Rest-of-World	2434	−11	1279	2386	31	0	14	19	16
Total Classified Uses of Funds	7794	6161	8641	12551	100	100	100	100	100

Source: Tables 1, 2, 3, and 4.

cent or more of the aggregate flow from businesses and individuals, but this shift was most pronounced during the 1945–49 cycle when nonmonetary liabilities were 56 per cent of the total of monetary and nonmonetary liabilities. This high percentage for nonmonetary liabilities during the 1945–49 cycle resulted from an extraordinarily small aggregate flow of money rather than from an extraordinarily large aggregate flow of nonmonetary liabilities. The money supply of Mexico actually declined during 1946 and 1947 as a result both of post-war repatriation of funds deposited in Mexico during the war and capital flight in anticipation of the peso devaluation which occurred in 1948 and 1949. When the exchange rate was finally stabilized in 1949, a return flow began, but the bulk of this flow occurred in 1950 and, hence, added to the increase in monetary liabilities during the 1950–54 cycle. Were it possible to adjust the figures for these distortions, it is likely that the picture would be one of gradually increasing public preferences for nonmonetary liabilities over money rather than the erratic behavior indicated in Table 9.

With respect to the allocation of funds to businesses and individuals, changes in the financial sector's portfolio distribution were even more significant. At the end of 1944 approximately half of the total assets of the financial sector were claims on businesses and individuals; at the end of 1959 approximately three-fourths of total assets were such claims. Long-term loans and investments were only 29 per cent of financial sector claims on businesses and individuals in 1944, but by the end of 1959 they were 51 per cent. Thus during the 1945–1959 period, claims on businesses and individuals were increasing at a much more rapid rate than total assets of the financial sector, and long-term loans and investments were increasing at a much more rapid rate than short-term loans. This latter was especially true of the 1945–49 cycle, when the financial sector increased its long-term claims by approximately two pesos for each peso of increase in short-term claims, but during the 1955–59 cycle the amounts of increase in the long-term and short-term claims were approximately equal. When one considers that long-term loans and investments of the financial sector are more likely than short-term loans to finance fixed investment, and that short-term loans are more likely than long-term claims to finance consumer purchases and inventory speculation, then it is seen that these financial sector portfolio changes during the 1945–1959 period might have been significant factors in minimizing inflationary pressures while promoting developmental investment. This matter is analyzed at greater length in Chapter V, below.

Important changes occurred during this period in the relative importance of financial sector claims on and liabilities to the government sector. At the end of 1944 one-fifth of the financial sector's financial assets were government securities, but at the end of 1959 they accounted for only one-tenth of these assets. Only during the 1945–49 cycle did the financial sector's government securities holdings increase more rapidly than total financial claims. But during this cycle increases in financial sector liabilities and capital held by the government sector offset a little more than one-half of these increases in government securities holdings. At the end of 1944 the government sector held approximately one peso of financial sector liabilities and capital for every three pesos of financial sector holdings of government securities; by the end of 1959 this ratio was one for every one and one-fifth. Thus, after 1949 the financial sector was providing almost no net funds to the government sector.

During the 1945–1959 period the relative importance of gold, silver, and foreign exchange holdings was reduced by approximately one-half. At the end of 1944 almost one-third of the financial sector's classified assets were such holdings, but at the end of 1959 they accounted for only 16 per cent. Even more important is the fact that at the end of 1944 financial sector liabilities to the rest-of-world sector were negligible while at the end of 1959 they were one-eighth greater than the financial sector's holdings of gold, silver, and foreign exchange. Analysis of the flows of funds between the financial sector and the rest-of-world sector during this period shows that, even with the writing up of the peso value of exchange holdings accompanying the 1948–49 and 1954 devaluations, foreign loans to intermediaries were much greater in the 1945–49 cycle, somewhat less during the 1950–54 cycle, and slightly greater during the 1955–59 cycle than financial sector additions to gold, silver, and foreign exchange holdings.

The statistical discrepancy for the financial sector arises not only from differences between unclassified assets and unclassified liabilities, but also from differences between the quantities shown as owing to other intermediaries and due from other intermediaries. This latter difference accounts for approximately three-fourths of the statistical discrepancy

of the 1945–49 cycle—a discrepancy equal to two-fifths of total classified uses of funds. Since liabilities owing to intermediaries were not
classified by nationality of the intermediaries, it is likely that a major
portion of the large excess of liabilities due to intermediaries over claims
on intermediaries (which are foreign exchange holdings if the intermediary is foreign) was foreign short-term lending to Mexican intermediaries.

In summary, then, the major trends during the 1945–1959 period
were (1) an increased relative importance of nonmonetary relative to
monetary liabilities, (2) an increased relative importance of the rest-of-
world sector as a source of funds, (3) an increased relative importance
of the business and individual sector compared to the government and
rest-of-world sectors as a recipient of financial sector funds, and (4) a
greatly increased importance of long-term compared to short-term
lending to businesses and individuals.

CHAPTER IV

A Comparison of the Financial Sector with the Nonfinancial Sectors

IN ORDER TO assess the importance of the Mexican financial intermediaries in Mexican economic development, it is necessary to describe
the Mexican nonfinancial sectors in some detail. For this purpose flow-
of-funds tables for the nonfinancial sectors were compiled for the 1945–
1960 period; these are presented as Appendix Tables 21, 23, and 25.
The statistical procedures used in summarizing the flow of funds of the
financial sector were also used to summarize the flow of funds of the
nonfinancial sectors; these procedures are described in the preceding
chapter. Summaries of the real funds flows of the business and individual sector, the government sector, and the rest-of-world sector are
presented in this chapter. As each flow is discussed, its major limitations
are noted.[1] In these flow of funds tables theoretical precision in the
definitions was sometimes sacrificed in the interest of obtaining series
which covered the entire period.[2]

---

[1] The three major sources of the data in the flow-of-funds tables of the nonfinancial sectors are (1) the annual reports of Banco de Mexico and Nacional
Financiera; (2) the Spanish version of the Combined Mexican Working Party's
1953 study of Mexico—Raúl Ortiz Mena, *et al.*, *El desarrollo económico de
México y su capacidad para absorber capital del exterior* (México: Nacional
Financiera, S. A., 1953)—hereafter referred to as *CM*; and (3) Mexico's general
statistical yearbook, *Anuario Estadístico de los Estados Unidos Mexicanos*, published and compiled by the Secretaría de Industria y Comercio, Dirección General
de Estadística in Mexico.

[2] This consideration, for instance, was of decisive significance in defining financial intermediaries to exclude insurance companies. It also dictated leaving businesses and individuals together as one sector.

The statistical procedures described above gave data which are used here to accomplish two tasks. First, they are used to measure the importance of and trends in the importance of financial flows in Mexico in relation to output. Second, they are used as a step in the process of measuring the importance of and trends in the importance of Mexican financial intermediaries in relation to total finance in Mexico. For these purposes it was found convenient to express the real flows of a cycle as percentages of that cycle's real gross national product. Substantial margins of error are present in many of the series; however, for these purposes substantial margins of error are tolerable.

THE BUSINESS AND INDIVIDUAL
SECTOR FLOW OF FUNDS

An analysis of the real funds flows of the business and individual sector is presented in Table 10 for the 1945–1959 period.[3] The sources of this sector's funds include four categories: (1) nontransfer disposable income, (2) government transfers, (3) direct foreign investment, and (4) primary securities issues. Business and individual nontransfer disposable income was calculated by deducting the government sector's tax and miscellaneous receipts from gross national product. Government transfers are defined as all government spending not classified as investment spending, purchases of other goods and services, purchases of indirect securities, or repayments of the principal of government debt; less all government revenue not classified as tax and miscellaneous receipts or income from increases in indebtedness. Direct foreign investment was taken directly from the Mexican balance of payments published by Banco de Mexico in *BMIA* and hence is given no special definition here.

Ideally, primary securities issues would include several categories of financial claims which are not included here. The special definition of primary securities used here includes only (1) claims on businesses and individuals (including equities) owned by financial intermediaries; (2) long-term claims on businesses and individuals held by the rest-of-

[3] For sources and more detailed definitions of specific items see the notes to Appendix Table 21.

TABLE 10

BUSINESS AND INDIVIDUAL SECTOR: ANALYSIS OF SELECTED REAL SOURCES AND USES OF FUNDS

End-of-1944 and 1945–1959

	End 1944	Millions of 1950 Pesos			Per Cent of Gross National Product		
		1945–49	1950–54	1955–59	1945–49	1950–54	1955–59
Real Sources of Funds							
Nontransfer Disposable Income		165471	199788	272784	91.3	90.3	90.2
Government Transfers		2336	5601	8740	1.3	2.5	2.9
New Direct Foreign Investment (1944 is aggregate)	4262	1219	3055	4027	.7	1.4	1.3
Long-Term Loans and Open-Market Securities Issues	1348	3323	4369	6465	1.8	2.0	2.1
Short-Term Loans from Financial Sector	2647	1554	3158	4725	.9	1.4	1.6
Total Classified Sources of Funds	8257	173903	215971	296741	95.9	97.6	98.2
Real Uses of Funds							
Consumer Expenditures and Inventory Accumulation		149463	182385	247439	82.5	82.4	81.8
Fixed Investment							
Gross Private		15410	17638	28365	8.5	8.0	9.4
Government Enterprises		4063	6768	8321	2.2	3.1	2.8
Total Fixed Investment		19473	24406	36686	10.7	11.0	12.1
Financial Claims Purchases							
Open-Market Business and Individual (Excluding Equities)	272	288	644	1821	.2	.3	.6
Government Securities	221	−166	43	346	−.1	.0	.1
Nonmonetary Indirect Securities	2135	1882	2856	3835	1.0	1.2	1.3
Money	5624	1512	4336	4282	.8	2.0	1.4
Total Financial Claims Purchases	8252	3516	7879	10284	1.9	3.5	3.4
Statistical Discrepancy		1451	1301	2332	.9	.7	.8
Total Classified Uses of Funds		173903	215971	296741	95.9	97.6	98.2

Source: Table 9 and Appendix Tables 21–26.

world sector which were obtained through the intervention of government intermediaries; and (3) open-market fixed-interest claims on businesses and individuals held by other businesses and individuals. Thus, equities issued by businesses and individuals are included in the definition of primary securities only if they were owned by financial intermediaries. Were this a study of a country with a high degree of intrasectoral and intersectoral shifting of ownership of equities, this omission would be a serious limitation to the usefulness of the study. However, in Mexico trading in the equities of corporations does not occur in an appreciable amount.[4] Beginning in 1956 open-end investment companies were encouraged in Mexico, and three were functioning in 1960. These represent an attempt to stimulate investment in equities as a use of savings rather than for purposes of control.[5] Trade credit is also excluded from our definition of primary securities, and no attempt was made to measure the relative importance of this type of credit.

Uses of business and individual funds were divided into purchases of goods and services and purchases of financial assets. The former is divided into private investment, government enterprise investment, and consumer spending and inventory accumulation. Both categories of investment are defined here as they are defined in the sources from which they were taken directly, and they exclude inventory accumulation.[6] Inventory accumulation is included with consumer spending since separate estimates of these two types of spending were available only for the last few years of the 1944–1960 period. Consumer spending and inventory accumulation for the period 1944–1954 was computed as a residual by subtracting public purchases of goods and services, private fixed investment, and net foreign investment from gross national product. No special definition of government securities is used here; for business and individual primary securities as a use of funds, the special definition

[4] Nacional Financiera reported that, for the period January through April of 1960, only 3 per cent of the peso value of transactions on the Mexico City Securities Exchange (the largest in the country) were transactions in equities; for the same period a slightly smaller percentage obtained on the other Mexican securities exchanges if their transactions are combined. "El mercado de valores en los primeros cuatro meses," *El Mercado de Valores* (June 5, 1961), p. 276.

[5] For a description of the Mexican equities market in terms intended to be understood by those familiar with the United States securities markets, see John Morris Ryan, ed., *Handbook for the Foreign Investor in Mexico* (Second edition; Mexico: John Morris Ryan, 1961), pp. 118–153.

[6] See notes to Appendix Table 21.

of primary securities given above is used. Nonmonetary indirect securities and money are defined in the preceding chapter.

Business and personal disposable income (the sum of lines 1 and 2 in Table 10) rose slightly as a result of increased government transfers, from 92.6 per cent of gross national product to 93.1 per cent in the 1955–59 cycle. On the other hand, consumer purchases and inventory accumulation declined slightly from 82.5 per cent to 81.8 per cent. The investment spending of this sector increased from 10.7 per cent of gross national product in the 1945–49 cycle to 12.1 per cent during the 1955–59 cycle. Private investment accounted for approximately four-fifths of this investment in the 1945–49 and 1955–59 cycles and somewhat less than this during the 1950–54 cycle.

Table 10 shows important trends in the relative importance of various categories of financial claims as sources and uses of business and individual funds. Figures on the end of 1944 stock of financial claims included in this study are presented to give a rough indication of their relative importance as sources and uses of business and individual funds prior to 1945. From Table 10 it is seen that direct foreign investment and short-term loans from the financial sector were each more important, and together far more important, than long-term borrowing and open-market securities issues prior to 1945. But in each of the three cycles studied here long-term loans and securities issues were the most important financial source of funds, and during the 1945–49 cycle they accounted for more than 50 per cent of the total. Long-term loans and open-market securities issues rose from 1.8 per cent of gross national product during the 1945–49 cycle to 2.1 per cent during the 1955–59 cycle. New direct foreign investment nearly doubled between these two cycles as a percentage of gross national product—going from 0.7 per cent to 1.3 per cent. Short-term loans from the financial sector rose from 0.9 per cent of gross national product in 1945–49 to 1.6 per cent in 1955–59. Together these sources of business and individual funds roughly measure changes in the ratio of external finance to gross national product for this sector—it rose from 3.4 per cent in 1945–49 to 4.8 per cent in 1950–54 and to 5.0 per cent in 1955–59. Since domestic financial claims purchases by businesses and individuals were 1.9, 3.5, and 3.4 per cent during these periods, respectively, it is clear that the business and individual sector was consistently a net recipient of funds from other sectors from 1945–1959, whereas prior to 1945 it had been on average a balanced budget sector or possibly a surplus sector.[7]

Prior to 1945 businesses and individuals held more than two-thirds of their domestic financial claims in the form of money. However, during the 1945–49 and 1955–59 cycles less than 45 per cent of their real increments in holdings of domestic financial claims were money.[8] Holdings of government securities—always a minor use of Mexican business and individual funds—were actually reduced during the 1945–49 cycle, and real increments in government securities holdings were still only 0.1 per cent of gross national product during the 1955–59 cycle. Nonmonetary indirect securities acquisitions rose from 1.0 per cent of gross national product in 1945–49 to 1.3 per cent in 1955–59. Although business and individual holdings of open-market issues of other businesses and individuals were initially quite minor in importance, they increased steadily in importance from 0.2 per cent of gross national product in 1945–49 to 0.6 per cent in 1955–59.

As a use of business and individual funds to purchase financial claims, indirect securities purchases were of very great but declining importance during the 1945–1959 period in Mexico. During both the 1945–49 and the 1950–54 cycles, purchases of indirect securities accounted for more than 90 per cent of financial claims purchases, but during the 1955–59 cycle they were only approximately 80 per cent. From these statistics it is evident that, during this early period of rapid development, indirect finance was quite important in Mexico.

THE GOVERNMENT SECTOR FLOW OF FUNDS

Annual data on the government sector flow of funds are presented in Appendix Tables 23 and 24; sources and definitions of these series are found in the notes to Appendix Table 23. A summary of the government sector's real flow-of-funds tables is presented in Table 11. Only two sources of funds—nontransfer current income and government

---

[7] Since business and individual holdings of financial claims on the rest-of-world sector are not measured in this study, if they were added to the end of 1944 stocks of financial claims these latter would then exceed the stocks of liabilities.

[8] See the preceding chapter for an explanation of the erratic behavior of money in Mexico during the 1945–49 and 1950–54 cycles.

TABLE 11

GOVERNMENT SECTOR: ANALYSIS OF SELECTED REAL SOURCES AND USES OF FUNDS

End-of-1944 and 1945–1959

	End 1944	Millions of 1950 Pesos			Per Cent of Gross National Product		
		1945–49	1950–54	1955–59	1945–49	1950–54	1955–59
Real Sources of Funds							
Nontransfer Current Income (Taxes and Misc.)		15781	21566	29540	8.7	9.7	9.8
Government Securities Issues	2092	1099	185	732	.6	.1	.2
Statistical Discrepancy		328	151	−263	.2	.1	−.1
Total Sources of Funds		17208	21892	30009	9.5	9.9	9.9
Real Uses of Funds							
Government Fixed Investment		4814	5224	7840	2.7	2.4	2.6
Other Goods and Services Purchases		9201	10642	12354	5.1	4.8	4.1
Total Goods and Services Purchases		14015	15866	20194	7.7	7.2	6.7
Net Government Transfers		2336	5601	8740	1.3	2.5	2.9
Purchases of Financial Sector Liab. and Capital	549	857	425	1075	.5	.2	.4
Total Uses of Funds		17208	21892	30009	9.5	9.9	9.9

Source: Table 9 and Appendix Tables 21–26.

securities issues—are shown for the government sector in the flow-of-funds tables. Transfer income of the government sector is included as a deduction from transfer spending and is not shown separately. Government participation in dividend payments of government enterprises is included in current income, but government participation in the retained earnings of those enterprises and of government intermediaries is not included in government income. Government sources of funds are understated relative to uses of funds to the extent that the government participated in the retained earnings of financial intermediaries, since these retained earnings are treated as government purchases of the equities of financial intermediaries.

In the government's uses of funds, purchases of investment goods and purchases of other goods and services are shown separately. Government purchases of investment goods include expenditures for resource conservation as well as expenditures for fixed investment. Government transfers are defined to include all government spending reported but not elsewhere classified in the government's flow-of-funds tables, less all government income reported but not elsewhere classified. Government purchases of financial assets include only purchases of indirect securities; government purchases of business and individual securities (including those of government enterprises) are included in government transfers, since sufficient data to permit showing these separately for the entire period were not available.

Table 11 indicates that the government's tax and miscellaneous receipts increased as a percentage of gross national product from 8.7 per cent in 1945–49 to 9.8 per cent in 1955–59, but compared with more developed countries these percentages are still quite small. Government purchases of goods and services and government transfers together were slightly more than tax and miscellaneous receipts in 1945–49, approximately equal in 1950–54, and slightly less in 1955–59; hence, the government went from a deficit to a balanced budget to a surplus spending unit during the 1945–1959 period. Government fixed investment declined slightly as a fraction of gross national product from 2.7 per cent in 1945–49 to 2.6 per cent in 1955–59. Other government purchases of goods and services declined more substantially as a fraction of gross national product from 5.1 per cent in 1945–49 to only 4.1 per cent in 1955–59, while over the same period government transfers rose from 1.3 per cent to 2.9 per cent.

At the beginning of the 1945–1959 period, for each peso of Mexican government debt outstanding, the government sector owned one-fourth of a peso of claims on the financial sector. Real increments in government indebtedness were 0.6 per cent of gross national product in the 1945–49 cycle and afterwards between 0.1 and 0.2 per cent; however, real increments in government sector holdings of indirect securities (almost all nonmonetary indirect securities rather than money) used five-sixths of the 1945–49 funds and used substantially more than the 1950–59 funds received from government securities issues.

The above facts show that although the flow of funds to the government sector permitted an ever greater fraction of gross national product to be allocated by the government sector during this period, direct purchases of goods and services by the government declined in relative importance. Indirect government allocation through government enterprises and through other transfer payments increased rapidly in relative importance, while indirect allocation through government financial intermediaries declined somewhat as a percentage of gross national product.

THE REST-OF-WORLD SECTOR FLOW OF FUNDS

Appendix Tables 25 and 26 are annual data on the rest-of-world sector flow of funds; the notes to Appendix Table 25 indicate the sources of these data. Table 12 is a summary of the real flow of funds for the rest-of-world sector during the 1945–1959 period. Although data on exports and imports were taken directly from the Mexican balance of payments published by Banco de Mexico, the various capital account flows are given special definitions which do not necessarily coincide with similar concepts in the balance of payments. The two capital account flows from Mexico to the rest-of-world sector shown in the present study are (1) changes in Mexican financial sector holdings of gold, silver, and foreign exchange (which were taken from the financial intermediary balance sheets rather than from the balance of payments) and (2) reductions in foreign holdings of Mexican government debt (which were taken from figures on total external government debt outstanding less that held by Mexican financial intermediaries).

Direct foreign investment was taken from the balance of payments data. The financial claims flow from the rest-of-world sector to the

TABLE 12

REST-OF-WORLD SECTOR: ANALYSIS OF SELECTED SOURCES AND USES OF FUNDS

End-of-1944 and 1945–1959

	End 1944	Millions of 1950 Pesos			Per Cent of Gross National Product		
		1945–49	1950–54	1955–59	1945–49	1950–54	1955–59
Real Sources of Funds							
Mexican Imports		24866	37980	53064	13.7	17.2	17.6
Financial Sector Gold, Silver, and Exchange	2434	−11	1279	2386	.0	.6	.8
Statistical Discrepancy		−158	834	2150	−.1	.4	.7
Total Sources of Funds		24697	40131	57600	13.6	18.1	19.1
Real Uses of Funds							
Mexican Exports		23170	36677	51070	12.8	16.6	16.9
Direct Foreign Investment	4262	1219	3055	4027	.7	1.4	1.3
Mexican Government Securities	231*	−342	−459	−285	−.2	−.2	−.1
Long-Term Loans with Govt. Intermediary Guarantee	0	43	420	1865	.0	.2	.6
Loans Directly to Financial Sector	64	607	438	923	.3	.2	.3
Total Uses of Funds		24697	40131	57600	13.6	18.1	19.1

Source: Table 9 and Appendix Tables 21–26.

* Since no funds transfers were immediately involved, changes in debt due to renegotiations and due to devaluations of the peso are not in-cluded in the flows. This makes it appear as though the debt repayments were greater than the initial end-of-1944 stock.

business and individual sector includes only long-term claims on businesses and individuals that were acquired through the intervention of Mexican government nonmonetary intermediaries. This financial claims flow is a net flow in that repayments of these obligations were deducted; it is a gross flow in that Mexican acquisitions of similar securities were not deducted. Rest-of-world loans directly to the financial sector are defined to include only total nondeposit liabilities of Mexican government nonmonetary intermediaries stated in foreign currencies.

In view of the above special definitions the statistical discrepancy shown in Table 12 includes the following: (1) errors and omissions from the merchandise and invisibles accounts of the balance of payments; (2) capital account flows from the rest-of-world sector to Mexican financial intermediaries other than government nonmonetary intermediaries; (3) long-term and short-term capital flows from the rest-of-world sector other than the two flows specifically included, and (4) all long-term and short-term capital flows from the business and individual sector to the rest-of-world sector (except for repayments of the debts specifically included). This discrepancy shows a net flow of purchasing power from Mexico to the rest-of-world sector of −0.1 per cent of gross national product in 1945–49, 0.4 per cent in 1950–54, and 0.7 per cent in 1955–59. It appears reasonable to consider this as a net flow from the business and individual sector to the rest-of-world sector—largely a flow on capital account.

From Table 12 it is seen that Mexican exports as a percentage of gross national product increased significantly from 12.8 per cent in 1945–49 to 16.6 per cent and 16.9 per cent during 1950–54 and 1955–59, respectively. Imports moved with exports but at a higher level, so that the trade balance deficit was 0.9 per cent in 1945–49, 0.6 per cent in 1950–54, and 0.7 per cent in 1955–59. The remaining investigated flows of purchasing power from Mexico to the rest-of-world sector were financial sector exchange purchases, repayments of the principal of foreign-held Mexican government debt, and the statistical discrepancy. There was a strong upward trend during this 1945–1959 period in financial sector increments to foreign exchange holdings as a percentage of gross national product; although they were negligible in 1945–49, they were 0.6 per cent in 1950–54 and 0.8 per cent in 1955–59. Repayments of foreign-held Mexican government debt declined from 0.2 per cent of gross national product in 1945–49 to 0.1 per cent in 1955–59.

The statistical discrepancy rose from −0.1 per cent in 1945–49 to 0.4 per cent in 1950–54 and to 0.7 per cent in 1955–59. The sum of the trade balance deficit, increments in precious metal and exchange holdings, principal payments on government foreign-held debt, and the unclassified flow equaled 1.0 per cent of gross national product in 1945–49, 1.8 per cent in 1950–54, and 2.3 per cent in 1955–59. These last percentages also measure the investigated purchases by the rest-of-world sector of financial claims on the financial and the business and individual sectors.

In this study the three investigated financial flows from the rest-of-world sector to the other sectors are direct foreign investment, loans directly to the financial sector, and long-term loans to businesses and individuals with government intermediary guarantees. As a percentage of gross national product, the loans directly to the financial sector remained almost constant between 0.2 and 0.3 per cent. Loans with the financial sector's guarantee increased significantly in importance, rising from negligible amounts in 1945–49, to 0.2 per cent of gross national product in 1950–54 and to 0.6 per cent in 1955–59. Thus the funds from the rest-of-world sector that were liabilities or contingent liabilities of Mexican government intermediaries increased from 0.3 per cent of gross national product in 1945–49 to 0.9 per cent in 1955–59. This indirect finance, however, was never as important quantitatively as direct foreign investment, which increased from 0.7 per cent of gross national product in 1945–49 to 1.4 per cent in 1950–54 and to 1.3 per cent in 1955–59.

THE FINANCIAL SECTOR FLOW OF FUNDS COMPARED

In Table 13 the sources and uses of funds of the financial sector are shown as percentages of gross national product. Trends in the relative importance of the various sources of financial sector funds were discussed in the sections of this chapter which dealt with the sectors supplying these funds.

Let us first consider the activities of financial intermediaries in the government securities market. When government indirect securities pur-

TABLE 13

FINANCIAL INTERMEDIARY SECTOR:
REAL SOURCES AND USES OF FUNDS AS PERCENTAGE
OF GROSS NATIONAL PRODUCT

	1945–49	1950–54	1955–59
Real Sources of Funds			
Businesses and Individuals			
Nonmonetary	1.0	1.2	1.3
Money	.8	2.0	1.4
Total	1.9	3.2	2.7
Rest-of-World			
Intermediary Liabilities	.3	.2	.3
Intermediary Contingent Liabilities	.0	.2	.6
Government	.5	.2	.4
Statistical Discrepancy	.7	.1	.2
Total Sources of Funds	3.4	3.9	4.2
Real Uses of Funds			
Businesses and Individuals			
Long-Term Loans and Securities	1.7	1.7	1.5
Short-Term Loans	.9	1.4	1.6
Total	2.5	3.1	3.1
Government Securities	.9	.2	.3
Rest-of-World (Gold, Silver, and Foreign Exchange)	.0	.6	.8
Total Uses of Funds	3.4	3.9	4.2

Source: Table 9 and Appendix Tables 21–26.

chases are deducted from financial sector purchases of government securities, it is seen that the government sector was a net recipient of funds from financial intermediaries to the extent of 0.4 per cent of gross national product in 1945–49, but that the percentages were 0.0 in 1950–54 and −0.1 in 1955–59. It is helpful in interpreting the activities of the financial sector in the government securities market to summarize the activities of all sectors with respect to government debt. For the various sectors, real changes in government securities holdings as a percentage of gross national product were as follows:

Sector	1945–49	1950–54	1955–59
Rest-of-World	−0.2	−0.2	−0.1
Business and Individual	−0.1	0.0	0.1
Financial	0.9	0.2	0.3
Total	0.6	0.0	0.3

When the financial sector increased its holdings of government securities while the nonfinancial sectors were reducing their holdings, then in reality the financial sector was supplying funds to the business and individual sector or to the rest-of-world sector rather than to the government sector. Correcting for this factor to arrive at a measure of the financial sector's net financing of the government sector shows net financing as a percentage of gross national product to have been as follows:

1945–49	1950–54	1955–59
0.6	0.0	0.2

Finally, if from this net government financing by the financial sector the return flow of funds from the government to the financial sector in the form of purchases of indirect securities is deducted, then the financial sector's net government financing becomes the following percentages of gross national product:

1945–49	1950–54	1955–59
0.1	−0.2	−0.2

These data show that even though throughout the entire 1945–1959 period the financial sector was the most important purchaser of government securities in Mexico, (1) government deficit financing through the banking system does not explain a significant portion of Mexican inflation during the 1945–1959 period, and (2) government deficit financing through the banking system does not explain a significant portion of Mexican economic development during this period.

Although the financial sector as a whole was supplying only negligible net amounts of funds to the government sector during the entire 1945–1959 period, during the 1955–59 cycle the private financial subsector's real increments in government securities holdings were 0.4 per cent of gross national product. On the other hand the government intermediaries were receiving funds from the government sector equal to 0.4 per cent of gross national product and were selling government securities equal to 0.1 per cent of gross national product. These facts may be of significance in explaining Mexican price and production experience if significant differences existed between the allocation decisions of government intermediaries and those of private intermediaries. The government intermediaries were, in effect, allocating funds totaling 0.5 per cent of gross national product and coming almost entirely from the private intermediaries ultimately. During this 1955–59 cycle the rate of inflation was only approximately half of that during the two previous cycles, and the rate of increase in gross national product was somewhat higher.

Let us now consider the net transactions of the financial and government sectors with the rest-of-world sector. From Table 12 it is seen that the rest-of-world sector supplied to the financial sector, either directly or with financial sector guarantee, the following flow of funds as a percentage of gross national product:

1945–49	1950–54	1955–59
0.3	0.4	0.9

However, the rest-of-world sector drained funds from Mexican development financing by reducing its holdings of Mexican government debt. When repayments of Mexican government foreign-held debt are deducted from the above figures, the rest-of-world sector's contribution to the financing of Mexican development plans (as a percentage of gross national product) becomes the following:

1945–49	1950–54	1955–59
0.1	0.2	0.8

Funds were also drained from Mexican development financing through increases in Banco de Mexico's holdings of gold, silver, and foreign exchange. Adjustment for this factor leaves a net contribution of the rest-of-world sector as follows:

1945–49	1950–54	1955–59
0.1	−0.4	0.0

These figures show clearly that during the 1950–54 and 1955–59 cycles Mexico could have financed as many imports by refraining from accumulating foreign exchange reserves as could have been financed with the net loans from the rest-of-world sector to the government and financial sectors.

Just as comparison of the participation of the various sectors in the government securities market revealed that financial intermediaries dominated the demand side of that market, so also comparison of the various sectors' participation in the market for business and individual securities shows that the financial sector's influence was dominant. The following figures summarize real increases in holdings of business and individual securities as percentages of gross national product:

Sector	1945–49	1950–54	1955–59
Business and Individual	0.2	0.3	0.6
Financial (Short-Term)	(0.9)	(1.4)	(1.6)
(Long-Term)	(1.7)	(1.7)	(1.5)
(Total)	2.5	3.1	3.1
Total Issues	2.7	3.4	3.7

These figures indicate that the financial sector absorbed 93 per cent of business and individual securities issues in 1945–49, but that this percentage declined to 91 per cent in 1950–54 and to 84 per cent in 1955–59. If only long-term open-market securities issues are considered, a more pronounced trend in the same direction is observed in the relative importance of indirect finance—it went from 89 per cent in 1945–49 to 85 per cent and 71 per cent in the 1950–54 and 1955–59 cycles, respectively. Not only is it important to note from the above figures the declining importance of indirect compared to direct finance, it is also important to note the rather sharp increase in the percentage relationship between total issues and gross national product. This rising issues-income ratio is one measure of the success in developing a capital market in Mexico during the 1945–1959 period, and the declining relative importance of the financial sector in that market is an indication of the success in inducing the participation of businesses and individuals in the demand side of that securities market.

Finally we consider the importance of the financial sector in investment spending in Mexico. The following figures show real investment spending as a percentage of real gross national product for the three cycles:

Sector	1945–49	1950–54	1955–59
Private	8.5	8.0	9.4
Government Enterprise	2.2	3.1	2.8
Government	2.7	2.4	2.6
Total	13.4	13.5	14.8

It is clear from these figures that government enterprise investment was responsible for preventing a substantial decline in the investment ratio during the 1950–54 cycle and that private investment was responsible for the large increase in the investment ratio during the 1955–59 cycle. The following figures summarize various sources of investment financing in Mexico:

Source	1945–49	1950–54	1955–59
Business and Individual Issues			
Direct	0.2	0.3	0.6
Indirect	2.5	3.1	3.1
Total	2.7	3.4	3.7
Government Indirect Issues	0.1	..	..
Taxes (at least)	2.6	2.4	2.6
Other Domestic Savings	7.1	7.1	7.8
Total Domestic Savings	12.5	12.9	14.1
Trade Balance Deficit	0.9	0.6	0.7
Total Investment	13.4	13.5	14.8

Thus from 1945–1959 the rest-of-world sector financed between 4 and 7 per cent of gross investment, and domestic savings financed the rest. The above figures indicate that between 15 and 20 per cent of gross investment was financed through taxation; however, this is an understatement of the relative importance of taxes, since these figures do not take into consideration that portion of government enterprise investment financed through government transfer payments. The financial sector, through supplying funds to businesses and individuals and to the government, financed approximately one-fifth of gross investment in each of the cycles. This leaves slightly more than one-half of gross investment financed during this period by retained earnings, depreciation allowances, and direct finance. If it is assumed that replacement investment was 6 per cent of gross national product during these cycles, then the financial sector financed between one-third and two-fifths of net investment during this 1945–1959 period.

Among the important aggregate economic statistics not included in the various tables of real sources and uses of funds are the incremental capital-output ratio and the rates of increase in output, population, and prices. Mexico's incremental capital-output ratio was quite low during the 1945–1959 period and apparently was rising slowly. Based on data from Table 14, this ratio was as follows:

1945–49	1950–54	1955–59
2.66	2.80	2.96

The average compound rate of increase in real gross national product was high and rising somewhat during this period in Mexico. Industrial production (including manufacturing, mining, petroleum, construction, electricity, and transportation) showed a sharply rising rate of increase, while that of agricultural production was declining sharply. Total industrial and agricultural production was rising at an increasing rate during the 1945–1959 period. Based on data from Appendix Table 29, the average annual compound rates of increase in production were as follows:

	1945–49	1950–54	1955–59
Industrial	4.4	5.0	7.3
Agricultural	7.0	6.0	3.0
Industrial and Agricultural	5.3	5.4	5.7
Gross National Product	5.1	4.9	5.4

As is shown in Appendix Table 32, agricultural production accounted for approximately 20 per cent of gross national product, while industrial production accounted for approximately 30 per cent. Population increased by an average of approximately 3 per cent per year during the 1945–1959 period, and there was a weak upward trend in this rate of increase. The rate of increase in the price level was high but declined sharply during the 1945–1959 period. From Appendix Table 33 it is seen that the following percentage increases in the Mexico City General Wholesale Price Index occurred during the indicated cycles.

	1945–49	1950–54	1955–59
Entire cycle	59.0	51.0	31.0
Annual average	9.6	8.3	4.7

Although the figures presented in this chapter in many respects are incomplete measures of financial flows in Mexico during the 1945–1959 period, one may safely conclude that financial intermediaries during this period dominated the market for government securities, the market for short-term funds for businesses and individuals, and the market for long-term funds for businesses and individuals. One may also conclude that government deficit financing was relatively insignificant, as was net financing by the rest-of-world sector. Hence, the significant changes which occurred in the structure of the financial sector in Mexico were quite important to total finance in Mexico. Having established this fact, let us now examine evidence that the high and increasing share of government intermediary and nonmonetary intermediary allocation of financial sector funds was related significantly to Mexico's experience of rising rates of real growth and declining rates of inflation.

CHAPTER V

Financial Intermediaries and Economic Development in Mexico

THE broad and sweeping picture of Mexican financial intermediaries and of the Mexican economy during a period of rapid industrialization which has been presented in the earlier chapters provides a background for observations of possible causal relationships. The historical background presented in Chapter II showed Mexico during the late 1920's and the following decade regularly attempting to remove financial impediments to economic development by establishing specialized, government-owned financial intermediaries. The wholesale revisions in Mexico's financial system during the early 1940's were followed by frequent new changes as additional financial impediments developed and as old financial impediments were revealed. This financial development process tended more and more toward the use of discretionary control rather than specific legal dictates. By 1960 the Mexican financial system was an efficient, coordinated group of highly diversified institutions which could be mobilized quickly for financing development plans. Emphasis during the late 1950's appeared to center on improvements in the organizational techniques necessary for efficiency in such a diversified system.

The statistical descriptions in Chapter III of the funds flows of the various financial subsectors showed each to have been relatively specialized in the performance of particular financial functions. The most noticeable degrees of specialization were present in the deposit and savings subsector and the government nonmonetary intermediary subsector. Deposit and savings banks were quite specialized as recipients of funds from businesses and individuals. Private nonmonetary intermediaries were specialized both in receiving funds from and supplying funds to the business and individual sector. During the period acquisitions of government securities shifted from Banco de Mexico to the private intermediaries. With the high and increasing levels of specialization went an increasing importance of inter-intermediary flows of funds. These flows were of special significance as evidence that the Mexican financial intermediary was not limited in its allocations of funds by its ability to sell liabilities to the public. Inter-intermediary funds flows were presented as evidence of the possibility in Mexico of reallocating funds within the financial sector so as to eliminate financial impediments to economic development.

The description in Chapter III of the relative importance of the various financial subsectors to particular flows showed major trends in the declining importance of deposit and savings banks and the increasing importance of private nonmonetary intermediaries. Like most of the other trends observed, these trends to a significant extent were the results of policy decisions. The control mechanisms available to the financial authorities were sufficient either to permit or prevent the progress of significant trends.

In Chapter IV the descriptions of the nonfinancial sectors showed low but increasing levels of taxation and investment compared to income. That chapter also showed the active participation of the government in the process of economic development, through the government enterprises included in the business and individual sector as well as through the government sector proper. Together the government enterprises and the government sector accounted for approximately one-third of investment expenditures during the 1945–1959 period. Nevertheless, a vigorous and growing private sector was evidenced by the fact that private investment as a fraction of total investment was almost constant during the period. With respect to purchases on the goods and services markets, the rest-of-world sector was shown to have been more than twice as important a purchaser and seller as the government sector.

The comparison of the various sectors with respect to flows of financial claims revealed the financial sector as the overwhelmingly dominant influence in the government securities market, the money market, and the market for business and individual securities. However, this dominance showed a downward trend with respect to the market for business and individual securities, since both other businesses and individuals and the rest-of-world sector were providing increasing portions of this type of financing.

Finally, it was shown that Mexico during this period from 1945–1959 experienced high and rising rates of increase in industrial and agricultural production. Mexico also experienced a high but sharply declining rate of inflation during this period. Evidence was presented that suggested low and relatively constant incremental capital-output ratios for industrial and agricultural output.

The relationships and trends of the Mexican economy presented in broad outline in the preceding chapters show the historical experience of the financial intermediaries during economic development. All the trends present in the various series of data presented in these chapters were consistent with high and increasing rates of growth of industrial and agricultural production and with high and declining rates of inflation. When a theory of the relation of finance to economic development is applied in interpreting these data, they may tend to support or to oppose the theory.

The theory which was presented in Chapter I postulated that the allocation decisions of financial intermediaries were of primary significance to economic development; hence, we proposed to concentrate this analysis on the allocation function of intermediaries. The entire picture of Mexican intermediaries drawn in the earlier chapters shows that they were a group of specialists. In many cases this specialization by private intermediaries resulted from legal requirements and policy prescriptions. The specialized government intermediaries were created in most cases specifically with a view to their performing special functions.

One might argue that if legal requirements and policy prescriptions had been removed, private intermediaries would have been less specialized in their allocation of loanable funds. It is quite probable that in the absence of a legal categorization of private intermediaries, categories of private intermediaries would have been less distinct. Deposit and savings banks would probably have issued securities similar to those issued by nonmonetary intermediaries; the nonmonetary intermediaries would probably have held a relatively larger quantity of demand deposits. The deposit and savings banks would probably have made a greater quantity of long-term loans and investments; the nonmonetary intermediaries would probably have made a relatively larger quantity of short-term loans. This greater diversification in the sources and uses of funds of particular private intermediaries may have increased the profitability of particular private intermediaries and of private intermediaries as a group. Had all these events occurred in Mexico, then an analysis of intrafinancial-sector funds transfers between private intermediaries would have not been so necessary in the present study. An analysis more nearly resembling that of Gurley and Shaw, which assumes an intermediary's sales of liabilities to the business and individual sector to fix the amount of its primary securities purchases from the public, could have been used to discuss the private intermediaries in Mexico.

However, the facts are that Mexican private intermediaries were specialized during this 1945–1959 period, as they have always been specialized in Mexico. With a view toward developing a market for long-term securities, the pattern and level of interest rates on indirect securities and primary securities were set by Banco de Mexico and Nacional Financiera. In view of this, one cannot assume that the quantity of its liabilities which an intermediary could entice the public to hold would provide the optimum quantity of funds for financing the businesses and individuals to whom that intermediary specialized in lending. The specialization of intermediaries with respect to borrowers, the specialization of borrowers with respect to intermediaries, and the specialization of intermediaries and lenders with respect to indirect securities were important Mexican institutional characteristics which were not subject to sudden change. Intrafinancial-sector funds flows served in this environment to make possible an allocation of funds to businesses and individuals by private intermediaries on a basis determined by variables other than the allocation of funds by businesses and individuals among various types of indirect securities.

When one assumes a highly competitive, nonspecialized financial market structure, the interruption of an intrafinancial-sector flow of funds could be assumed to have only minor and short-lasting effects on the allocation of funds by intermediaries. In such an assumed situation the source of supply of funds to a particular intermediary that had been interrupted could be assumed to be replaced quickly by appropriate adjustments in the interest rates on other liabilities of that intermediary (among other adjustments). In the Mexican case, the interruption of these intrasector flows could not reasonably be expected to have such minor effects. A policy decision, for instance, to prevent deposit and savings banks from purchasing the liabilities of *financieras* would reasonably be expected in Mexico to have resulted in a more or less permanent reduction in the funds available to *financieras*. Hence, it is reasonable to assume that in such an event the specialized group financed by these *financieras* would experience a rather long-lasting relative scarcity of loanable funds. The type of funds allocation decisions made by *financieras* would be reduced compared to other funds allocation decisions.

These points are particularly relevant to the present theory of the relationship between Mexican financial intermediaries and Mexican economic development. This theory rests on the premise that marginal adjustments in prices and interest rates did not make and could not have made the observed specialization of financial intermediaries trivial. This theory assumes that, with a smaller quantity of funds available to it, a Mexican financial intermediary would have continued to allocate its available funds to various uses in approximately the same proportions as the larger quantity was allocated. This theory also assumes that alternative sources of supply of loanable funds were available to borrowers only after the lapse of a time interval of sufficient length, or at rates of interest sufficiently higher, to influence significantly the time pattern and quality of investment spending.

Since government intermediaries in Mexico did not depend for their continued operation on the accounting relationships between their net income and their expenses on current account, their decisions were especially important in economic development. These government intermediaries could consider social costs and social benefits in their allocations of loanable funds—their allocation decisions could be decisions planned for contribution to national product rather than profit.

The government intermediaries also were not limited in the quantity of funds which they allocated by the market demand for those funds. If development plans indicated that a particular manufacturing plant would be desirable, Mexican customs permitted any one of several alternative approaches to be used in establishing and financing that plant. If a private demand for that type of plant existed, Nacional Financiera probably would have provided funds to a private group or arranged for a private *financiera* to provide the funds. If no private demand existed, then a demand from one of the corporations in which Nacional Financiera was majority stockholder could have been created or the government could have established a new government enterprise for carrying out the task. These are all examples of techniques which were used during this 1945–1959 period to prevent prices and interest rates from determining the quantity of funds allocated by government intermediaries.

Thus, both on the side of demand by businesses and individuals and on the side of supply by the intermediaries, the allocations of loanable funds by the government intermediaries were not necessarily determined by market prices and interest rates. This fact means that these intermediaries were in a position to act as the source of financing for new firms, for investment in social overhead capital, and for investments in basic industries—in short, for risky and privately unprofitable projects.

The funds available to these government intermediaries were from government tax revenues, from the rest-of-world sector, from sales of liabilities to the business and individual sector, and from other financial intermediaries. Given the quantity of funds from the government and rest-of-world sectors, in the absence of inter-intermediary funds flows the quantity of funds available to government intermediaries would have been determined by the public's demand for their liabilities. The government intermediaries engaged in a substantial amount of indirect security diversification and interest rate manipulation in an attempt to increase the public's demand for government intermediary liabilities.

However, the final step in severing the connection between the quantity of funds allocated by government intermediaries and market prices and interest rates, just as in the case of private intermediaries in Mexico, was inter-intermediary funds flows subject to determination by policy prescriptions. With these intrasector flows of funds the institutional impediments to a developmental allocation of financial intermediary funds were reduced significantly. In effect the aggregate real flow of funds to the entire financial sector could be reallocated among the intermediaries, instead of matching allocations by one intermediary with a specific portion of that flow. Hence, the preferences of businesses and individuals for particular indirect securities did not necessarily determine the quantity of funds which were allocated by any financial institution. That intermediaries specialized with respect to borrowers, that borrowers specialized with respect to intermediaries, that some developmental projects involved substantial risks, that some developmental projects resulted in inappropriable products—all these did not for this reason necessarily impede economic development owing to inadequate financing.

Without intrafinancial-sector funds transfers all of the above institutional characteristics of the Mexican economy would have been financial impediments to economic development. Finance would have provided a bottleneck in the economic development of Mexico, since some projects which were technically feasible and which were necessary for further development would not have been adequately financed. Within the government intermediary subsector, Banco de Mexico could still have created money for financing development projects. However, without sterilization of these funds through intrafinancial-sector transfers (100 per cent reserves on increments in deposit liabilities of deposit and savings banks, for instance), an undesirable inflationary situation might have resulted from this money creation.

On the basis of the statistical data presented in this study it is possible to estimate roughly the size of the adverse effect on economic development of a decision to eliminate the transfers of funds among intermediaries in Mexico during the 1945–1959 period. One of the measurable differences in the allocation decisions of financial intermediaries is the quantity of long-term compared to total financing of businesses and individuals that an intermediary chooses to provide. The institutional patterns of Mexico, as of other capitalistic economies, make long-term financing a requirement for establishing new going concerns, for adding in a major way to old going concerns, and for carrying out any spending project that is large in relation to the spender's income. This financing may come from the accumulated savings of the spending unit carrying out the spending project, or it may come through a flow of long-term funds to spending units. Abstracting from cyclical effects and from income redistribution in the long period, one would expect the aggregate quantity of financing from the accumulated savings of the spender to be largely determined by past income. If aggregate income had been increasing, then one would expect the quantity of such financing to be growing at approximately the same rate. There would be little reason to expect this long-term financing of individual spending plans from the individual spenders' savings to raise the growth rate of output.[1]

However, particularly in a country less developed industrially than

[1] Downward trends in either the long-run propensity to consume or the incremental capital-output ratio would be exceptions to this statement.

some others, there would exist a continuously increasing backlog of technically feasible spending projects requiring long-term financing and not matched with spending units that had accumulated the necessary savings. Long-term direct finance, long-term funds from the rest-of-world sector, or long-term funds from financial intermediaries could remove this financial impediment to economic development. If the backlog of technically feasible spending projects were large relative to the spending projects which could be financed with the spending unit's accumulated savings, then one would expect output to be quite responsive to changes in the flow of long-term funds to businesses and individuals.[2] If the flow of long-term funds to businesses and individuals were large compared to the backlog of projects, then output would be significantly more responsive to a decrease than to an increase in the flow. If the backlog were large compared to the flow of long-term funds, then output would be quite responsive to both an increase and a decrease in the flow.

Traditional financing—depreciation allowances, retained earnings, direct investment of accumulated savings and short-term loans from the financial sector—was assumed in Chapter I to be a function of real income; hence, if the capital-output ratio is constant, this traditional financing would finance traditional investment sufficient to maintain a constant per capita output. Innovation financing includes the following: (1) the real flow of long-term funds to the business and individual sector from issues of bonds, open-market issues of equities, and long-term loans from the financial sector; (2) real new direct foreign investment; (3) real government securities issues; and (4) real increases in tax collections more than sufficient to maintain a constant level of real per capita taxation.[3]

In Chapter I it was also assumed that significant increases in per capita output require innovation financing. Innovation financing can affect per capita output either through increasing the rate of capital accumulation or through changing the capital-output ratio, or both. To test the rele-

---

[2] If the backlog were not relatively large (which is unlikely in an underdeveloped economy), then by assuming that projects with significantly lower incremental capital-output ratios were chosen by the former savers, (1) the flow of long-term funds might finance projects with relatively high incremental capital-output ratios, and (2) the total number of available projects might be quickly exhausted.

[3] This latter assumes that traditional government spending is customarily equal to tax collections, so that increases in per capita tax collections are only temporarily available as a source of innovation financing.

vance of the hypothesis that innovation financing is required for significant increases in per capita output, let us call the increase in output more than sufficient to maintain a constant per capita output O^* and let us call real innovation financing adjusted for changes in the incremental capital-output ratio between observations F^*. In a traditional economy, since O^* is at or near zero, the hypothesis is that F^* is also at or near zero. The early years of the industrialization effort are accompanied in this theory by an elasticity of O^* with respect to F^* of approximately unity, so that during this period a relatively constant relationship exists between increments in O^* and increments in F^*. This theory is presented diagramatically in Figure 1, and it is suggested that

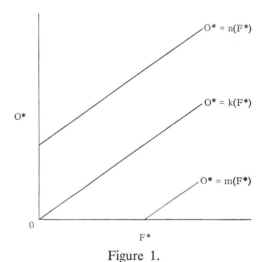

Figure 1.

observations for various periods during the early years of industrialization would fall on a straight line through the origin similar to $O^* = k(F^*)$. If observations fell on a line similar to $O^* = n(F^*)$, this would support the hypothesis that traditional financing (reinvested profits, depreciation allowances, and direct investment of accumulated savings) is more than sufficient to maintain a constant per capita output. However, if observations fell on a line similar to $O^* = m(F^*)$ the hypothesis that traditional financing is less than sufficient to maintain a constant per capita output would be supported.

In applying this theory to observations of Mexican experience, the following equation was used for $O^* = kF^*$:

$$\Delta 0 - \left(\frac{0_{t-n} + 0_{t-n+1}}{2} \cdot \frac{N_t - N_{t-n}}{N_{t-n}} \right) = k \left[\frac{\Delta 0}{I} \cdot \frac{I_b}{\Delta 0_b} \right]$$

$$\left[\sum_{i=t-n+1}^{t} \frac{B_i + G_i + F_i + \Delta T_i}{p_i} - \left(\frac{T_{t-n}}{p_{t-n}} \cdot \frac{N_t - N_{t-n}}{N_{t-n}} \right) \right]$$

where

0   is real gross national product,

N is population,

$\Delta 0$ is $\dfrac{0_t + 0_{t+1}}{2} - \dfrac{0_{t-n} + 0_{t-n+1}}{2}$,

I is aggregate real gross investment spending for a cycle,

B is the annual change in the outstanding stock of long-term business and individual indebtedness and new open-market issues of equities,

G is the annual change in the outstanding stock of government securities,

F is new direct foreign investment,

T is government tax receipts,

p is an index of prices divided by one hundred,

t is the final year included in a business cycle,

n is the number of years in the cycle in question,

b denotes the value of a variable in a base cycle, and

k is the relation between innovation financing and increases in output more than sufficient to provide the initial population and increments in the population the initial per capita output.

In words, the left side of the equation is the change during a business cycle in aggregate annual output more than sufficient to provide a per capita output equal to that at the end of the previous cycle. The factor immediately following k is the incremental output-capital ratio of the cycle divided by that of a base cycle; this factor corrects for changes between cycles in the incremental capital-output ratio. The final factor is total innovation financing during the cycle.

Data for Mexico permit one to obtain values for the above variables for the three short cycles—1945–49, 1950–54, and 1955–59. The average annual percentage change in real gross national product was 4.9 per cent for 1945–49, 5.0 per cent for 1950–54, and 5.8 per cent for 1955–59. Though the increase in Mexican population averaged approximately three per cent per year during the 1945–59 period, and though there was a slight upward trend in the rate of population increase, these growth rates of output are evidence of substantial and rising rates of increase in per capita output. The Mexico City General Wholesale Price Index increased 59 per cent from 1945–49, 51 per cent from 1950–54, and 31 per cent from 1955–59.

Values for the various cycles necessary for determining k are presented in Table 14. It is seen from Table 14 that k was 0.71 for 1945–49,

TABLE 14

VALUES OF VARIABLES

MEXICO, 1945–1959

(millions of 1950 pesos)

Variable		1945–49	1950–54	1955–59
1. $\Delta 0$		8761	10564	15050
2. $\dfrac{0_{t-n} + 0_{t-n+1}}{2}$		30825	39586	50150
3. $\dfrac{N_t - N_{t-n}}{N_{t-n}}$	(ratio)	.15	.155	.16
4. I		23287	29630	44526
5. $\dfrac{\Delta 0}{I} \cdot \dfrac{I_b}{\Delta 0_b}$	(ratio)	1.11	1.06	1.00
6. $\sum \dfrac{B}{p}$		3323	4369	6465
7. $\sum \dfrac{G}{p}$		243	−240	−343
8. $\sum \dfrac{F}{p}$		791	1888	2946
9. $\sum \dfrac{\Delta T}{p} - \left(\dfrac{T_{t-n}}{p_{t-n}} \cdot \dfrac{N_t - N_{t-n}}{N_{t-n}} \right)$		865	158	1004
10. k	(ratio)	.71	.69	.70

Sources and definitions:

1. Real gross national product from *BMIA*, 1960, p. 73.

3. Based on 1940, 1950, and 1960 census figures from *México: Cinquenta años de revolución*, II, 4.

4. From Appendix Tables 22, 24, and 26. Money figures deflated with Mexico City General Wholesale Price Index (1950 = 100).

6, 7, 8, and 9. Same sources as 4, above. 6 is deflated net annual changes in fixed-interest open-market liabilities, loans of maturities greater than one year from financial intermediaries, long-term loans from rest-of-world guaranteed by Mexican government intermediaries, and equities held by financial intermediaries. 7 is government acquisitions of financial intermediary liabilities and equities deducted from government securities issues. 8 includes only new direct foreign investment.

0.69 for 1950–54, and 0.70 for 1955–59 in Mexico. The relative constancy of this relationship supports the hypothesis that innovation financing as measured for Mexico was a requirement of increases in Mexican per capita output during this period. In the discussion which follows it is assumed that a change of $1.00 in innovation financing would have resulted in a change in the same direction of $0.70 in output so long as per capita output did not decline.

Table 15 indicates the relative importance of the various sectors providing innovation financing during the three cycles used in this study. From these figures it is possible to observe trends in the relative impor-

TABLE 15
RELATIVE IMPORTANCE OF SOURCES OF INNOVATION FINANCING
MEXICO, 1945–1959
(per cent)

	1945–49	1950–54	1955–59
To businesses and individuals from:			
Banco de Mexico	6	−1	1
Government nonmonetary intermediaries	36	49	31
Deposit and savings banks	5	8	3
Private nonmonetary intermediaries	11	6	10
Total long-term indirect finance	58	62	46
Direct finance	6	11	18
Total from domestic sources ($\Sigma B/p$)	64	73	64
New direct foreign investment ($\Sigma F/p$)	15	31	29
Total to businesses and individuals	79	104	93
To government sector from:			
Government intermediaries	11	−1	−14
Deposit and savings banks	2	2	8
Private nonmonetary intermediaries	0	0	4
Total indirect finance	13	1	−2
Business and individual sector	−3	1	3
Rest-of-world sector	−7	−8	−3
Total deficit financing ($\Sigma G/p$)	3	−6	−2
Increases in per capita taxes	17	3	10
Total to government sector	20	−3	8
Total to domestic nonfinancial sectors	100	100	100

Source: Appendix Tables 1–26.
Components may not equal totals owing to rounding.

tance of these sources of funds. Indirect finance accounted for 71 per cent of the aggregate in 1945–49, 63 per cent in 1950–54, and 44 per cent in 1955–59. The business and individual sector through direct finance provided 3 per cent in 1945–49, 12 per cent in 1950–54, and 21 per cent in 1955–59. The rest-of-world sector through transactions in Mexican government securities and new direct foreign investment provided the following percentages of aggregate innovation financing: 1944–49, 8 per cent; 1950–54, 23 per cent; 1955–59, 26 per cent. Increases in per capita tax collections accounted for 17 per cent in 1944–49, 3 per cent in 1950–54, and 10 per cent in 1955–59. These figures show a pattern of high and sharply declining relative importance of the financial sector, low and sharply increasing relative importance of the business and individual sector, moderate and moderately increasing relative importance of the rest-of-world sector, and low and mixed relative importance of increases in per capita taxes. The relative importance of government deficit financing is seen to have been a very small percentage of total innovation financing—3 per cent in 1945–49, −6 per cent in 1950–54, and −2 per cent in 1955–59.

When only that portion of innovation financing that was provided to the business and individual sector by the financial sector or other businesses and individuals is considered, it accounted for approximately two-thirds of total innovation financing. The financial sector accounted for 91, 85, and 72 per cent of this financing, while the business and individual sector accounted for the remaining 9, 15, and 28 per cent during the 1945–49, 1950–54, and 1955–59 cycles, respectively.

Let us now narrow the focus of our attention to the flow of funds from the financial sector and its subsectors to the business and individual sector. During the 1945–49 and 1950–54 cycles the long-term portion of this flow accounted for roughly 60 per cent of total innovation financing in Mexico, while this percentage dropped to 46 per cent during the 1955–59 cycle. In accordance with the theory described above and with the remaining sources of innovation financing given, a particular quantity of long-term funds from the financial sector to businesses and individuals is required for a particular level of per capita output increase. However, the total flow of funds from the financial sector to the business and individual sector is an inflationary force, either through increasing the real quantity of money or through increasing the real quantity of indirect securities and (with a given pattern of interest rates) thus reducing the demand for money. Financial policy makers presumably face the task of permitting a target rate of economic development while minimizing the inflationary impact of its financing.

As a means of emphasizing the importance in Mexico during the 1945–1949 period of qualitative aspects of financial sector uses of funds, let us assume that the observed 2 per cent per year increase in per capita output was a target at the end of 1944, that the observed incremental capital-output ratio had been accurately predicted, that the observed fiscal policies had been known and their results accurately predicted, that the observed new direct foreign investment had been known, and that the observed financial sector flows of funds to and from the government securities market had been known. Under these assumptions the observed 3,035 million 1950 pesos of long-term funds from the financial sector to the business and individual sector were required during the 1945–1949 period. What financial policies and innovations were required for attaining this goal while minimizing the inflationary impact of its attainment?

Table 16 contains information relevant to this question. It is seen from

TABLE 16

ANALYSIS OF FINANCIAL SECTOR FLOWS OF FUNDS TO BUSINESSES AND INDIVIDUALS

MEXICO, 1945–1959

L = Long-Term
S = Short-Term

	End of 1944 Stock in Millions of 1950 Pesos		$\frac{L}{L+S}$ (100)				$\frac{L+S}{\Sigma(L+S)}$ (100)			
	L	L+S	End 1944	1945–49	1950–54	1955–59	End 1944	1945–49	1950–54	1955–59
Banco de Mexico	38	833	5	3310	−1	11	22	0.2	7	10
Government Nonmonetary Intermediaries	452	643	70	73	74	68	17	55	57	49
Total Government Intermediaries	490	1476	33	87	66	58	40	55	64	59
Deposit and Savings Banks	63	1454	4	23	25	25	39	25	27	15
Private Nonmonetary Intermediaries	521	788	66	67	56	45	21	20	9	26
Total Private Intermediaries	584	2242	26	42	33	37	60	45	36	41
Total Financial Sector	1074	3718	29	66	54	50	100	100	100	100

Source: Appendix Tables 1–26. Components may not equal totals owing to rounding.

Table 16 that the observed modest increase in per capita output of 2 per cent per year required an increase of 281 per cent in the stock of long-term claims on businesses and individuals held by the financial sector during the five-year period—more than a 30 per cent per year increase in this stock. Prior to 1945 the Mexican financial sector had, on the average, increased its short-term loans approximately seven pesos for each three pesos of increase in long-term financing. Thus if each financial subsector had maintained its ratio of long-term to total business and individual securities constant at the December 31, 1944, figure and if each financial subsector had shared the required 1945–49 aggregate flow as the December 31, 1944, aggregate stock was shared, both long and short-term financing would have increased 281 per cent from 1945–49 over the end of 1944 stock. Had there been no change in the money value of the stock of short-term loans from 1945–49, the required increase in the total of long-term and short-term holdings would have been 82 per cent of the end of 1944 stock. As it actually happened in Mexico the increase in the total of long-term and short-term holdings was limited to 123 per cent of the end of 1944 stock. Whereas the long-term ratio (the ratio of long-term to total business and individual financing by the financial sector) of the financial sector had been 0.29 for the end of 1944 stock, it was raised to 0.66 for the 1945–1949 flow of funds. This large and important qualitative change in the Mexican financial sector allocation of funds was a primary determinant of Mexico's success during this period in maintaining a 2 per cent per year increase in the level of per capita output while restraining the rate of inflation to slightly under 10 per cent per year.

One method of raising the long-term ratio for the financial sector was attempting to raise the long-term ratio of the individual financial subsectors. Comparison of Column 3 with Column 4 of Table 16 shows that the already high long-term ratios of government and private nonmonetary intermediaries were in fact raised slightly. The long-term ratio for deposit and savings banks was raised substantially—from 0.04 to 0.23—during this period; and for Banco de Mexico it rose phenomenally from 0.05 to 33.10. The long-term ratio for the aggregate government intermediary subsector rose from 0.33 at the end of 1944 to 0.87 for the 1945–49 period, while that of the private subsector rose from 0.26 to 0.42. These figures are evidence of changes of heroic proportions, and these changes were the results of policy decisions of the government intermediaries with respect to their own portfolios and policy decisions of the Ministry of Finance and its dependencies with respect to the freedom of deposit and savings banks to engage in long-term lending activities.

The second method of raising the long-term ratio for the aggregate financial sector was to permit nonmonetary intermediaries (whose long-term ratios were higher than those of monetary intermediaries) to allocate a larger fraction of the total flow of funds from the financial sector to businesses and individuals. Comparison of Columns 7 and 8 of Table 16 indicates the extent to which this method was used in Mexico from 1945 through 1949. Government nonmonetary intermediaries, which at the end of 1944 held only 17 per cent of the financial sector's aggregate claims on businesses and individuals, allocated 55 per cent of the 1945–49 flow of funds. The relative share of deposit and savings banks fell from 39 per cent to 25 per cent, and the relative share of Banco de Mexico fell from 22 per cent to 0.2 per cent. The share of government intermediaries rose from 40 per cent to 55 per cent, while that of the private intermediaries fell from 60 per cent to 45 per cent. These changes reflected an increase in the public's real demand for nonmonetary indirect securities compared to money, an increase in the flow of funds from the rest-of-world sector to government nonmonetary intermediaries, and an increase in the flow of funds from the government sector to government nonmonetary intermediaries. But possibly more important than any of the above explanations was the extraordinary drain of funds from deposit and savings banks to the rest-of-world sector during this period in which a devaluation of the Mexican peso occurred. This drain had an effect on deposit and savings bank lending analogous to the effect of an increase in their required reserve deposits in Banco de Mexico as a fraction of their liabilities. The quality of the aggregate financial sector's portfolio was changed during the 1945–49 period in these ways much more than through changing the long-term ratios of the individual subsectors.

Trends shown in Table 15 indicate that after 1949, while the government's deficit financing and tax policies acted to increase the relative importance of financial sector innovation financing, this effect was approximately offset during the 1950–54 cycle and was more than offset during the 1955–59 cycle by an increased importance of both new direct foreign investment and direct finance. And since the financial sector portfolio qualities for the end of 1949 and the end of 1954 reflected the increased relative importance of long-term finance during the 1945–49 and the 1950–54 cycles, respectively, the qualitative changes in the lending activities of the financial sector necessary for attaining substantial increases in per capita output while minimizing inflationary pressures were substantially less than those of 1945–49. Thus, while the 1945–49 increase of 2 per cent per year in per capita output required a flow during the period of innovation financing by the financial sector equal to 281 per cent of the initial stock, the same rate of increase in per capita output in 1950–54 required an increase of only approximately 120 per cent, and the 2.8 per cent rate of increase in 1955–59 required an increase of approximately 110 per cent. During these later periods the lending power of deposit and savings banks was curtailed compared to that of the other financial subsectors by directing the uses of deposit and savings bank funds toward the liabilities of other intermediaries and the government. The lending power of government nonmonetary intermediaries was increased primarily through increased sales of their liabilities to the rest-of-world sector and to other intermediaries, although the 1950–54 period witnessed substantial sales of their liabilities to businesses and individuals. During the 1955–59 cycle even though the long-term ratios of both nonmonetary intermediary subsectors declined somewhat, the relative importance of these subsectors to the aggregate flow of funds from intermediaries to businesses and individuals increased so significantly that the aggregate financial sector's long-term ratio dropped only from 0.54 in 1950–54 to 0.50 in 1955–59. The annual rate of inflation in Mexico dropped from approximately 10 per cent during the 1945–54 period to approximately 6 per cent from 1955–59.

This analysis has shown that the requirements of economic development in Mexico initially necessitated extraordinary quantitative changes in the financial sector's assets, while controlling the rate of inflation required extraordinary qualitative changes in the distribution of these assets—both among and within financial subsectors. Government nonmonetary intermediaries were the principal institutions through which these changes were effected in Mexico during the early years of the development effort. How necessary were government intermediaries for attaining the observed rates of development while restricting the rate of inflation? If the Mexican financial sector in 1944 had consisted entirely of private intermediaries having an aggregate long-term ratio equal to 0.29 (that observed for the actual financial sector in 1944), could this ratio for 1945–49 have been raised to 0.66 (the financial sector's actual 1945–49 long-term ratio) rather than from 0.26 to 0.42 (the actual private subsector's 1944 and 1945–49 ratios)? Probably not, nor would this hypothetical entirely private financial sector have been able to attract the funds from the rest-of-world sector attracted by the Mexican government nonmonetary intermediaries. Thus, the discontinuity of the changes required of the financial sector in the early stages of industrialization establishes the presumption that the role of government financial intermediaries is quite important in this process of development.

In Table 17 an attempt is made roughly to quantify the effect on per capita output of these observed changes in financial production functions.

TABLE 17

PERCENTAGE REDUCTIONS IN PER CAPITA OUTPUT INCREASES

UNDER THREE ASSUMPTIONS

MEXICO, 1945–1959

	1945–49	1950–54	1955–59
A. Financial Sector Long-Term Ratios			
Assumption I	.29	.29	.29
Assumption II	.606*	.336	.302
Assumption III	.291	.257	.267
B. Observed Long-Term Ratios	.66	.54	.50
C. Observed Financial Sector Percentage of Total			
Innovation Financing	.58	.62	.46
D. Percentage Reductions in Increase in Per Capita			
Output. $100C(1 - A/B)$			
Assumption I	38	29	19
Assumption II	5	24	18
Assumption III	38	33	22

Source: Tables 15 and 16 and Appendix Tables 1–26.

Assumption I: Observed aggregate financial sector funds allocated to businesses and individuals on basis of end-of-1944 financial subsector long-term ratios and per cent of aggregate.

Assumption II: Financial subsectors allocated to businesses and individuals funds received by them from businesses and individuals on basis of actual long-term ratios.

Assumption III: Financial subsectors allocated to businesses and individuals funds received by them from businesses and individuals on basis of end-of-1944 long-term ratios.

* In the interest of presenting reasonable results, the government nonmonetary intermediaries and Banco de Mexico were considered together. Considering them separately as in the other computations would have resulted in a financial sector long-term ratio of 7.95.

Utilizing the assumption that an increase in output more than sufficient to maintain a constant per capita output requires an increase in innovation financing equal to 1.43 times the increase in output, we can measure the sacrifice of this output which would have occurred in the absence of changes in the financial production functions. In these computations the total quantity and the quality of financial sector *liabilities* are assumed to have been those observed, and hence the rate of inflation is assumed to have been that observed.[4]

Under the assumption that each subsector in the three cycles allocated on the basis of its end-of-1944 long-term ratio the same fraction of each cycle's aggregate financial sector flow to businesses and individuals as that subsector's end-of-1944 fraction, increases in per capita output would have been reduced by 38 per cent in 1945–49, 29 per cent in 1950–54, and 19 per cent in 1955–59. Thus, under these assumptions, changes in the relative importance of the various financial subsectors to the total financial sector flow of funds to businesses and individuals and changes in the various financial subsectors' long-term ratios together contributed the above percentages of the observed increases in per capita output. Since the observed average annual rates of increase in per capita output were 2.0 for 1945–49, 2.0 for 1950–54, and 2.8 for 1955–59, the financial sector's changes in these parts of its production function accounted for approximately a 0.75 per cent increase in per capita output in 1945–49, a 0.6 per cent increase in 1950–54, and a 0.56 per cent increase in 1955–59.

The second and third assumptions in Table 17 are an attempt to measure the importance of inter-intermediary funds flows to increases in per capita output during these three cycles. Assumption II is that the quantity of funds allocated to businesses and individuals by each financial subsector on the basis of observed long-term ratios was determined by the quantity of that subsector's liabilities held by the public. Assumption III is the same as assumption II except that end-of-1944 long-term ratios are used. With the exception of the 1945–49 period under assumption II, the effects on increases in per capita output are slightly smaller under assumption II and slightly greater under assumption III than under assumption I. Assumption II indicates that for the 1945–49 period increases in per capita output would have been reduced only 5 per cent. This small reduction, compared with the results for the same period under the other assumptions, is the result of the extraordinary change in Banco de Mexico's portfolio distribution. As is shown in Table 1, Banco de Mexico reduced its holdings of business and

---

[4] It is likely, however, that more short-term loans would have resulted in more inflation.

individual short-term obligations by almost the same amount as the increase in its holdings of long-term obligations during this period. But virtually all of Banco de Mexico's funds were allocated to purchases of government securities (another form of innovation financing). Since government deficit financing by the financial sector was of very minor significance except during the 1945–49 period (see Table 15), it was decided to omit it in this discussion of the financial sector. But for these reasons it would be better to consider the results of assumption III for the 1945–49 period as a more accurate measure of the effect of inter-intermediary funds flows on increases in per capita output.

The time pattern of the magnitude of these effects on increases in per capita output is particularly significant. The declining relative importance of changes in financial production functions results largely from the increased relative importance of direct finance and new direct foreign investment in Mexico over time; this is shown in Table 15. But it also results from the downward trend over time in the long-term ratios of the private nonmonetary and the government intermediary subsectors shown in Table 16. Thus, it is seen from the above analysis that the activities of the financial sector in Mexico were more important in the earlier years of the development effort but were still quite important in 1959.

CHAPTER VI

Conclusions

Four different types of conclusions are warranted by the foregoing study of Mexican financial intermediaries during a period of rapid industrialization. First, the empirical data for Mexico permit conclusions concerning the appropriateness to the Mexican case of the theoretical approach outlined in Chapter I. Second, the study permits generalizations concerning the relative permissiveness of economic development evidenced by the allocation decisions of the various financial subsectors. Third, the study warrants conclusions concerning the time pattern of Mexican financial development. Finally, suggestions for financial planning in other underdeveloped countries follow from this study.

The theoretical approach of Chapter I assumed that institutional patterns in Mexico during the 1945–1959 period were such that marginal adjustments of prices and interest rates could not adequately explain Mexico's rapid industrialization. The market for capital funds was assumed to be quite personalized initially—only a special group of households and a special intermediary were assumed to be available as alternative outside sources of funds for a firm. Businesses and individuals were assumed to be able to allocate funds to purchases of the particular direct and indirect securities they chose. Either policy decisions or new financial intermediaries were assumed to be required in order to alter substantially the allocation decisions of the financial sector so as to provide financing for the innovations necessary for economic development. Flows of funds were assumed to be directed initially to their customary uses rather than to innovation financing; breaking with custom was required for economic development. Finally, it was asserted that this break with customary activities could be accomplished relatively quickly through planning the uses of financial intermediary funds. What light does the present analysis of Mexican experience throw on the appropriateness of such theoretical assumptions in the Mexican case?

Evidence was presented that indicated that marginal adjustments in prices and interest rates did not sufficiently explain Mexican experience during this period. It included the following considerations: The Mexican government and government-owned enterprises accounted for approximately one-third of real investment spending during this period. Government financial intermediaries allocated an average of more than 50 per cent of the financial sector's flow of funds to businesses and individuals. Interest rates on primary securities and indirect securities were usually held at fixed levels by the financial authorities. Finally, the control system of the Mexican financial sector permitted the financial authorities to determine to a significant extent the directions in which the entire financial sector's funds were allocated. In view of the above facts of Mexican experience, the question of why funds were allocated to particular uses in Mexico was avoided not by assuming optimum decisions based on profit-maximizing behavior but rather by concentrating on the decisions that were actually made.

The assumption that only a specialized group of households and a special intermediary were initially available as outside sources of funds for a firm was supported by the following facts. During the entire period studied here, a market for the equities of businesses and individuals was almost nonexistent in Mexico. This, together with the fact that non-financial sector purchases of open-market, fixed-interest securities of businesses and individuals were fairly insignificant in amount early in the period, suggests that outside finance from sources other than the financial sector was initially very scarce. Support for the rigid assumption that a particular firm could obtain funds only from a particular intermediary rests largely on intuitive bases, such as reasoning by analogy from Alhadeff's study of the banking system in the United States.[1] However, the assumption that only one intermediary provided funds to each firm was not necessary to the major portion of the analysis; it was

---

[1] David A. Alhadeff, *Monopoly and Competition in Banking* (Berkeley: University of California Press, 1954). See particularly Chapter III.

sufficient that only a particular financial subsector supplied funds to a particular firm or that a particular financial subsector specialized in loans for particular purposes. It was shown that government nonmonetary intermediaries initially were almost the sole source of long-term financing in Mexico. Together with the assumption that established firms required little outside long-term finance, this fact makes plausible the assumption that established firms dealt largely with the private financial subsectors. The Mexican pattern of legal restrictions on intermediary lending activities was additional evidence of intermediary specialization as to type of loans. Finally, the assumption of a close association between long-term finance and innovation financing establishes the government nonmonetary intermediaries as the most important source of innovation financing during the entire period and as almost the only source of such funds early in the period.

The absence in Mexico during this period of a control technique for requiring businesses and individuals to purchase particular types of indirect securities is sufficient evidence for the assumption that businesses and individuals were able to choose the particular indirect securities which they purchased. However, these choices were influenced by indirect security diversification and the permitted pattern of indirect security yields, both of which resulted largely from policy decisions during this period. A fruitful area for further investigation would be a study of the important variables which determined the initial distribution among intermediaries of funds from the business and individual sector. Such a study would be extremely important if in Mexico the value judgment that uses of intermediary funds should not be planned by the financial authority was, say, equally important as the value judgment that per capita output should be increased. However, the Mexican case gives every reason to suppose that the Mexicans felt that uses of intermediary funds should be planned for increases in per capita output. Assuming that this was the dominant Mexican value judgment with respect to financial intermediaries, the important analysis focuses on the uses of funds which promote increases in output and on the techniques that can be used to direct funds to those uses, whatever the public's preferences for particular indirect securities. Prediction of purchases of indirect securities by the public would be nonstrategic information as compared to information concerning appropriate uses of intermediary funds, actual uses of intermediary funds, and actual purchases of indirect securities by the public. This is not to say that prediction of the public's choices is unimportant; it is certainly important to predict the public's responses to alternative policy decisions. However, it is more important to have knowledge of the reasons why any policy decision is required and knowledge of the facts which any chosen policy would have to alter. For these causes the present analysis of Mexican financial experience has shown greater concern with the uses of intermediary funds and with techniques for controlling those uses than with the sources of funds available to particular intermediaries or classes of intermediaries.

With respect to breaking with traditional customs of the past, it was shown that the Mexican Revolution resulted in substantial alterations in the Mexican distribution of property ownership and political power. One result was the increased importance of government intermediaries in the financial sector. In 1925 when Banco de Mexico was established, government intermediaries were allocating no funds to businesses and individuals in Mexico; by 1945 and through 1959, government intermediaries were allocating more than half of the financial sector's total flow of funds to the business and individual sector. During this 1945–59 period a strong group of private nonmonetary intermediaries developed in Mexico; this is additional evidence of financial innovations and policy decisions which further removed the Mexican financial sector from its traditional uses of funds. Two developments during this period in addition to the development of private nonmonetary intermediaries further changed the traditional flows of funds in the Mexican economy. These were the development of direct long-term finance as an important source of business and individual funds and the development of the rest-of-world sector as an important source of both direct and indirect finance. It is important to note that the development of the government intermediaries was the most significant initial break with the Mexican economy's traditional flows of funds. This suggests that during the early years of industrialization, institutions not necessarily limited by profit and loss accounting relationships may have been required for financing sufficient innovations to permit development. The Mexican experience also suggests that later (as innovation financing became more a traditional flow of funds) the private intermediaries, the business and individual sector, and the rest-of-world sector came forward as important suppliers of funds for innovation. Thus, in Mexico the government and government-owned financial intermediaries were apparently the financial innovators; the other sectors acted more as followers in this respect.

All of these characteristics of the Mexican economy lead to the conclusions that the theoretical assumptions of Chapter I are reasonable approximations to Mexican financial experience and that these assumptions recognize institutional patterns which were important determinants of Mexican financial experience.

While the descriptive portions of this study provide a body of statistical data basic to any informed analysis of Mexican financial flows during a critical period in her industrial development, the theoretical and analytical portions of this study are primarily concerned with the allocation function of Mexican financial intermediaries. Aside from the nonfinancial activities of these intermediaries, their choices of the spending units which could finance spending projects with funds provided by financial intermediaries are their closest points of contact with the process of economic development. More indirectly, through affecting the rate of inflation (and through thereby affecting the distribution of income), financial intermediaries may affect economic development. But each allocation decision made by a financial intermediary reallocates the effective purchasing power of the economy. Different intermediaries permit the demands for commodities of different prospective purchasers to become effective demands. It is imperative, then, that in studies of the role of financial intermediaries in economic development an increased emphasis be placed on differences among intermediaries in their allocation decisions and on differences in the degree in which these decisions permit economic development. Such analysis of differences presumes a disaggregative approach to the study of financial intermediaries and an approach that focuses attention primarily on the uses of intermediary funds.

Several steps were taken in the direction of disaggregation of the financial sector and disaggregation of its uses of funds in the present study. Differences between monetary and nonmonetary intermediaries and between government and private intermediaries were discussed. The financial sector was further disaggregated into the central bank, government nonmonetary intermediaries, deposit and savings banks, and private nonmonetary intermediaries. For each of these financial subsectors the sources and uses of funds were disaggregated into flows of funds to and from the government sector, the business and individual sector, the rest-of-world sector, and other financial intermediaries. The flows of funds to the business and individual sector were disaggregated into a short-term flow and a long-term flow. Even with this amount of disaggregation, the level of aggregation in the analysis remains excessive; additional studies should be directed toward still further disaggregation, for instance, of the broad category called long-term financing.

It was shown in this study that in Mexico during the 1945–1959 period a relatively constant amount of increase in per capita output was associated with a given amount of increase in the real flow of long-term funds to businesses and individuals and the government. Initially the financial sector provided almost all of this net flow, but during the period the business and individual sector and the rest-of-world sector became increasingly important sources of long-term financing. By the end of the period the business and individual sector and the rest-of-world sector were supplying almost half of this long-term financing. Thus, during this period the relative importance of planned flows of long-term funds from the financial sector declined.

Not only was long-term financing by the financial sector of declining relative importance from 1945–1959 but also within that sector long-term financing by government nonmonetary intermediaries was declining in importance in relation to that of private nonmonetary intermediaries. Government nonmonetary intermediaries in Mexico were the primary initial sources of innovation financing, but as industrialization progressed the private nonmonetary intermediaries' lending, rather than the directly planned lending of government nonmonetary intermediaries, became increasingly important.

This pattern of Mexican financial development, evidencing private decision-making replacing government decision-making in relative importance as the development process gained momentum, raises many significant questions which deserve further investigation. Did the observed pattern of Mexican financial development occur as a result of an increased effectiveness of indirect controls of private decisions, such as improved techniques for controlling the primary securities available for purchase in Mexico or improved techniques for directing the allocation decisions of private intermediaries? Or did this pattern result from changes in the demand side of the loanable funds market—such changes as relatively higher profit expectations on the part of businesses and individuals from investments in new and improved plant and equipment?

If changes originated primarily in the conditions of supply of funds by financial intermediaries, were these primarily changes in the cost or in the availability of funds? Questions such as these have received little attention in this study. However, the trends have been described here and much information bearing on these questions has been presented. Further investigation is needed to permit more precise statements concerning the causal relationships present in the trend away from direct government decision-making; such information as was presented here suggests both that indirect control techniques were increasingly effective and that private demand for new and improved plant and equipment increased as a percentage of gross national product.

A second group of questions raised by this analysis has to do with the technique required for initiating the flow of long-term funds to businesses and individuals. Was it necessary that the new specialized government-owned intermediaries be established in order to provide a flow of long-term funds sufficient to permit substantial increases in per capita output? Could incentives have been provided that would have been sufficient to elicit the required funds from private sources? If so, then would the real cost of these incentives—such costs as devising a program of subsidies, policing the use of subsidies, etc.—have been sufficiently insignificant to permit consideration of this approach as an alternative to government intermediaries? Further investigation would probably reveal that government intermediaries in Mexico created a large portion of the demand for their services through such nonfinancial activities as acting as entrepreneur in establishing many operating plants. Would private intermediaries have performed these nonfinancial functions in the early years of Mexico's industrialization effort? Finally, are these questions really important in economies such as Mexico's, where government participation in the economy is popularly regarded as a legitimate and valuable institutional pattern?

Several questions are raised with respect to the relationship between the Mexican financial development pattern and Mexico's inflationary experience. Did the provision of relatively large flows of long-term funds from financial intermediaries early in the period explain a large portion of the concomitantly high rate of inflation? If so, would the rate of inflation have been lower had other lending by intermediaries been reduced more? Most important, would a reduction in the other lending by Mexican intermediaries have been accompanied by a decline in the output growth rate? During this 1945–1959 period, short-term lending by intermediaries was increasing at a faster rate than the total flow of long-term finance. However, virtually all the increase in the amount of the flow of short-term finance was accounted for by financial subsectors other than deposit and savings banks. This suggests the possibility that short-term finance by deposit and savings banks was largely inflationary. Further research along these lines of investigation is warranted to determine in greater detail the differences among the financial subsectors in the uses made of their short-term funds. It is true that the government intermediaries made substantial quantities of short-term loans in an effort to control food prices. Were substantial quantities of deposit-and-savings-bank short-term funds used for speculative inventory accumulations, etc.? Certainly such questions deserve further investigation; the results of such investigation might show that a substantial amount of Mexico's forced saving early in the period could have been avoided without reducing the growth rate of output.

All of the preceding questions for further analysis are directed toward obtaining information from the Mexican experience that would be of value to other countries interested in higher output growth rates and lower rates of inflation. In addition to searching for answers to the above questions concerning Mexican experience, comparative studies of other countries—studies using the general approach presented in this study of Mexico—are required. Has the success of development efforts been less spectacular than that of Mexico in countries which used a less bold and imaginative approach to the planned use of financial intermediary funds? Is the pattern of early investment financing by intermediaries and somewhat later development of alternative sources of financing found generally? Has the early use of financial intermediaries as sources of development financing been generally accompanied by high rates of inflation? These questions are important today; this study is only a step toward more informed answers.

Appendix

Sources for Tables 5, 6, 7, and 8 (balance sheets for the financial subsectors) are the Tables entitled "Recursos y obligaciones del systema bancario, Activos líquidos de empresas y particulares," and "Recursos y obligaciones de las instituciones de crédito privadas," found in *BMIA* for the years 1947–1960. For 1951 and 1960 the figures in these tables are unrevised figures from the source; for other years the figures are revised from the source, except as noted below. The balance sheets for private nonmonetary intermediaries (Table 9) were derived by subtracting those of deposit and savings banks (Table 8) from those of total private intermediaries (Table 5); the balance sheets for total government intermediaries (Table 4) were derived by adding those of Banco de Mexico (Table 6) to those of government nonmonetary intermediaries (Table 7); the balance sheets of total nonmonetary intermediaries (Table 3) were derived by adding those of government nonmonetary intermediaries (Table 7) to those of private nonmonetary intermediaries (Table 9); the balance sheets of total monetary intermediaries (Table 2) were derived by adding those of Banco de Mexico (Table 6) to those of deposit and savings banks (Table 8); the balance sheets of the aggregate financial sector (Table 1) were derived by adding those of monetary intermediaries (Table 2) to those of nonmonetary intermediaries (Table 3).

The major divergence of the figures presented here from those published in the source results from the fact that prior to 1953 the source did not include the common funds of Nacional Financiera's Participation Certificates; after 1953 these were included. Comparison of the difference between the above sources and the series published by Banco de Mexico entitled "Financiamiento total concedido por el sistema bancario" (*BMIA*, 1960, p. 94) with figures on the investment of these common funds prior to 1953 (*NFIA*, 1954, pp. 50 and 111) reveals that, except in minor respects, the difference is explained by the common funds. Hence, the figures on total financing extended by the banking system computed from the sources shown in the last paragraph were subtracted from those from Banco de Mexico's series mentioned in this paragraph, and the difference was added algebraically to the appropriate assets and liabilities of government nonmonetary intermediaries. This procedure was used for investments in government securities and in liabilities of businesses and individuals (the latter were assumed to have been long-term loans exclusively). The sum of these differences for government securities and business and individual securities was added to government nonmonetary intermediary securities owned by businesses and individuals and to total liabilities and capital of government non-monetary intermediaries. This method of treating the common funds prior to 1953 excludes the portion of those funds invested in indirect securities.

A second divergence of the figures presented here from those of the sources also results from the Nacional Financiera Participation Certificates. Prior to 1955 for all the financial subsectors, and to the present for the private subsectors, the source includes investments in Participation Certificates with investments in government securities. Such investments are here considered to be investments in indirect securities; hence, they are excluded from investments in government securities and included in investments in obligations of "banks."

The third adjustment made in the figures published by Banco de Mexico was that the "Time and Sight Obligations in Foreign Currencies" (Obligaciones a la vista y a plazo, ME) of government nonmonetary intermediaries are shown as owned by the rest-of-world sector here; in the source they are shown as owned by the business and individual sector in the table entitled "Assets and Liabilities of the Banking System" and are not shown in the table entitled "Liquid Assets of Businesses and Individuals."

Finally, for all the subsectors' assets and liabilities in foreign currencies or precious metals in 1953, the revised figures in the source were multiplied by 8.65/12.5 in order to state them in terms of exchange rates prevailing at the end of 1953. In the source these data for 1953 are stated in terms of exchange rates prevailing at the end of 1954. Capital accounts were adjusted to correct for differences between total assets and total liabilities and capital resulting from this adjustment for all subsectors except Banco de Mexico (where the discrepancy was on the order of one billion pesos).

Column headings of the balance sheets presented here are defined as follows in terms of other column headings in these balance sheets (in which case no Spanish in parentheses appears) or in terms of categories in the source tables "Assets and Liabilities of the Banking System" (ALS), or "Liquid Assets of Businesses and Individuals" (LA) (in which case the Spanish name of the category appears in parentheses).

I. "Assets" (Total Assets are not shown separately since they equal Total Liabilities and Capital).
    A. "Total Classified Assets" is "Total Assets" (ALS, Recursos Totales) less "Other Assets" (ALS, Otros conceptos de activo).
        1. "Rest-of-World" is gold, silver, and foreign exchange reserves of Mexican intermediaries (ALS, Disponibilidades en oro, plata, y divisas).
        2. "Government" is government security holdings (excluding Participation Certificates of Nacional Financiera) (ALS, Gubernamentales) and loans to the federal government (ALS, Crédito al Gobierno Federal).
        3. "Banks" is "Total Classified Assets" less "Rest-of-World," "Government," and "Total Businesses and Individuals."
        4. "Total Businesses and Individuals" is "Total Securities" plus "Total Loans."
            a. "Total Securities" is "Stocks" plus "Other."
                (1) "Stocks" is "Stocks of Businesses and Individuals" (ALS, Valores de empresas y particulares, Acciones).
                (2) "Other" is "Business and Individual Securities" (ALS, Valores de empresas y particulares) less "Stocks."
            b. "Total Loans" is "Short-Term" plus "Long-Term."
                (1) "Short-Term" is "Loans to Businesses and Individuals" (ALS, Crédito, A empresas y particulares) less those with maturities greater than 360 days (ALS, a más de 360 días) and less Nacional Financiera's common funds (ALS, Fondos communes de Nacional Financiera).
                (2) "Long-Term" is loans with maturities greater than 360 days (ALS, Crédito, a empresas y particulares a más de 360 días) plus the common funds (ALS, Fondos communes de Nacional Financiera).
            c. "Total Long-Term" is "Total Securities" plus "Long-Term Loans."

II. "Total Liabilities and Capital" is (ALS, Recursos totales).
    A. "Total Classified" is "Total Liabilities and Capital" less "Other Liabilities" (ALS, Otros conceptos de pasivo).
        1. "Banks" is "Total Classified" less "Rest-of-World," "Total Government," and "Total Businesses and Individuals."
        2. "Rest-of-World" is "Sight and Time Obligations in Foreign Currencies" (ALS, Obligaciones a la vista y a plazo M/E)

of government nonmonetary intermediaries (Otras Instituciones Nacionales).

3. "Total Government" is "Government Deposits" and "Government Capital."

   a. "Deposits" is checking accounts of the Treasury (ALS, Cuenta de cheques M/N, de la Tesorería) and Treasury foreign currency sight deposits (ALS, Depósitos a la vista M/E, de la Tesorería).

   b. "Capital" is the ratio of government-owned capital stock (ALS, Capital, Exhibido, Aportado por el Gobierno Federal y por los gobiernos locales) to total capital stock (ALS, Capital, Exhibido), multiplied by the sum of capital stock (ALS, Capital) and reserves (ALS, Resultados y Reservas).

4. "Businesses and Individuals, Total" is the sum of a, b, c, and d below.

   a. "Money" is the sum held by businesses and individuals (ALS, empresas y particulares) of paper money (ALS, Billetes), coins (ALS, Moneda metálica), checking accounts (ALS, Cuenta de cheques M/N), other demand deposits (ALS, Otros depósitos a la vista M/N), and demand deposits in foreign currencies (ALS, Depósitos a la vista M/E).

   b. "Other Deposits, etc." is the sum held by businesses and individuals (ALS, empresas y particulares) of savings deposits (ALS, Depósitos de ahorro M/N), other time deposits (ALS, Otros depósitos a plazo M/N, y depósitos a plazo M/E), and sight and time obligations (ALS, Obligaciones a la vista y a plazo M/N y M/E) less "Restof-World" (II, 2 above).

   c. "Securities" is reserves for capitalizer securities (LA, Reservas técnicas de Títulos de Capitalización) plus fixedinterest open-market securities issued by financial intermediaries (LA, Tenencia de valores de renta fija, Bancarios menos Bonos del Ahorro Nacional). Since this series included holdings of government-owned enterprises prior to 1956, holdings of these enterprises from *BMIA* 1957–1960, Table entitled "Circulation and Holdings of FixedInterest Securities" (Circulación y tenencia de valores de renta fija) were added for the years 1956–1960.

   d. "Capital" for businesses and individuals was calculated in the same manner as Government Capital in 3b above, using capital stock held by businesses and individuals (ALS, Capital, Aportado por empresas y particulares).

NOTE 2

The tables of Selected Real Sources and Uses of Funds (Tables 10–18) are each derived by taking first differences of the Balance Sheet table of the respective subsector. Except as noted below, "Sources" are first differences of the corresponding liability or capital category and "Uses" are first differences of the corresponding asset category. These asset and liability categories are defined in Note 1 above.

In 1948 the peso/dollar exchange rate went from 4.65/1 to 6.88/1; in 1949 this latter was changed to 8.65/1; in 1954 this was changed to 12.5/1. Sources and uses in foreign currencies or precious metals were adjusted for these devaluations by using the difference between 1947, 1948, and 1953 foreign currency assets and liabilities evaluated at exchange rates prevailing at the end of 1948, 1949, and 1954, respectively, and observed values of these assets and liabilities for 1948, 1949, and 1954, respectively.

Before computing sources and uses for government nonmonetary intermediaries (and total government intermediaries, total nonmonetary intermediaries, and the total financial sector) "Long-Term Loans" (hence "Total Long-Term," "Total Businesses and Individuals," and "Total Classified Assets") for 1960 were reduced $1,456,000,000 (pesos) to adjust for the purchase by the Mexican government of foreign-owned electric companies. The figure used is not a precise measure of the participation of government nonmonetary intermediaries in financing this transfer; it is the amount of net foreign disinvestment involved in the transfer of ownership, as shown in the Mexican Balance of Payments (*BMIA*, 1960, p. 84).

After the above adjustments were made, the resulting sources and uses of funds were deflated with the Mexico City General Wholesale Price Index from Table 33.

Column headings in the sources and uses tables which differ from those of balance sheet tables are defined as follows in terms of balance sheet categories:

1. "Businesses and Individuals, Nonmonetary" is defined as the sum of "Other Deposits, etc.," "Securities," and "Capital."
2. "Used to Purchase Primary Securities, Total" is the sum of "Government" and "Businesses and Individuals, Total."
3. "Long-Term" is "Total Long-Term."

TABLE 1

FINANCIAL INTERMEDIARY SECTOR: BALANCE SHEET

MEXICO, 1945–1960

(End of year stocks in millions of pesos)

Assets: By Debtor Sector

Year	Total Classified Assets	Rest of World	Government	Banks	Businesses and Individuals Total	Securities Total	Securities Stocks	Securities Other	Loans Total	Loans Short Term	Loans Long Term	Total Long Term
1945	8162	1920	1248	2166	2828	374	196	178	2454	1756	696	1070
1946	8408	1438	1447	2120	3403	493	288	205	2910	2098	812	1305
1947	8850	879	1572	2152	4247	668	328	340	3579	2635	947	1615
1948	10150	990	1905	2197	5058	751	420	331	4307	2939	1367	2118
1949	11701	1588	2229	2088	5796	1057	457	600	4739	2752	1988	3045
1950	15089	2756	2179	3360	6794	943	465	478	5851	3161	2691	3634
1951	17250	2796	1823	3687	8944	1099	466	633	7845	4222	3623	4722
1952	18770	2790	2017	4092	9871	1340	508	832	8531	4348	4183	5523
1953	20936	2585	2380	4853	11118	1490	691	799	9628	5715	3912	5402
1954	24616	2927	2901	4878	13910	1961	847	1114	11949	6699	5252	7213
1955	28293	5449	3084	5171	14589	1658	915	743	12931	7296	5635	7293
1956	31636	6195	3002	5783	16656	1854	1083	771	14802	8574	6226	8080
1957	35369	6403	3625	6502	18839	2221	1212	1009	16618	9501	7118	9339
1958	40073	5959	4580	7531	22003	2962	1535	1427	19041	10634	8407	11369
1959	46515	6771	4269	8475	27000	3151	2025	1126	23849	14953	8898	12049
1960	55277	5995	5745	9788	33749	3446	2420	1026	30303	17349	12955	16401

TABLE 1—Continued

Liabilities and Capital: By Owning Sector

Year	Total Liabilities and Capital	Total Classified	Banks	Rest of World	Government			Businesses and Individuals				
					Total	Deposits	Capital	Total	Money	Other Deposits, Etc.	Securities	Capital
1945	8478	8205	2455	73	332	1	331	5346	3718	853	419	356
1946	8753	8461	2498	228	361	1	360	5374	3663	848	445	418
1947	9358	8986	2563	307	429	31	398	5686	3608	1046	527	505
1948	10854	10176	2477	506	567	30	537	6626	4238	1241	584	563
1949	12466	11628	2288	780	1084	52	1032	7476	4735	1481	683	577
1950	16120	15301	3648	743	1138	76	1062	9772	6349	1621	1128	674
1951	18711	17732	4092	959	1190	73	1117	11491	7234	2111	1368	778
1952	20589	19395	4568	1114	1243	119	1124	12470	7687	2341	1571	871
1953	23084	21644	5139	1302	1496	35	1461	13707	8240	2841	1392	1234
1954	27556	25687	5365	1924	1617	47	1570	16781	10114	4214	1302	1151
1955	31528	29509	5764	1890	2139	242	1897	19717	11904	4923	1560	1330
1956	35273	32844	5964	2014	2936	290	2646	21929	13204	5592	1637	1496
1957	38648	36140	6966	2225	2916	269	2647	24033	14410	6524	1413	1686
1958	43668	40693	8455	2968	2764	82	2682	26506	15825	7701	1327	1653
1959	50255	46957	9358	3564	3403	123	3280	30632	17363	9801	1462	2006
1960	59471	55492	10647	6135	3647	188	3459	35063	18771	12023	2213	2056

For sources and definitions, see Note 1.

147

TABLE 2

TOTAL MONETARY INTERMEDIARIES: BALANCE SHEET
MEXICO, 1945–1960
(End of year stocks in millions of pesos)

Assets: By Debtor Sector

Year	Total Classified Assets	Rest of World	Government	Banks	Businesses and Individuals Total	Securities Total	Stocks	Other	Loans Total	Short Term	Long Term	Total Long Term
1945	6150	1912	811	1916	1511	51	16	35	1460	1428	32	83
1946	5911	1433	939	1842	1697	146	97	49	1551	1512	37	183
1947	5886	871	1086	1786	2143	237	76	161	1906	1839	67	304
1948	6697	974	1542	1751	2430	285	100	185	2145	2055	89	374
1949	7646	1552	2076	1784	2234	426	159	267	1808	1698	111	537
1950	10115	2729	1859	2862	2665	389	190	199	2276	2099	179	568
1951	10897	2763	1803	2982	3349	394	192	202	2955	2663	292	686
1952	11605	2751	1809	3320	3725	456	244	212	3269	2860	411	867
1953	12917	2528	2087	3810	4492	437	273	164	4055	3584	471	908
1954	14657	2889	2673	4032	5063	502	284	218	4561	3984	577	1079
1955	17650	5407	2605	4291	5347	515	264	251	4832	4283	549	1064
1956	19579	6136	2393	4627	6423	549	274	275	5874	5246	628	1177
1957	21434	6368	2914	5523	6629	696	336	360	5933	5270	665	1361
1958	23225	5695	3574	6189	7767	1169	358	811	6598	5766	832	2001
1959	25873	6573	3250	6866	9184	1054	647	407	8130	7319	813	1867
1960	27639	5865	3971	7530	10273	1131	702	429	9142	8369	774	1905

TABLE 2—Continued

Liabilities and Capital: By Owning Sector

Year	Total Liabilities and Capital	Total Classified	Banks	Rest of World	Government Total	Government Deposits	Government Capital	Businesses and Individuals Total	Money	Other Deposits, Etc.	Securities	Capital
1945	6321	6173	1745	(no entries)	90	1	89	4338	3637	553	(no entries)	148
1946	6062	5939	1564		81	1	80	4294	3612	526		156
1947	6156	5984	1462		130	31	99	4392	3570	665		157
1948	7122	6681	1421		156	30	126	5104	4132	786		186
1949	8094	7525	1599		179	52	127	5747	4602	936		209
1950	10668	10197	2620		212	76	136	7365	6189	929		247
1951	11607	11026	2294		220	73	147	8512	7068	1116		328
1952	12487	11791	2373		271	119	152	9146	7516	1242		388
1953	13839	13084	2791		239	35	204	10054	8027	1445		582
1954	16067	14959	2885		255	47	208	11819	9650	1645		524
1955	19029	17908	3418		471	242	229	14020	11448	1952		620
1956	21017	19815	3506		698	290	408	15611	12708	2215		688
1957	22797	21498	3630		695	269	426	17172	13907	2528		737
1958	24822	23384	4384		518	82	436	18482	15171	2780		531
1959	27480	25891	4770		564	123	441	20557	16831	3035		691
1960	29459	27577	4600		628	188	440	22350	18158	3483		709

For sources and definitions, see Note 1.

149

TABLE 3

TOTAL NONMONETARY INTERMEDIARIES: BALANCE SHEET

MEXICO, 1945–1960

(End of year stocks in millions of pesos)

Assets: By Debtor Sector

Year	Total Classified Assets	Rest of World	Government	Banks	Businesses and Individuals Total	Securities Total	Stocks	Other	Loans Total	Short Term	Long Term	Total Long Term
1945	2012	8	437	250	1317	323	180	143	994	328	664	987
1946	2497	5	508	278	1706	347	191	156	1359	586	775	1122
1947	2964	8	486	366	2104	431	252	179	1673	796	880	1311
1948	3453	16	363	446	2628	466	320	146	2162	884	1278	1744
1949	4055	36	153	304	3562	631	298	333	2931	1054	1877	2508
1950	4974	27	320	498	4129	554	275	279	3575	1062	2512	3066
1951	6353	33	20	705	5595	705	274	431	4890	1559	3331	4036
1952	7165	39	208	772	6146	884	264	620	5262	1488	3772	4656
1953	8019	57	293	1043	6626	1053	418	635	5573	2131	3441	4494
1954	9959	38	228	846	8847	1459	563	896	7388	2715	4675	6134
1955	10643	42	479	880	9242	1143	651	492	8099	3013	5086	6229
1956	12057	59	609	1156	10233	1305	809	496	8928	3328	5598	6903
1957	13935	35	711	979	12210	1525	876	649	10685	4231	6453	7978
1958	16848	264	1006	1342	14236	1793	1177	616	12443	4868	7575	9368
1959	20642	198	1019	1609	17816	2097	1378	719	15719	7634	8085	10182
1960	27638	130	1774	2258	23476	2315	1718	597	21161	8980	12181	14496

TABLE 3—Continued

Liabilities and Capital: By Owning Sector

Year	Total Liabilities and Capital	Total Classified	Banks	Rest of World	Government			Businesses and Individuals				
					Total	Deposits	Capital	Total	Money	Other Deposits, Etc.	Securities	Capital
1945	2157	2032	709	73	242		242	1008	81	300	419	208
1946	2691	2522	933	228	280		280	1080	51	322	445	262
1947	3202	3002	1101	307	300		300	1295	38	381	527	349
1948	3732	3495	1056	506	411		411	1522	106	455	584	377
1949	4372	4103	689	780	905		905	1729	133	545	683	368
1950	5452	5104	1028	743	925	(no entries)	925	2407	160	692	1128	427
1951	7104	6706	1798	959	970		970	2979	166	995	1368	450
1952	8102	7604	2195	1114	971		971	3324	171	1099	1571	483
1953	9245	8560	2348	1302	1258		1258	3653	213	1396	1392	652
1954	11489	10728	2480	1924	1362		1362	4962	464	2569	1302	627
1955	12499	11601	2346	1890	1668		1668	5697	456	2971	1560	710
1956	14256	13029	2458	2014	2238		2238	6319	496	3377	1637	809
1957	15851	14642	3336	2225	2220		2220	6861	503	3996	1413	949
1958	18846	17309	4071	2968	2246		2246	8025	654	4921	1327	1123
1959	22775	21066	4588	3564	2839		2839	10075	532	6766	1462	1315
1960	30012	27915	6047	6135	3020		3020	12713	613	8540	2213	1347

For sources and definitions, see Note 1.

151

TABLE 4

TOTAL GOVERNMENT INTERMEDIARIES: BALANCE SHEET

MEXICO, 1945–1960

(End of year stocks in millions of pesos)

Assets: By Debtor Sector

Year	Total Classified Assets	Rest of World	Government	Banks	Businesses and Individuals							Total Long Term
					Total	Securities			Total	Loans		
						Total	Stocks	Other		Short Term	Long Term	
1945	4545	1807	1095	512	1131	199	69	130	932	565	366	565
1946	4652	1314	1310	567	1461	258	125	133	1203	797	405	663
1947	4892	781	1408	783	1920	358	106	252	1562	1071	493	851
1948	5705	850	1750	736	2369	402	149	253	1967	1098	868	1270
1949	6854	1429	2052	488	2885	681	154	527	2204	845	1359	2040
1950	8816	2867	1862	751	3336	535	151	384	2801	839	1962	2497
1951	10005	2666	1559	1090	4690	630	136	494	4060	1505	2555	3185
1952	10775	2587	1805	1268	5115	768	179	589	4347	1377	2970	3738
1953	12296	2389	2062	1765	6080	1020	378	642	5060	2371	2687	3707
1954	14588	2594	2589	1452	7953	1394	463	931	6559	2762	3798	5192
1955	15983	5120	2407	997	7459	985	491	494	6474	2359	4115	5100
1956	17509	5886	2122	1271	8230	1000	559	441	7230	2825	4404	5404
1957	19007	6128	2516	1145	9218	1124	574	550	8094	3049	5045	6169
1958	21397	5132	3025	1506	11734	1686	718	968	10048	4115	5933	7619
1959	24325	5938	1939	1865	14583	1697	1099	598	12886	6998	5889	7586
1960	29748	5771	2808	2294	18875	1821	1350	471	17054	7993	9062	10883

TABLE 4—Continued

Liabilities and Capital: By Owning Sector

Year	Total Liabilities and Capital	Total Classified	Banks	Rest of World	Government			Businesses and Individuals				
					Total	Deposits	Capital	Total	Money	Other Deposits, Etc.	Securities	Capital
1945	4712	4541	1886	73	332	1	331	2250	1795	257	180	18
1946	4814	4642	1762	228	361	1	360	2291	1842	267	162	20
1947	5193	4965	1751	307	429	31	398	2477	1849	414	182	32
1948	6171	5663	1607	506	567	30	537	2983	2272	497	186	28
1949	7332	6694	1424	780	1084	52	1032	3406	2574	572	236	24
1950	9479	8887	2666	743	1138	76	1062	4341	3129	575	596	41
1951	11050	10346	2997	959	1190	73	1117	5200	3706	764	688	42
1952	12129	11245	3353	1114	1243	119	1124	5535	3878	802	849	6
1953	13934	12833	4043	1302	1496	35	1461	5991	4167	1010	725	90
1954	17002	15528	3988	1924	1617	47	1570	7999	5161	1962	806	70
1955	18580	17070	4511	1890	2139	242	1897	8530	5615	2091	771	53
1956	20456	18636	4468	2014	2936	290	2646	9217	6339	2041	777	60
1957	21412	19601	5183	2225	2916	269	2647	9277	6735	1912	566	64
1958	24084	21905	5832	2968	2764	82	2682	10341	7557	2138	585	61
1959	27069	24740	6321	3564	3403	123	3280	11452	8043	2658	672	79
1960	32754	29936	7238	6135	3647	188	3459	12915	8704	3146	981	84

For sources and definitions, see Note 1.

153

TABLE 5

TOTAL PRIVATE INTERMEDIARIES: BALANCE SHEET

MEXICO, 1945–1960

(End of year stocks in millions of pesos)

Assets: By Debtor Sector

Year	Total Classified Assets	Rest of World	Government	Banks	Businesses and Individuals							
					Total	Securities			Loans			Total Long Term
						Total	Stocks	Other	Total	Short Term	Long Term	
1945	3617	113	153	1654	1697	175	127	48	1522	1191	330	505
1946	3756	124	137	1553	1942	235	163	72	1707	1301	407	642
1947	3958	98	164	1369	2327	310	222	88	2017	1564	454	764
1948	4445	140	155	1461	2689	349	271	78	2340	1841	499	848
1949	4847	159	177	1600	2911	376	303	73	2535	1907	629	1005
1950	6273	−111	317	2609	3458	408	314	94	3050	2322	729	1137
1951	7245	130	264	2597	4254	469	330	139	3785	2717	1068	1537
1952	7995	203	212	2824	4756	572	329	243	4184	2971	1213	1785
1953	8641	197	318	3088	5038	470	313	157	4568	3344	1225	1695
1954	10028	333	312	3426	5957	567	384	183	5390	3937	1454	2021
1955	12310	329	677	4174	7130	673	424	249	6457	4937	1520	2193
1956	14127	309	880	4512	8426	854	524	330	7572	5749	1822	2676
1957	16362	275	1109	5357	9621	1097	638	459	8524	6452	2073	3170
1958	18676	827	1555	6025	10269	1276	817	459	8993	6519	2474	3750
1959	22190	833	2330	6610	12417	1454	926	528	10963	7955	3009	4463
1960	25529	224	2937	7494	14874	1625	1070	555	13249	9356	3893	5518

TABLE 5—Continued

Liabilities and Capital: By Owning Sector

Year	Total Liabilities and Capital	Total Classified	Banks	Rest of World	Government			Businesses and Individuals				
					Total	Deposits	Capital	Total	Money	Other Deposits, Etc.	Securities	Capital
1945	3766	3664	568					3096	1923	596	239	338
1946	3939	3819	735					3084	1821	581	283	399
1947	4165	4021	812					3209	1759	632	345	473
1948	4683	4513	870					3643	1966	744	398	535
1949	5134	4934	863					4071	2161	909	447	554
1950	6641	6414	982		(no entries)			5432	3220	1046	532	634
1951	7661	7386	1095					6291	3528	1347	680	736
1952	8460	8150	1215					6935	3809	1539	722	865
1953	9151	8812	1096					7716	4074	1832	667	1144
1954	10554	10159	1377					8782	4953	2252	496	1081
1955	12948	12439	1252					11187	6289	2832	789	1277
1956	14817	14208	1496					12712	6865	3551	860	1436
1957	17236	16539	1783					14756	7675	4612	847	1622
1958	19584	18788	2623					16165	8268	5563	742	1592
1959	23186	22217	3037					19180	9320	7143	790	1927
1960	26717	25556	3408					22148	10067	8877	1232	1972

For sources and definitions, see Note 1.

TABLE 6

BANCO DE MEXICO, S.A.: BALANCE SHEET

MEXICO, 1945–1960

(End of year stocks in millions of pesos)

Assets: By Debtor Sector

Year	Total Classified Assets	Rest of World	Government	Banks	Businesses and Individuals								Total Long Term
					Total	Securities			Loans				
						Total	Stocks	Other	Total	Short Term	Long Term		
1945	3328	1801	693	360	474	33	5	28	441	441	0	33
1946	3147	1313	837	389	608	99	65	34	509	508	0	99
1947	3093	778	960	522	833	152	21	131	681	682	0	152
1948	3493	839	1424	397	833	188	32	156	645	644	0	188
1949	4088	1401	1935	297	455	292	48	244	163	163	0	292
1950	5257	2846	1578	398	435	240	72	168	195	195	0	240
1951	5446	2647	1579	561	659	228	77	151	431	431	0	228
1952	5690	2563	1627	716	784	281	117	164	503	503	0	281
1953	6132	2349	1794	955	1034	248	139	109	786	785	0	248
1954	6853	2587	2382	843	1041	267	129	138	774	774	0	267
1955	8021	5103	1952	432	534	227	98	129	307	307	0	227
1956	8927	5858	1536	472	1061	186	96	90	875	875	0	186
1957	9620	6122	1821	660	1017	212	102	110	805	806	0	212
1958	10355	5128	2437	840	1950	644	102	542	1306	1306	0	644
1959	11521	5911	1601	1163	2846	466	340	126	2380	2381	0	466
1960	12115	5750	1900	1163	3302	562	409	153	2740	2739	2	564

TABLE 6—Continued

Liabilities and Capital: By Owning Sector

Year	Total Liabilities and Capital	Total Classified	Banks	Rest of World	Government			Businesses and Individuals				
					Total	Deposits	Capital	Total	Money	Other Deposits, Etc.	Securities	Capital
1945	3417	3330	1457		90	1	89	1783	1731	49		3
1946	3206	3152	1215		81	1	80	1856	1799	54		3
1947	3272	3183	1072		130	31	99	1981	1814	167		0
1948	3813	3472	927		156	30	126	2389	2173	211		5
1949	4401	3950	1062		179	52	127	2709	2454	250		5
1950	5621	5282	2014		212	76	136	3056	2988	68		0
1951	5934	5512	1652	(no entries)	220	73	147	3640	3549	91	(no entries)	0
1952	6320	5808	1715		271	119	152	3822	3724	98		0
1953	6782	6241	1955		239	35	204	4048	3961	86		0
1954	7952	7121	2039		255	47	208	4827	4749	78		0
1955	9009	8217	2476		471	242	229	5270	5204	66		0
1956	9935	9136	2446		698	290	408	5992	5886	106		0
1957	10429	9587	2508		695	269	426	6383	6265	114		4
1958	11329	10408	2845		518	82	436	7045	6910	135		0
1959	12421	11444	3228		564	123	441	7652	7516	136		0
1960	13205	12027	3117		628	188	440	8282	8097	185		0

For sources and definitions, see Note 1.

157

TABLE 7

GOVERNMENT NONMONETARY INTERMEDIARIES: BALANCE SHEET

MEXICO, 1945–1960

(End of year stocks in millions of pesos)

Assets: By Debtor Sector

Year	Total Classified Assets	Rest of World	Government	Banks	Businesses and Individuals Total	Securities Total	Stocks	Other	Loans Total	Short Term	Long Term	Total Long Term
1945	1217	6	402	152	657	166	64	102	491	124	366	532
1946	1505	1	473	178	853	159	60	99	694	289	405	564
1947	1799	3	448	261	1087	206	85	121	881	389	493	699
1948	2212	11	326	339	1536	214	117	97	1322	454	868	1082
1949	2766	28	117	191	2430	389	106	283	2041	682	1359	1748
1950	3559	21	284	353	2901	295	79	216	2606	644	1962	2257
1951	4559	19	−20	529	4031	402	59	343	3629	1074	2555	2957
1952	5085	24	178	552	4331	487	62	425	3844	874	2970	3457
1953	6163	39	268	810	5046	772	239	533	4274	1586	2687	3459
1954	7735	7	207	609	6912	1127	334	793	5785	1988	3798	4925
1955	7962	17	455	565	6925	758	393	365	6167	2052	4115	4873
1956	8582	28	586	799	7169	814	463	351	6355	1950	4404	5218
1957	9387	6	695	485	8201	912	472	440	7289	2243	5045	5957
1958	11042	4	588	666	9784	1042	616	426	8742	2809	5933	6975
1959	12804	27	338	702	11737	1231	759	472	10506	4617	5889	7120
1960	17633	21	908	1131	15573	1259	941	318	14314	5254	9060	10319

TABLE 7—Continued

Liabilities and Capital: By Owning Sector

Year	Total Liabilities and Capital	Total Classified	Banks	Rest of World	Government			Businesses and Individuals				
					Total	Deposits	Capital	Total	Money	Other Deposits, Etc.	Securities	Capital
1945	1295	1211	430	73	242		242	466	64	208	180	14
1946	1608	1490	547	228	280		280	435	43	213	162	17
1947	1921	1782	679	307	300		300	496	35	247	182	32
1948	2358	2191	680	506	411		411	594	99	286	186	23
1949	2931	2744	362	780	905		905	697	120	322	236	19
1950	3858	3605	652	743	925		925	1285	141	507	596	41
1951	5116	4834	1345	959	970	(no entries)	970	1560	157	673	688	42
1952	5809	5437	1638	1114	971		971	1713	154	704	849	6
1953	7151	6591	2088	1302	1258		1258	1944	205	923	725	90
1954	9050	8407	1949	1924	1362		1362	3172	412	1884	806	70
1955	9571	8853	2035	1890	1668		1668	3260	411	2025	771	53
1956	10521	9500	2022	2014	2238		2238	3225	453	1935	777	60
1957	10983	10014	2675	2225	2220		2220	2894	470	1798	566	60
1958	12755	11497	2987	2968	2246		2246	3296	647	2003	585	61
1959	14648	13296	3092	3564	2839		2839	3800	527	2522	672	79
1960	19549	17909	4121	6135	3020		3020	4633	607	2961	981	84

For sources and definitions, see Note 1.

159

TABLE 8

DEPOSIT AND SAVINGS BANKS: BALANCE SHEET

MEXICO, 1945–1960

(End of year stocks in millions of pesos)

Assets: By Debtor Sector

Year	Total Classified Assets	Rest of World	Government	Banks	Businesses and Individuals Total	Securities Total	Securities Stocks	Securities Other	Loans Total	Loans Short Term	Loans Long Term	Total Long Term
1945	2822	111	118	1556	1037	18	11	7	1019	987	32	50
1946	2764	120	102	1453	1089	47	32	15	1042	1004	37	84
1947	2793	93	126	1264	1310	85	55	30	1225	1157	67	152
1948	3204	135	118	1354	1597	97	68	29	1500	1411	89	186
1949	3558	151	141	1487	1779	134	111	23	1645	1535	111	245
1950	4858	−117	281	2464	2230	149	118	31	2081	1904	179	328
1951	5451	116	224	2421	2690	166	115	51	2524	2232	292	458
1952	5915	188	182	2604	2941	175	127	48	2766	2357	411	586
1953	6785	179	393	2855	3458	189	134	55	3269	2799	471	660
1954	7804	302	291	3189	4022	235	155	80	3787	3210	577	812
1955	9629	304	653	3859	4813	288	166	122	4525	3976	549	837
1956	10652	278	857	4155	5362	363	178	185	4999	4371	628	991
1957	11814	246	1093	4863	5612	484	234	250	5128	4464	665	1149
1958	12870	567	1137	5349	5817	525	256	269	5292	4460	832	1357
1959	14352	662	1649	5703	6338	588	307	281	5750	4938	813	1401
1960	15524	115	2071	6367	6971	569	293	276	6402	5630	772	1341

TABLE 8—Continued

Liabilities and Capital: By Owning Sector

Year	Total Liabilities and Capital	Total Classified	Banks	Rest of World	Government			Businesses and Individuals				
					Total	Deposits	Capital	Total	Money	Other Deposits, Etc.	Securities	Capital
1945	2904	2843	289					2554	1906	504		144
1946	2856	2787	349					2438	1813	472		153
1947	2884	2801	390					2411	1756	498		157
1948	3309	3209	494					2715	1959	575		181
1949	3693	3575	537					3038	2148	686		204
1950	5047	4915	606					4309	3201	861		247
1951	5673	5514	642		(no entries)			4872	3519	1025	(no entries)	328
1952	6167	5983	659					5324	3792	1144		388
1953	7057	6843	836					6006	4066	1359		582
1954	8115	7838	846					6992	4901	1567		524
1955	10020	9691	941					8750	6244	1886		620
1956	11082	10679	1060					9619	6822	2109		688
1957	12368	11911	1122					10789	7642	2414		733
1958	13493	12976	1539					11437	8261	2645		531
1959	15059	14447	1542					12905	9315	2899		691
1960	16254	15550	1482					14068	10061	3298		709

For sources and definitions, see Note 1.

161

Table 9

TOTAL PRIVATE NONMONETARY INTERMEDIARIES: BALANCE SHEET

MEXICO, 1945–1960

(End of year stocks in millions of pesos)

Assets: By Debtor Sector

Year	Total Classified Assets	Rest of World	Government	Banks	Businesses and Individuals								
						Securities			Loans			Total Long Term
					Total	Total	Stocks	Other	Total	Short Term	Long Term	
1945	795	2	35	98	660	157	116	41	503	204	298	455
1946	992	4	35	100	853	188	131	57	665	297	370	558
1947	1165	5	38	105	1017	225	167	58	792	407	387	612
1948	1241	5	37	107	1092	252	203	49	840	430	410	662
1949	1289	8	36	113	1132	242	192	50	890	372	518	760
1950	1415	6	36	145	1228	259	196	63	969	418	550	809
1951	1794	14	40	176	1564	303	215	88	1261	485	776	1079
1952	2080	15	30	220	1815	397	202	195	1418	614	802	1199
1953	1856	18	25	233	1580	281	179	102	1299	545	754	1035
1954	2224	31	21	237	1935	332	229	103	1603	727	877	1209
1955	2681	25	24	315	2317	385	258	127	1932	961	971	1356
1956	3475	31	23	375	3064	491	346	145	2573	1378	1194	1685
1957	4548	29	16	494	4009	613	404	209	3396	1988	1408	2021
1958	5806	260	418	676	4452	751	561	190	3701	2059	1642	2393
1959	7838	171	681	907	6079	866	619	247	5213	3017	2196	3062
1960	10005	109	866	1127	7903	1058	777	279	6847	3726	3121	4177

TABLE 9—Continued

Liabilities and Capital: By Owning Sector

Year	Total Liabilities and Capital	Total Classified	Banks	Rest of World	Government Total	Government Deposits	Government Capital	Businesses and Individuals Total	Money	Other Deposits, Etc.	Securities	Capital
1945	862	821	279					542	17	92	239	194
1946	1083	1032	386					646	8	109	283	246
1947	1281	1220	442					798	3	134	345	316
1948	1374	1304	376					928	7	169	398	354
1949	1441	1359	326					1033	13	223	447	350
1950	1594	1499	376					1123	19	185	532	387
1951	1988	1872	453		(no entries)			1419	9	322	680	408
1952	2293	2167	556					1611	17	395	722	477
1953	2094	1969	260					1709	8	472	667	562
1954	2439	2321	530					1791	52	685	496	558
1955	2928	2748	311					2437	45	946	789	657
1956	3735	3529	436					3093	43	1442	860	748
1957	4868	4628	661					3967	33	2198	847	889
1958	6091	5812	1083					4729	7	2918	742	1062
1959	8127	7770	1495					6275	5	4244	790	1236
1960	10463	10006	1926					8080	6	5579	1232	1263

For sources and definitions, see Note 1.

163

TABLE 10

TOTAL FINANCIAL INTERMEDIARY SECTOR: SELECTED REAL SOURCES AND USES OF FUNDS

MEXICO, 1944–1960

(Millions of 1950 pesos)

Year	Total Uses Classified	Sources of Funds					Used to Purchase Primary Securities			
		Govern-ment	Businesses and Individuals			Total	Govern-ment	Businesses and Individuals		
			Total	Non-monetary	Money			Total	Long Term	Short Term
1944	2235	—	1551	364	1164	1254	232	1023	420	603
1945	2016	—	1122	609	484	1293	397	895	656	239
1946	335	39	39	113	−76	1054	271	783	320	465
1947	569	88	400	471	−71	1245	161	1085	398	690
1948	1115	165	1022	333	689	1370	399	971	603	364
1949	1412	565	842	355	485	1161	355	807	1014	−205
1950	3386	54	2294	681	1613	948	−50	998	589	409
1951	1741	42	1386	673	713	1446	−287	1734	876	855
1952	1182	41	762	408	352	872	151	720	623	97
1953	1718	201	980	542	439	1276	287	988	−95	1084
1954	1833	87	1732	553	1221	2402	378	2024	1312	713
1955	2346	333	1873	730	1141	549	117	433	51	381
1956	2037	486	1348	555	793	1210	−50	1259	479	779
1957	2181	−12	1231	525	704	1640	365	1275	736	542
1958	2632	−85	1384	592	792	2306	535	1772	1137	634
1959	3564	353	2282	1431	851	2592	−171	2764	376	2389
1960	3852	129	2335	1593	742	3569	778	2791	1528	1263

For sources and definitions, see Note 2.

TABLE 11

TOTAL MONETARY INTERMEDIARIES: SELECTED REAL SOURCES AND USES OF FUNDS

MEXICO, 1944-1960

(Millions of 1950 pesos)

Year	Total Uses Classified	Government	Sources of Funds			Used to Purchase Primary Securities				
			Businesses and Individuals					Businesses and Individuals		
			Total	Non-monetary	Money	Total	Government	Total	Long Term	Short Term
1944	1409	—	1233	111	1122	761	193	568	16	552
1945	1288	—	598	218	396	423	227	196	34	161
1946	-325	-13	-59	-26	-34	427	174	253	136	114
1947	-32	63	126	179	-54	762	189	573	155	421
1948	533	32	762	154	607	890	546	344	84	257
1949	763	25	625	168	457	369	584	-214	178	-390
1950	2467	33	1617	31	1586	214	-217	431	31	401
1951	630	6	925	217	708	506	-45	552	95	454
1952	551	40	493	144	348	297	4	292	141	153
1953	1040	-26	720	315	405	829	220	608	33	574
1954	446	12	1057	17	1039	838	425	414	124	290
1955	1909	138	1404	257	1147	137	-43	182	-10	191
1956	1175	138	970	201	768	527	-130	656	69	587
1957	1084	-1	913	212	700	425	305	120	107	14
1958	1002	-99	732	25	707	1006	370	637	358	278
1959	1465	25	1148	230	918	604	-179	784	-74	859
1960	931	34	945	246	699	954	380	574	20	554

For sources and definitions, see Note 2.

TABLE 12

TOTAL NONMONETARY INTERMEDIARIES: SELECTED REAL SOURCES AND USES OF FUNDS

MEXICO, 1944-1960

(Millions of 1950 pesos)

Year	Total Uses Classified	Sources of Funds					Used to Purchase Primary Securities				
		Govern-ment	Businesses and Individuals			Total	Govern-ment	Total	Businesses and Individuals		
			Total	Non-monetary	Money				Total	Long Term	Short Term
1944	826	—	318	253	42	493	38	493	455	404	51
1945	728	—	524	392	88	870	171	870	700	621	78
1946	660	52	98	139	-42	627	97	627	530	184	351
1947	601	25	274	292	-17	483	-28	483	512	243	269
1948	582	133	260	178	81	480	-147	480	627	519	107
1949	649	540	216	187	28	792	-229	792	1021	836	185
1950	919	21	677	650	27	734	167	734	567	558	8
1951	1111	36	461	456	5	940	-242	940	1182	781	401
1952	631	1	269	264	4	575	147	575	428	482	-56
1953	678	227	260	227	34	447	67	447	380	-128	510
1954	1387	75	676	535	182	1564	-47	1564	1610	1188	423
1955	437	195	469	473	-6	412	160	412	251	61	190
1956	862	348	378	354	25	683	80	683	603	410	192
1957	1097	-11	318	313	4	1215	60	1215	1155	629	528
1958	1630	14	652	567	85	1300	165	1300	1135	779	356
1959	2099	328	1134	1201	-67	1988	8	1988	1980	450	1530
1960	2921	95	1390	1347	43	2615	398	2615	2217	1508	709

For sources and definitions, see Note 2.

166

TABLE 13

TOTAL GOVERNMENT INTERMEDIARIES: SELECTED REAL SOURCES AND USES OF FUNDS

MEXICO, 1944-1960

(Millions of 1950 pesos)

Year	Total Uses Classified	Sources of Funds					Used to Purchase Primary Securities			
		Govern-ment	Businesses and Individuals			Total	Govern-ment	Businesses and Individuals		
			Total	Non-monetary	Money			Total	Long Term	Short Term
1944	1075	—	617	45	549	676	153	523	171	352
1945	804	—	154	209	−85	648	280	368	419	−52
1946	146	39	56	−9	63	743	293	450	134	315
1947	309	88	239	230	9	716	126	590	241	352
1948	581	165	600	97	503	947	410	537	502	32
1949	1016	565	454	128	326	894	331	564	842	−277
1950	1961	54	934	379	555	261	−190	451	457	−6
1951	958	42	693	229	465	847	−244	1092	554	537
1952	599	41	261	126	134	522	191	330	430	−100
1953	1206	201	361	133	229	968	203	764	−24	788
1954	891	87	1192	519	714	1740	382	1358	1076	283
1955	890	333	339	49	289	−432	−116	−315	−59	−257
1956	930	486	419	−23	442	296	−174	469	185	284
1957	875	−12	36	−196	231	808	231	577	447	131
1958	1337	−85	595	135	460	1694	285	1409	812	597
1959	1620	353	615	346	269	975	−600	1576	−18	1595
1960	2092	129	771	423	348	1954	458	1496	972	525

For sources and definitions, see Note 2.

TABLE 14

TOTAL PRIVATE INTERMEDIARIES: SELECTED REAL SOURCES AND USES OF FUNDS

MEXICO, 1944-1960

(Millions of 1950 pesos)

Year	Total Uses Classified	Sources of Funds					Used to Purchase Primary Securities			
		Govern-ment	Businesses and Individuals			Total	Govern-ment	Businesses and Individuals		
			Total	Non-monetary	Money			Total	Long Term	Short Term
1944	1160	(no entries)	934	319	615	578	78	500	249	251
1945	1211		969	401	568	645	117	527	236	291
1946	189		−17	122	−139	311	−22	333	186	150
1947	260		161	241	−80	529	35	495	157	338
1948	534		422	236	186	423	−11	434	101	332
1949	396		388	227	160	267	24	243	172	72
1950	1425		1360	302	1058	687	140	547	132	415
1951	783		693	444	248	599	−43	642	322	318
1952	583		501	282	218	350	−40	390	193	197
1953	512		619	409	210	308	84	224	−71	296
1954	942		541	33	507	662	−4	666	236	430
1955	1456		1534	681	852	981	233	748	110	638
1956	1107		929	578	351	914	124	790	294	495
1957	1306		1195	721	473	832	134	698	289	411
1958	1295		789	457	332	612	250	363	325	37
1959	1944		1667	1085	582	1617	429	1188	394	794
1960	1760		1564	1170	394	1615	320	1295	556	738

For sources and definitions, see Note 2.

TABLE 15

BANCO DE MEXICO, S.A.: SELECTED REAL SOURCES AND USES OF FUNDS

MEXICO, 1944-1960

(Millions of 1950 pesos)

| | | Sources of Funds | | | | Used to Purchase Primary Securities | | | | |
| | | | Businesses and Individuals | | | | | Businesses and Individuals | | |
Year	Total Uses Classified	Govern-ment	Total	Non-monetary	Money	Total	Govern-ment	Total	Long Term	Short Term
1944	561	—	456	−61	517	460	106	354	16	338
1945	407	—	−172	8	−164	85	133	−49	16	−64
1946	−246	−13	99	6	92	378	196	182	90	91
1947	−69	63	161	141	19	447	158	289	68	224
1948	87	32	483	56	426	556	556	0	43	−46
1949	414	25	343	39	304	145	559	−413	114	−526
1950	1168	33	347	−187	534	−377	−357	−20	−52	32
1951	152	6	471	19	452	181	1	181	−10	190
1952	190	40	142	5	136	135	37	97	41	56
1953	351	−26	179	−9	188	331	132	198	−26	224
1954	−236	12	548	−17	564	431	426	5	14	−8
1955	745	138	283	−8	290	−598	−274	−323	−26	−298
1956	552	138	440	24	416	68	−254	321	−25	346
1957	405	−1	229	7	221	141	167	−26	15	−40
1958	411	−99	370	9	361	867	345	522	242	280
1959	645	25	336	1	335	33	−462	496	−98	595
1960	313	34	332	26	306	398	158	240	52	189

For sources and definitions, see Note 2.

TABLE 16

GOVERNMENT NONMONETARY INTERMEDIARIES: SELECTED REAL SOURCES AND USES OF FUNDS

MEXICO, 1944–1960

(Millions of 1950 pesos)

Year	Total Uses Classified	Sources of Funds					Used to Purchase Primary Securities			
		Govern-ment	Businesses and Individuals			Total	Govern-ment	Businesses and Individuals		
			Total	Non-monetary	Money			Total	Long Term	Short Term
1944	514	—	161	106	31	216	47	169	155	14
1945	397	—	326	201	80	563	147	416	404	13
1946	392	52	-43	-15	-29	365	97	268	44	224
1947	378	25	78	89	-10	269	-32	301	173	128
1948	493	133	117	41	77	391	-146	537	459	78
1949	602	540	110	89	22	749	-228	977	728	249
1950	793	21	587	566	21	638	167	471	509	-38
1951	806	36	222	210	13	666	-245	911	564	347
1952	409	1	119	121	-2	387	154	233	389	-156
1953	855	227	182	142	41	637	71	566	2	564
1954	1126	75	644	536	149	1309	-44	1353	1062	291
1955	145	195	56	57	-1	166	158	8	-33	41
1956	378	348	-21	-47	26	228	80	148	210	-62
1957	470	-11	-193	-203	10	667	64	603	432	171
1958	926	14	225	126	99	827	-60	887	570	317
1959	975	328	279	345	-66	942	-138	1080	80	1000
1960	1779	95	439	397	42	1556	300	1256	920	336

For sources and definitions, see Note 2.

TABLE 17

DEPOSIT AND SAVINGS BANKS: SELECTED REAL SOURCES AND USES OF FUNDS

MEXICO, 1944–1960

(Millions of 1950 pesos)

Year	Total Uses Classified	Sources of Funds					Used to Purchase Primary Securities				
		Govern-ment	Businesses and Individuals			Total	Total	Govern-ment	Businesses and Individuals		
			Total	Non-monetary	Money				Total	Long Term	Short Term
1944	848		777	172	605	301	301	87	214	0	214
1945	881		770	210	560	338	338	94	244	19	225
1946	−79		−158	−32	−126	49	49	−22	71	46	23
1947	37		−35	38	−73	315	315	31	284	87	197
1948	446		279	98	181	334	334	−10	344	41	303
1949	349		282	129	153	224	224	25	199	64	136
1950	1299		1270	218	1052	591	591	140	451	83	369
1951	478	(no entries)	454	198	256	325	325	−46	371	105	264
1952	361		351	139	212	162	162	−33	195	100	97
1953	689		541	324	217	498	498	88	410	59	350
1954	681		509	34	475	407	407	−1	409	110	298
1955	1164		1121	265	857	735	735	231	505	16	489
1956	623		530	177	352	459	459	124	335	94	241
1957	679		684	205	479	284	284	138	146	92	54
1958	591		362	16	346	139	139	25	115	116	−2
1959	820		812	229	583	571	571	283	288	24	264
1960	618		613	220	393	556	556	222	334	−32	365

For sources and definitions, see Note 2.

TABLE 18

TOTAL PRIVATE NONMONETARY INTERMEDIARIES: SELECTED REAL SOURCES AND USES OF FUNDS

MEXICO, 1944–1960

(Millions of 1950 pesos)

Year	Total Uses Classified	Sources of Funds					Used to Purchase Primary Securities			
		Govern-ment	Businesses and Individuals			Total	Govern-ment	Businesses and Individuals		
			Total	Non-monetary	Money			Total	Long Term	Short Term
1944	312		157	146	10	277	−9	286	249	37
1945	330		199	191	8	307	23	283	218	66
1946	268		141	154	−13	262	0	262	140	127
1947	223		196	203	−7	214	4	211	70	141
1948	89		143	138	5	89	−1	90	60	29
1949	47		106	98	7	43	−1	44	108	−64
1950	126	(no entries)	90	84	6	96	0	96	49	46
1951	305		239	246	−8	274	3	271	217	54
1952	222		150	143	6	188	−7	195	93	100
1953	−177		78	85	−7	−190	−4	−186	−130	−54
1954	261		32	−1	33	255	−3	257	126	132
1955	292		413	416	−5	246	2	243	94	149
1956	484		399	401	−1	455	0	455	200	254
1957	627		511	516	−6	548	−4	552	197	357
1958	704		427	441	−14	473	225	248	209	39
1959	1124		855	856	−1	1046	146	900	370	530
1960	1142		951	950	1	1059	98	961	588	373

For sources and definitions, see Note 2.

TABLE 19

FINANCIAL INTERMEDIARY SECTOR

SELECTED LOANS AND INVESTMENTS: BY INDUSTRY, MEXICO, 1942–1960

(End of year stocks in millions of pesos)

			Businesses and Individuals			
Year	Total	Government	Total	Commerce	Industry and Mining	Agriculture and Ranching
1942	2024	789	1235	337	470	428
1943	2530	861	1669	499	641	529
1944	3250	994	2256	531	969	756
1945	4076	1248	2828	960	1284	584
1946	4850	1447	3403	1088	1730	585
1947	5819	1572	4247	1226	2313	708
1948	6963	1905	5058	1344	2944	770
1949	8025	2229	5796	1508	3372	916
1950	8973	2179	6794	1968	3764	1062
1951	10767	1823	8944	2246	5446	1252
1952	11888	2017	9871	2449	5892	1530
1953	13498	2380	11118	2499	6566	2053
1954	16811	2901	13910	3033	8741	2136
1955	17673	3084	14589	3354	8428	2807
1956	19658	3002	16656	4304	9113	3239
1957	22464	3625	18839	4709	10525	3605
1958	26583	4580	22003	5326	12634	4043
1959	31269	4269	27000	6842	15122	5036
1960	39494	5745	33749	8030	19750	5969

Source: BMIA, 1960, p. 94.

TABLE 20

FINANCIAL INTERMEDIARY SECTOR

SELECTED REAL USES OF FUNDS: BY INDUSTRY, MEXICO, 1943–1960

(Net annual flow in millions of 1950 pesos)[1]

			Businesses and Individuals			
Year	Total	Government	Total	Commerce	Industry and Mining	Agriculture and Ranching
1943	1082	154	928	346	366	216
1944	1254	231	1023	56	571	395
1945	1293	398	895	671	493	−269
1946	1052	270	782	174	606	1
1947	1245	161	1084	177	749	158
1948	1370	399	971	141	756	74
1949	1161	354	807	179	468	160
1950	948	−50	998	460	392	146
1951	1446	−287	1733	224	1356	153
1952	872	151	721	158	347	216
1953	1276	287	989	40	534	415
1954	2401	378	2023	387	1576	60
1955	550	17	433	205	−200	428
1956	1210	−50	1260	579	417	263
1957	1640	364	1276	237	825	214
1958	2305	535	1770	345	1180	245
1959	2592	−172	2764	839	1376	549
1960	3569	778	2791	626	1673	492

Source: Table 19.
[1] Deflated with Mexico City General Wholesale Price Index.

TABLE 21

BUSINESS AND INDIVIDUAL SECTOR: SELECTED SOURCES AND USES OF FUNDS

MEXICO, 1940–1960

(Millions of pesos)

| | Sources of Funds | | | | | Uses of Funds | | | | | | | | | |
| | | | | | | Goods and Services Purchases | | | | Financial Asset Purchases | | | | | |
Year	Current Non-Transfer Disposable Income[1]	Government Transfers[2]	Direct Foreign Investment[3]	Primary Security Issues[4]	Total Uses Classified[5]	Total	Private Investment[6]	Government Ent. Investment[7]	Consumption & Inventory Acc.[8]	Total	Government Securities[9]	Bus. & Ind. Primary Sec.[10]	Non-Monetary Indirect[11]	Money[12]	Discrepancy Col. 6 − (Cols. 2, 3, 4, & 5)
1940	6575	11	45	(no entries)	(no entries)	6361	457	146	5758	(no entries)	(no entries)	(no entries)	(no entries)	(no entries)	(no entries)
1941	7968	0	79			7917	608	115	7194						
1942	9760	17	167			9453	524	146	8783						
1943	12388	31	43			11849	659	184	11006						
1944	16175	90	194	611	16908	16064	1016	259	14789	844	−27	24	183	668	−162
1945	18841	125	223	622	19216	18579	1348	385	16846	637	−86	50	330	309	−595
1946	23898	158	56	731	25042	24852	2156	429	22267	190	−20	141	84	−55	199
1947	26619	358	181	867	27937	27635	2726	634	24275	302	−10	0	367	−55	−188
1948	29018	495	229	817	30558	29718	2917	766	26035	840	−26	14	277	575	−1
1949	31612	798	263	742	32768	32010	3087	1048	27875	758	−13	1	325	444	−647
1950	37659	782	626	1212	40383	38113	3294	1468	33351	2270	−163	147	682	1614	104
1951	46464	1565	1043	2163	51235	49373	3855	1472	44046	1862	−26	117	834	885	0
1952	52466	1648	590	1255	55392	54266	4732	1746	47788	1126	−16	163	526	453	−567
1953	50997	1235	362	1677	54604	52861	4600	1554	46707	1743	172	334	684	553	333
1954	60010	1792	1165	3128	64670	61843	5400	2105	54338	2827	84	15	1044	1684	−1425
1955	75324	2109	1319	1704	80516	77155	7600	2090	67465	3361	86	339	1146	1790	60
1956	84384	2899	1580	3029	91096	88236	9060	2438	76738	2860	180	468	912	1300	−796
1957	93020	3514	1645	3468	100147	97849	10124	2496	85229	2298	−173	367	898	1206	−1500
1958	103505	3010	1253	4714	111972	108654	10770	3594	94290	3318	−20	865	1058	1415	−510
1959	110354	3417	1014	6493	119970	114190	10944	3673	99573	5780	530	1124	2588	1538	−1308
1960	121199	6272	1361	4754	132748	127853	12435	5604	109814	4895	868	−404	3023	1408	−838

[1] *Source:* *BMIA*, 1960, p. 73 and Column 2, Table 23. Calculated as GNP less government nontransfer income.

[2] *Source:* Column 8, Table 23.

[3] *Source:* Column 6, Table 25.

[4] *Source:* Column 13 of this table, Column 10 of Table 25, and Column 9, Table 10.

[5] Column 7 plus Column 11.

[6] *Source:* 1940–1951, *CM*, pp. 34–35; 1952–1959, *NFIA*, 1954–1960, Table entitled "Mexico's National Budget"; and 1960, *El Mercado de Valores*, (November 20, 1961), p. 589.

[7] *Source:* Same as Note 6, above.

[8] *Source:* 1940–1954 and 1960 computed as GNP less the sum of public fixed investment, private fixed investment, and net foreign investment. 1955–1959 *NFIA*, 1956–1960, Table entitled "Mexico's National Budget."

[9] *Source:* 1944–1945 computed as government securities less purchases of government securities by financial intermediaries and rest-of-world sector, 1946–1960, *BMIA*, 1950–1960, Tables entitled "Liquid Assets of Businesses and Individuals" and (only 1955–1960) "Circulation and Holdings of Fixed Interest Securities." The investments of decentralized agencies and government enterprises are added to the liquid assets figures for 1953–1960 since they are included in the pre-1953 figures.

[10] Includes only cédulas hipotecarias, obligaciones hipotecarias, and obligaciones no hipotecarias de Petroleos Mexicanos, all of which are fixed-interest securities.

Source: 1944–1945, *BMIA*, 1948, pp. 105–147, and Comisión Nacional de Valores, *Memoria*, 1960, p. 97 (computed as change in total private fixed-interest securities less change in private financial intermediary securities less private nonbank securities purchased by financial intermediaries). 1946–1960, see Note 9, above, for the same years.

[11] *Source:* Column 5, Table 10.

[12] *Source:* Column 6, Table 10.

TABLE 22

BUSINESS AND INDIVIDUAL SECTOR: SELECTED REAL SOURCES AND USES OF FUNDS

MEXICO, 1940–1960

(Millions of 1950 pesos)[1]

| | Sources of Funds | | | | | Uses of Funds | | | | | | | | |
| | | | | | | Goods and Services Purchases | | | | Financial Asset Purchases | | | | |
Year	Current Non-Transfer Disposable Income	Government Transfers	Direct Foreign Investment	Primary Security Issues	Total Uses Classified	Total	Private Investment	Government Ent. Investment	Consumption	Total	Government Securities	Bus. & Ind. Securities	Non-Monetary Indirect	Money
1940	19924	33	136	(no entries)	(no entries)	19276	1385	442	17448	(no entries)	(no entries)	(no entries)	(no entries)	(no entries)
1941	22636	0	224			22491	1727	327	20438					
1942	25155	44	430			24363	1351	376	22637					
1943	26470	66	92			25318	1408	393	23517					
1944	28179	157	338	1064	29456	27986	1770	451	25765	1470	-47	42	319	1164
1945	29485	196	349	973	30072	29075	2110	603	26363	997	-135	78	516	484
1946	32470	215	76	993	34024	33766	2929	583	30254	258	27	192	114	-75
1947	34215	460	233	1114	35909	35521	3504	815	31202	388	-13	0	472	-71
1948	34752	593	274	978	36596	35590	3493	917	31180	1006	-31	17	332	689
1949	34549	872	287	811	35812	34984	3374	1145	30464	828	-14	1	355	485
1950	37621	781	625	1211	40343	38075	3291	1467	33318	2268	-163	147	681	1612
1951	37441	1261	840	1743	41285	39785	3106	1186	35492	1500	21	94	672	713
1952	40798	1281	459	976	43073	42198	3680	1358	37160	876	-12	127	409	352
1953	40442	979	287	1330	43302	41920	3648	1232	37040	1382	136	265	542	439
1954	43486	1299	844	2267	46862	44814	3913	1525	39375	2049	61	11	757	1220
1955	48038	1345	841	1087	51349	49206	4847	1333	43026	2143	55	216	731	1142
1956	51422	1767	963	1846	55512	53770	5521	1486	46763	1743	110	285	556	792
1957	54366	2054	961	2027	58531	57188	5917	1459	49812	1343	-101	214	525	705
1958	57921	1684	701	2638	62659	60802	6027	2011	52764	1857	-11	484	592	792
1959	61037	1890	561	3591	66355	63158	6053	2032	55074	3197	293	622	1431	851
1960	63856	3305	717	2505	69941	67362	6552	2953	57858	2579	457	-213	1593	742

Source: Table 21.

[1] Deflated with Mexico City General Wholesale Price Index.

176

TABLE 23

GOVERNMENT SECTOR: SELECTED SOURCES AND USES OF FUNDS

MEXICO, 1940-1960

(Millions of pesos)

	Sources of Funds			Uses of Funds							Discrepancy Col. 4 − (Col. 2 + Col. 3)
				Goods and Services Purchases				Indirect Security Purchases			
Year	Non-Transfer Current Income[1]	Government Security Issues[2]	Total Classified[8]	Total	Investment[3]	Other[4]	Transfers[5]	Total	Non-Monetary[6]	Money[7]	
1940	725	83	830	819	170	649	11				22
1941	832	105	936	936	247	689	0	(no entries)			−1
1942	940	264	1102	1085	345	740	17				−102
1943	1312	7	1383	1349	434	915	31	3		3	64
1944	1525	37	1566	1478	455	1023	90	−2		−2	4
1945	1659	180	1934	1810	543	1267	125	−1		−1	95
1946	2202	−114	2120	1933	677	1256	158	29	29	0	32
1947	2381	132	2588	2161	744	1417	358	69	39	30	75
1948	2682	338	2976	2343	850	1493	495	138	139	−1	−44
1949	3588	363	4034	2719	979	1740	798	517	495	22	83
1950	3841	−177	3668	2833	884	1949	782	53	29	24	4
1951	5336	−198	5040	3423	1094	2329	1565	52	55	−3	−98
1952	5834	161	6055	4354	1516	2838	1648	53	7	46	60
1953	5303	37	5645	4156	1388	2768	1235	254	338	−84	305
1954	6468	508	6875	4962	1627	3335	1792	121	109	12	−101
1955	8676	275	8075	5444	2138	3306	2109	522	327	195	−876
1956	9616	274	9906	6209	2237	3972	2899	798	750	48	16
1957	9980	276	10571	7078	2924	4154	3514	−21	0	−21	315
1958	10495	187	10474	7616	2922	4694	3010	−152	35	−187	−208
1959	11646	225	12263	8207	3199	5008	3417	639	598	41	392
1960	13201	1954	15155	8638	3129	5509	6272	245	180	65	—

¹ *Source:* 1940–1949, *CM*, pp. 372–373 (only income for the federal, state, and local governments, including the Federal District). 1950–1960, *BMIA*, 1953–1960, Tables entitled "Economic Classification of the Income of the Federal Government" and "Economic Classification of the Income of the Governments of the Federal District, States and Territories, and Counties." From the last source the figures are the sum of income from taxes which affect income and spending, and income from government services and property.

² *Source:* Comisión Nacional de Valores, *Memoria*, 1959–1961, Table 1; Column 9, Table 25; and *BMIA*, 1948–1960, Table entitled "Assets and Liabilities of the Banking System." National Securities Commission figures are used for the government domestic bonded debt and treasury certificates outstanding; Banco de Mexico figures are used for loans to the federal government. To the figures on changes in net foreign indebtedness of the Mexican federal government from Table 25 are added that portion of the foreign debt owned by Mexican financial intermediaries.

³ *Source:* 1940–1949, *CM*, pp. 46–51 (does not include investments of decentralized organizations and government enterprises); 1950–1954, *BMIA*, 1953–1956, Tables entitled "Economic Classification of Spending of the Federal Government" and "Economic Classification of Spending of the Governments, etc." (includes only expenses in conservation of natural resources, expenses on public works and construction, and investments); 1955–1959, *NFIA*, 1956–1960, Table entitled "Gross Public Investment," and *BMIA*, 1959, p. 74; and 1960, *El Mercado de Valores*,"

November 20, 1961, p. 590 (does not include investments of decentralized agencies and government enterprises).

⁴ *Source:* 1940–1949, *CM*, pp. 46–51, 360–361, and 372–373 (the figures here are current expenses of the various governments less transfers by the federal government to decentralized agencies and government enterprises to finance their investments); 1950–1954, *BMIA*, 1953–1956, Tables cited in note (³) above (includes only administration expenses); 1955–1959, *NFIA*, 1956–1960, Table entitled "Mexico's National Budget," and 1960, *BMIA*, 1960, pp. 16–17 (this figure of 11 per cent increase over 1959 is not precise since the source cites this percentage as the increase for the combination of government operating expenses and consumer expenditures).

⁵ *Source:* 1940–1949, *CM*, pp. 372–373 (total net spending of the various levels of government less purchases of goods and services from Column 5 of this table); 1950–1959, *BMIA*, 1953–1960, Tables cited in notes (¹) and (³) above (transfer spending of all levels of government plus other deductions from total spending less the sum of other income and other deductions from total income); and 1960 computed as a residual from total income in this table less other categories of spending. Government purchases of nonmonetary indirect securities from Table 1 were deducted from transfer payments from the above sources.

⁶ *Source:* Column 7, Table 1.
⁷ *Source:* Column 6, Table 1.
⁸ *Source:* Column 5 plus Column 8 plus Column 9.

179

TABLE 24

GOVERNMENT SECTOR: SELECTED REAL SOURCES AND USES OF FUNDS

MEXICO, 1940–1960

(Millions of 1950 pesos)[1]

	Sources of Funds			Uses of Funds						
				Goods and Services				Indirect Security Purchases		
Year	Non-Transfer Current Income	Govt. Security Issues	Total Classified	Total	Investment	Other	Transfers	Total	Non-Monetary	Money
1940	2197	252	2515	2482	515	1967	33			
1941	2364	298	2659	2659	702	1957	0		(no entries)	
1942	2423	680	2840	2796	889	1907	44			
1943	2803	15	2955	2882	927	1955	66	6		6
1944	2657	64	2728	2575	793	1782	157	−3		−3
1945	2596	282	3027	2833	850	1983	196	−2		−2
1946	2992	−155	2880	2626	920	1707	215	39	39	0
1947	3060	170	3326	2778	956	1821	460	89	50	39
1948	3212	405	3564	2806	1018	1788	593	165	166	−1
1949	3921	397	4409	2972	1070	1902	872	565	541	24
1950	3837	−177	3664	2830	883	1947	781	53	29	24
1951	4300	−160	4061	2758	882	1877	1261	42	44	−2
1952	4537	125	4708	3386	1179	2207	1281	41	5	36
1953	4205	29	4477	3296	1101	2195	979	201	268	−67
1954	4687	368	4982	3596	1179	2417	1299	88	79	9
1955	5533	175	5150	3472	1364	2108	1345	333	209	124
1956	5860	167	6037	3784	1363	2420	1767	486	457	29
1957	5833	161	6178	4137	1709	2428	2054	−12	0	−12
1958	5873	105	5861	4262	1635	2627	1684	−85	20	−105
1959	6441	124	6783	4539	1769	2770	1890	353	331	23
1960	6955	1030	7985	4551	1649	2903	3305	129	95	34

Source: Table 23.

[1] Deflated with Mexico City General Wholesale Price Index.

TABLE 25

REST-OF-WORLD SECTOR: SELECTED SOURCES AND USES OF FUNDS

MEXICO, 1940–1960

(Millions of pesos)[1]

| | Sources of Funds | | | Uses of Funds | | | | | | | |
| | | | | | Direct Foreign Investment | | Financial Asset Purchases | | | | Discrepancy Col. 4 − (Col. 2 + Col. 3) |
Year	Mexican Imports[2]	Mexican Gold, Silver, & Foreign Exchange Purchases[3]	Total Classified Uses[4]	Mexican Exports[2]	Total[5]	New Direct Investments[5]	Total	Government Securities[6]	Business and Individual Securities[7]	Non-Monetary Indirect[8]	
1940	787	106	940	907	45	49	−12	−12	(no entries)	0	47
1941	1148	7	1148	1095	79	68	−26	−26		0	−7
1942	1011	215	1359	1173	167	78	19	−25		44	133
1943	1283	641	1736	1785	43	39	−92	−87		−5	−188
1944	1724	211	2010	1882	194	102	−66	−61		−5	75
1945	2050	445	2378	2161	223	107	−6	−40		34	−117
1946	3193	−482	2603	2508	56	39	39	−131	15	155	−108
1947	3908	−559	3338	3112	181	78	45	−57	23	79	−11
1948	5275	−257	5150	4914	229	275	7	−55	−8	70	132
1949	5472	344	6388	5943	263	130	182	35	3	144	572
1950	6543	1168	7618	7097	626	329	−105	−135	67	−37	93
1951	9222	40	9320	8226	1043	433	51	−61	−104	216	58
1952	8965	−6	9372	8645	590	320	137	−183	165	155	413
1953	9190	−205	9008	8473	362	320	173	−111	96	188	23
1954	13460	−808	14600	13133	1165	975	302	−62	321	43	1948
1955	14880	2522	18082	16281	1319	1063	482	−170	686	−34	680
1956	18200	746	19832	17755	1580	1038	497	−121	494	124	886
1957	19506	208	20215	17579	1645	1263	991	−138	918	211	401
1958	19284	−444	19742	17014	1253	788	1475	47	685	743	902
1959	18608	812	20106	18211	1014	825	881	−87	372	596	686
1960	21091	−776	22129	19000	1361	950	1863	−573	−135	2571	453

[1] Quantities stated in dollars in the sources indicated have been multiplied by the following to convert them to pesos: 1940–1947, 4.85; 1948, 6.88; 1949–1953, 8.65; 1954–1960, 12.5.

[2] *Source: BMIA*, 1950–1960, Table entitled "Balance of Payments of Mexico." For 1953 and 1954 remissions abroad on direct foreign investments were added to the figures for imports published in the source.

[3] *Source:* 1940–1945, *BMIA*, 1950, p. 183; 1946–1960, Table 1, Column 15. For 1948, 1949, and 1954 these figures were adjusted for devaluations by using the difference between the current year figures and the figures for the previous year evaluated at current exchange rates.

[4] Sum of Columns 5, 6, and 8.

[5] *Source: BMIA*, 1956, p. 82; and *BMIA*, 1960, p. 92.

[6] *Source: BMIA*, various years 1948–1960, Tables entitled "Circulation of the Foreign Public Debt of the Federal Government," "Estimate of the Surplus or Deficit of the Federal Government," and "Assets and Liabilities of the Banking System." Except as noted the figures are annual changes in the sum of bonded debt and debts to various creditors (in earlier years floating debt) less that portion of the foreign bonded debt owned by the Mexican banking system. Three hundred sixteen million pesos are deducted from the published 1943 change in order to eliminate the effect of a renegotiation of the amount of the debt. For 1949, 422 million pesos are deducted from the published figures for that year in order

to eliminate the effect of railroad debt, which in that year was included in the published figures for the first time but which had been contracted several years earlier. Though in the source the category of international credits is included in the federal government foreign debt, it is excluded here since in most cases the financial intermediaries through which the debt is channeled consider these as loans to businesses and individuals. Figures for the years 1948, 1949, and 1954 are adjusted for changes in exchange rates during those years.

[7] *Source: BMIA*, 1955–1960, Table entitled "Balance of Payments of Mexico," Table 1, and *NFIA*, 1954, p. 56, and 1960, p. 49.

For 1940–1945 this column is the difference between total net foreign credits of maturities one year or more through Nacional Financiera less those credits which were direct. For the years 1946–1952 the figures are foreign credits through Nacional Financiera and the National Mortgage Bank less Column 5 of Table 1. For 1953–1960 these figures are long-term foreign credits from the balance of payments less Column 5 of Table 1.

The figures are adjusted for devaluations in 1948, 1949, and 1954.

[8] *Source:* Column 5, Table 1, and *NFIA*, 1960, p. 49. 1940–1945 includes only long-term credits to Nacional Financiera; 1946–1960 includes only sight and time obligations in foreign currencies of government non-monetary intermediaries. 1948, 1949, and 1954 adjusted for devaluations.

TABLE 26

REST-OF-WORLD SECTOR: SELECTED REAL SOURCES AND USES OF FUNDS

MEXICO, 1940–1960

(Millions of 1950 pesos)[1]

| | Sources of Funds | | | | Uses of Funds | | | | | |
| | | | | | Direct Foreign Investment | | Financial Asset Purchases | | | |
Year	Mexican Imports	Mexican Gold, Silver, & Foreign Exchange Purchases	Total Classified Uses	Mexican Exports	Total	New Direct Investments	Total	Government Securities	Business and Individual Securities	Non-Monetary Indirect
1940	2385	321	2848	2748	136	148	−36	−36		0
1941	3261	20	3261	3111	224	193	−74	−74		0
1942	2606	554	3503	3023	430	201	49	−64		113
1943	2741	1370	3709	3814	92	83	−197	−186	(no entries)	−11
1944	3003	368	3502	3279	338	178	−115	−106		−9
1945	3208	696	3721	3382	349	167	−9	−63		53
1946	4338	−655	3537	3408	76	53	53	−178	20	211
1947	5023	−719	4290	4000	233	100	58	−73	30	102
1948	6317	−308	6168	5885	274	329	8	−66	−10	84
1949	5980	376	6981	6495	287	142	199	38	3	157
1950	6536	1167	7610	7090	625	329	−105	−135	67	−37
1951	7431	32	7510	6629	840	349	41	−49	−84	174
1952	6971	−5	7288	6722	459	249	107	−142	128	121
1953	7288	−163	7144	6719	287	254	137	−88	76	149
1954	9754	−586	10580	9517	844	707	219	−45	233	31
1955	9490	1608	11532	10383	841	678	307	−108	438	−22
1956	11091	455	12085	10820	963	633	303	−74	301	76
1957	11400	122	11815	10274	961	738	579	−81	537	123
1958	10791	−248	11048	9521	701	441	825	26	383	416
1959	10292	449	11121	10072	561	456	487	−48	206	330
1960	11112	−409	11659	10011	717	501	982	−302	−71	1355

Source: Table 25.

[1] Deflated with Mexico City General Wholesale Price Index.

TABLE 27

GROSS NATIONAL PRODUCT AT 1950 PRICES: BY INDUSTRY

MEXICO, 1939–1961

(Millions of 1950 pesos)

Year	Agriculture	Ranching	Mining	Petroleum	Manufactures	Construction	Electricity	Transportation	Other Activities	Total
1939	2926	1434	1220	383	3348	488	110	864	9732	20505
1940	2729	1526	1190	371	3529	460	112	871	9833	20721
1941	3185	1574	1209	398	4058	512	112	897	11344	23389
1942	3776	1652	1376	352	4637	594	117	1009	12860	26373
1943	3607	1639	1387	363	4882	672	122	1169	13517	27358
1944	3852	1598	1235	392	5257	761	122	1257	15216	29690
1945	3703	1494	1319	437	5732	846	137	1244	17047	31959
1946	3787	1639	948	490	5846	862	148	1367	18997	34084
1947	4250	1778	1239	551	5681	887	160	1378	18593	34517
1948	4768	1784	1127	566	6133	833	177	1345	19347	36080
1949	5249	1805	1117	611	6676	781	193	1557	19638	37627
1950	5912	1972	1223	656	7643	756	197	1780	21361	41500
1951	6273	1952	1162	724	8100	846	219	1852	23372	44500
1952	6039	2019	1249	787	7949	928	238	2007	23784	45000
1953	6385	2049	1209	825	7968	871	254	2064	22775	44400
1954	7570	2278	1107	870	8666	916	280	2274	23839	47800
1955	7750	2416	1198	1003	9623	1009	312	2388	26801	52500
1956	7863	2552	1297	1101	10567	1135	349	2599	28537	56000
1957	8178	2642	1345	1219	11234	1273	376	2786	28947	58000
1958	8925	2760	1240	1393	11775	1252	405	2854	29996	60600
1959	8700	2888	1297	1625	12644	1307	435	2945	31559	63400
1960	11634		1336	1731	13731	1477	479	3183	33329	67000
1961	11983		1296	1991	14212	1492	525	3199	34702	69400

Sources: 1939–1959, México: Cinquenta Años de revolucion I: La Economía (México: Fondo de Cultura Económica, 1961), pp. 588–589. 1960–1961, El Mercado de Valores (March 5, 1962), pp. 117–119.

TABLE 28

INDEX OF REAL GROSS NATIONAL PRODUCT

MEXICO, 1939–1961

(1950 = 1000)

Year	Agriculture	Ranching	Mining	Petroleum	Manu-factures	Con-struction	Electricity	Trans-portation	Other Activities	Total
1939	495	727	998	584	438	646	558	485	456	494
1940	462	774	973	566	475	608	569	489	460	499
1941	539	798	989	607	531	677	569	504	531	561
1942	639	838	1125	537	607	786	594	567	602	635
1943	610	831	1134	553	639	889	619	657	633	659
1944	652	810	1010	598	688	1007	619	706	712	715
1945	626	758	1078	666	750	1119	695	699	798	770
1946	641	831	775	747	765	1140	751	768	889	821
1947	719	902	1013	840	743	1173	812	774	870	832
1948	806	905	922	863	802	1102	898	756	906	869
1949	888	915	913	931	873	1033	980	875	919	907
1950	1000	1000	1000	1000	1000	1000	1000	1000	1000	1000
1951	1061	990	950	1104	1060	1119	1112	1040	1094	1072
1952	1021	1024	1021	1200	1040	1228	1208	1128	1114	1084
1953	1080	1039	989	1258	1043	1152	1289	1160	1066	1070
1954	1280	1155	905	1326	1134	1212	1421	1278	1116	1152
1955	1311	1225	980	1529	1259	1335	1584	1342	1255	1265
1956	1330	1294	1061	1678	1383	1501	1772	1460	1336	1349
1957	1383	1340	1100	1858	1470	1684	1909	1565	1355	1398
1958	1510	1400	1014	2123	1541	1656	2056	1603	1404	1460
1959	1472	1465	1061	2477	1654	1729	2208	1654	1477	1528
1960	1475		1092	2639	1797	1954	2431	1788	1560	1614
1961	1520		1060	3035	1860	1973	2665	1803	1625	1672

Source: Table 27.

TABLE 29

REAL GROSS NATIONAL PRODUCT: BY INDUSTRY, MEXICO, 1940–1961

(Millions of 1950 pesos)

Year	Real GNP	Business and Individual			
		Total	Commerce	Industry and Mining	Agriculture and Ranching
1940	20721	18209	7321	6633	4255
1941	23289	20630	8685	7186	4759
1942	26373	23577	10064	8085	5428
1943	27358	24299	10458	8595	5246
1944	29690	26692	12218	9024	5450
1945	31959	28485	13573	9715	5197
1946	34084	30797	15710	9661	5426
1947	34517	31172	15248	9896	6028
1948	36080	32973	16240	10181	6552
1949	37627	34586	16597	10935	7054
1950	41500	38667	18528	12255	7884
1951	44500	41726	20598	12903	8225
1952	45000	41520	20304	13158	8058
1953	44400	41062	19437	13191	8434
1954	47800	44266	20305	14113	9848
1955	52500	49041	23342	15533	10166
1956	56000	52188	24725	17048	10415
1957	58000	53817	24764	18233	10820
1958	60600	56218	25614	18919	11685
1959	63400	58761	26920	20253	11588
1960	67000	62420	28873	21959	11588
1961	69400	64659	29961	22715	11983

Source: Table 27.

TABLE 30

INDEX OF REAL GROSS NATIONAL PRODUCT: BY INDUSTRY, MEXICO,

1940–1960

(1949–1951 = 100)

Year	Real GNP	Business and Individual			
		Total	Commerce	Industry and Mining	Agriculture and Ranching
1940	50	48	39	55	55
1941	57	54	47	60	62
1942	64	62	54	67	70
1943	66	63	56	71	68
1944	72	70	66	75	71
1945	78	74	73	81	67
1946	83	80	85	80	70
1947	84	81	82	82	78
1948	88	86	87	85	85
1949	91	90	89	91	91
1950	101	101	100	102	102
1951	108	109	111	107	107
1952	109	108	109	109	104
1953	108	107	105	110	109
1954	116	115	109	117	128
1955	127	128	126	129	132
1956	136	136	133	142	135
1957	141	140	133	152	140
1958	147	147	138	157	151
1959	154	153	145	168	150
1960	163	163	155	183	150

Source: Table 29.

TABLE 31
REAL GROSS NATIONAL PRODUCT: BY INDUSTRY
ANNUAL PERCENTAGE CHANGE, MEXICO, 1941–1961
(Per cent)

| Year | Real GNP | Business and Individual | | | |
		Total	Commerce	Industry and Mining	Agriculture and Ranching
1941	12.4	13.3	18.6	8.3	11.8
1942	13.2	14.3	15.9	12.5	14.1
1943	3.7	3.1	3.9	6.3	−3.4
1944	8.5	9.8	16.8	5.0	3.9
1945	7.6	6.7	11.1	7.7	−4.6
1946	6.6	8.1	15.7	−0.6	4.4
1947	1.3	1.2	−2.9	2.4	11.1
1948	4.5	5.8	6.5	2.9	8.7
1949	4.3	4.9	2.2	7.4	7.7
1950	10.3	11.8	11.6	12.1	11.8
1951	7.2	7.9	11.2	5.3	4.3
1952	1.1	−0.5	−1.4	2.0	−2.0
1953	−1.3	−1.1	−4.3	0.3	4.7
1954	7.7	7.8	4.5	7.0	16.8
1955	9.8	10.8	15.0	10.1	3.2
1956	6.7	6.4	5.9	9.8	2.4
1957	3.6	3.1	0.2	7.0	3.9
1958	4.5	4.5	3.4	3.8	8.0
1959	4.6	4.5	5.1	7.1	−0.8
1960	5.7	6.2	7.3	8.4	0.0
1961	3.6	3.6	3.8	3.4	3.4

Source: Table 29.

TABLE 32
REAL GROSS NATIONAL PRODUCT: BY INDUSTRY
PER CENT OF TOTAL, MEXICO, 1940–1960
(Per cent)

| Year | Real GNP | Business and Individual | | | |
		Total	Commerce	Industry and Mining	Agriculture and Ranching
1940	100	88	35	32	21
1941	100	89	37	31	20
1942	100	89	38	31	21
1943	100	89	38	31	19
1944	100	90	41	30	18
1945	100	89	42	30	16
1946	100	90	46	28	16
1947	100	90	44	29	17
1948	100	91	45	28	18
1949	100	92	44	29	19
1950	100	93	46	30	19
1951	100	94	46	29	18
1952	100	92	45	29	18
1953	100	92	44	30	19
1954	100	93	42	30	21
1955	100	93	44	30	19
1956	100	93	44	30	19
1957	100	93	43	31	19
1958	100	93	42	31	19
1959	100	93	42	32	18
1960	100	93	43	33	17

Source: Table 29.

TABLE 33

MEXICO CITY WHOLESALE PRICE INDEX

MEXICO, 1940–1960

$(1950 = 100.0)$

Year	General Index	Consumer Goods Index	Producer Goods Index	Percentage Change in General Index
1940	33.0	33.0	32.6	2.6
1941	35.2	35.0	35.2	6.7
1942	38.8	38.9	38.8	10.2
1943	46.8	48.7	44.1	20.6
1944	57.4	62.8	49.3	22.7
1945	63.9	72.1	52.1	11.3
1946	73.6	83.8	58.8	15.1
1947	77.8	86.9	64.6	5.8
1948	83.5	89.1	75.4	7.3
1949	91.5	92.8	89.4	9.6
1950	100.0	100.0	100.0	9.4
1951	124.1	124.2	123.4	24.0
1952	128.6	130.7	125.1	3.7
1953	126.1	127.2	124.5	−1.9
1954	138.0	136.0	140.4	9.4
1955	156.8	155.3	157.4	13.6
1956	164.1	164.3	162.9	4.7
1957	171.1	172.2	169.2	4.3
1958	178.7	181.8	173.8	4.4
1959	180.8	183.2	176.9	1.2
1960	189.8	190.1	188.6	5.0

Source: *BMIA*, 1956, pp. 64–65, and 1960, p. 79.

BIBLIOGRAPHY

ANNUAL REPORTS, YEARBOOKS, AND STATISTICAL PUBLICATIONS

Asociación de Banqueros de México. *Anuario financiero de México.* México: Asociación de Banqueros de México, 1952 y 1961, XII y XXI.

Banco de México. *Asamblea general ordinaria de accionistas.* México: Banco de México, 1947–1961, XXVI-XL.

Banco Nacional de Comercio Exterior. *Comercio exterior de México.* México: Talleres de Imprenta y Offset "Policromica," 1960.

——. *Asamblea general ordinaria de accionistas.* México: Editorial Cultura, 1958–1960.

——. *Mexico 1960: Facts, Figures, Trends.* México: Banco Nacional de Comercio Exterior, 1961.

Comisión Nacional Bancaria. *El boletín estadístico de la Comisión Nacional Bancaria.* México: Comisión Nacional Bancaria, 1942–1960.

Comisión Nacional de Valores. *Memoria.* México: Comisión Nacional de Valores, 1958–1961.

International Monetary Fund. *International Financial Statistics.* Washington: International Monetary Fund, 1955–1961.

Nacional Financiera. *Asamblea general ordinaria de accionistas.* México: Nacional Financiera, 1949–1961, XV-XXVII.

Secretaría de Industria y Comercio, Dirección General de Estadística. *Anuario estadístico de los Estados Unidos Mexicanos.* México: Talleres Gráficos de la Nación, 1942–1959.

Secretaría de Industria y Comercio. *Memoria de labores.* México: Secretaría de Industria y Comercio, 1958–1960.

——. *Compendio estadístico.* México: Talleres Gráficos de la Nación, 1947–1958.

United Nations. *Statistical Yearbook.* New York: Statistical Office of the United Nations, 1948–1960.

PERIODICALS

Ackley, Gardner. "Liquidity Preference and Loanable Funds Theories of Interest: Comment," *American Economic Review* (September, 1957).

ASCHEIM, J. "Commercial Banks and Financial Intermediaries," *Journal of Political Economy* (February, 1959).

CHANDLER, LESTER V. "Monopolistic Elements in Commercial Banking," *Journal of Political Economy* (February, 1938).

"Los créditos del exterior en 1960," *El Mercado de Valores* (January 16, 1961).

CULBERTSON, J. M. "Financial Intermediaries and Monetary Theory," *American Economic Review* (March, 1958).

DIAMOND, WILLIAM. "Development Banks," *Investigación Económica* (Second Quarter, 1959).

Diario Oficial. (December 31, 1940).

"Evaluación de Nacional Financiera y su impacto en el desarrollo económico de México," *El Mercado de Valores* (August 7, 1961).

FERNÁNDEZ MORENO, HECTOR. "Intervención estatal en el crédito agrícola y ejidal," *Revista de Economia* (November, 1960).

FERNÁNDEZ Y FERNÁNDEZ, RAMÓN. "El crédito ejidal, préstamos y recuperaciones y cartera," *El Trimestre Económico* (April-June, 1958).

GURLEY, JOHN G., and SHAW, EDWARD S. "Financial Aspects of Economic Development," *American Economic Review* (September, 1955).

———. "Financial Intermediaries and the Saving-Investment Process," *Journal of Finance* (May, 1956).

———. "The Growth of Debt and Money in the United States, 1800–1950: A Suggested Interpretation," *Review of Economics and Statistics* (August, 1957).

JOHNSON, HARRY G. "Monetary Theory and Policy," *American Economic Review* (June, 1962).

MCDONALD, STEPHEN L. "Term Structure of Yields, Financial Intermediaries, and Contracyclical Monetary Policy," *Southwestern Social Science Quarterly* (Supplement, 1959).

MARTÍNEZ DOMÍNGUEZ, GUILLERMO. "Crédito al pequeño comercio: Banco sobre ruedas," *Investigación Económica* (Third Quarter, 1954).

"El Mercado de valores en los primeros quatro meses," *El Mercado de Valores* (June 5, 1961).

OSHIMA, H. T. "Share of Government in Gross National Product for Various Countries," *American Economic Review* (June, 1957).

PATINKIN, DON. "Financial Intermediaries and the Logical Structure of Monetary Theory," *American Economic Review* (March, 1961).

SCHULTZ, THEODORE W. "Investment in Human Capital," *American Economic Review* (March, 1961).

SMITH, WARREN L. "Financial Intermediaries and Monetary Controls," *Quarterly Journal of Economics* (November, 1959).

SOLÍS M., LEOPOLDO. "Controles Seléctivas del crédito: Un nuevo enfoque," *El Trimestre Económico* (October-December, 1961).

"XXV años del Banco Nacional Hipotecario Urbano y de Obras Públicas, S. A.," *El Mercado de Valores* (June 2, 1958).

"XVIII junta de mesa redonda de bancos de capitalización," *Revista Bancaria* (July-August, 1957).

BOOKS

ADLER, JOHN H. *Recursos financieros y reales para el desarrollo.* México: Centro de Estudios Monetarios Latinoamericanos, 1961.
ALCOCER, MARIANO. *Historia económica de México.* México: Editorial América, 1952.
ALHADEFF, DAVID A. *Monopoly and Competition in Banking.* Berkeley: University of California Press, 1954.
AYRES, C. E. *The Divine Right of Capital.* Boston: Houghton Mifflin Company, 1946.
————. *The Industrial Economy.* Boston: Houghton Mifflin Company, 1952.
————. *The Theory of Economic Progress.* Chapel Hill, N. C.: The University of North Carolina Press, 1944.
BANCO DE MÉXICO. *Instructivo sobre el depósito obligatorio y sus inversiones autorizadas.* México: Banco de México, 1950.
————. *Directorio de empresas industriales beneficiades con exenciones fiscales 1940–1960.* México: Talleres Gráficos Victoria, 1961.
————. *La estructura industrial de México en 1950.* México: Banco de México, 1959.
BANCO NACIONAL DE CRÉDITO AGRÍCOLA Y GANADERO. *Legislación sobre crédito agrícola.* México: Banco Nacional de Crédito Agrícola y Ganadero, 1951.
————. *Veinticinco años del Banco Nacional de Crédito Agrícola y Ganadero, S. A., 1926–1951.* México: Oficina de Biblioteca y Publicaciones del Banco Nacional de Crédito Agrícola y Ganadero, 1951.
BANCO NACIONAL DE CRÉDITO EJIDAL, CONTADURÍA GENERAL, SECCIÓN DE ESTADÍSTICA. *Obras de Riego 1935–1958.* México: Banco Nacional de Crédito Ejidal, 1959.
BANCO NACIONAL HIPOTECARIO URBANO Y DE OBRAS PÚBLICAS. *Promoción y financiamientos, January-June, 1960.* México: Editorial Style, 1960.
BANCO NACIONAL OBRERO DE FOMENTO INDUSTRIAL. *Actividades del Banco Obrero, 1938.* México: Banco Nacional Obrero de Fomento Industrial, 1939.
BANCO OBRERO, MÉXICO. *Un año de actividades del Banco Obrero.* México: Talleres Gráficos de la Nación, 1938.
BECERRA, RENÉ A. *La capitalización en cifras.* México: Editorial Servicio Impreso, 1953.
BETT, VIRGIL M. *Central Banking in Mexico: Monetary Policies and Financial Crises, 1864–1940.* Ann Arbor, Mich.: University of Michigan Press, 1957.

BOSKEY, SHIRLEY. *Bancos de fomento industrial: Problemas y políticas.* México: Centro de Estudios Monetarios Latinoamericanos, 1961.

CAMERON, RONDO E. *France and the Economic Development of Europe, 1800–1914.* Princeton, N. J.: Princeton University Press, 1961.

CENTRO DE ESTUDIOS MONETARIOS LATINOAMERICANOS. *Aspectos monetarios de las economías latinoamericanos, 1960.* México: Centro de Estudios Monetarios Latinoamericanos, 1961.

Ciclo de Conferencias en la Bolsa de Valores de México. México: Libros de México, 1958.

COMBINED MEXICAN WORKING PARTY, INTERNATIONAL BANK FOR RECONSTRUCTION AND DEVELOPMENT. *The Economic Development of Mexico.* Baltimore: The Johns Hopkins Press, 1953.

COMISIÓN NACIONAL BANCARIA. *Directorio de instituciones de crédito y organizaciones auxiliares.* México: Secretaría de Hacienda y Crédito Público, 1961.

CONFERENCE ON INCOME AND WEALTH. *Studies in Income and Wealth.* Volume XIII. Washington: National Bureau of Economic Research, 1951.

———. *Studies in Income and Wealth.* Volume XV. Washington: National Bureau of Economic Research, 1953.

Constitución Política de los Estados Unidos Mexicanos. Decimasexta edición. México: Editorial Porrua, 1961.

COSTANZO, G. A. *Programas de estabilización económica en America Latina.* México: Centro de Estudios Monetarios Latinoamericanos, 1961.

DEWEY, JOHN. *Theory of Valuation.* Chicago: University of Chicago Press, 1939.

Discursos pronunciados por los CC. Secretarias de Hacienda y Crédito Público en las Convenciones Bancarias celebradas del año 1934 a 1958. México: Secretaría de Hacienda y Crédito Público, Dirección General de Presna, Memoria, Bibliotecas y Publicaciones, 1958.

DUEÑES, HELIODORO. *Los bancos y la Revolución.* México: Editorial Cultura, 1945.

ELLIS, HOWARD S. (ed.). *El desarrollo económica y América Latina.* México: Fondo de Cultura Económica, 1960.

FLORES DE LA PENA, HORACIO, *et al. Problemas del desarrollo económico mexicano.* México: Universidad Nacional Autónoma de México, Escuela Nacional de Economía, 1958.

FRIEDMAN, MILTON (ed.). *Studies in the Quantity Theory of Money.* Chicago: University of Chicago Press, 1956.

GALBRAITH, JOHN KENNETH. *The Affluent Society.* Boston: Houghton Mifflin Company, 1958.

GLADE, WILLIAM PATTON, JR. "Las empresas gubernamentales descentralizadas," *Problemas Agrícolas e Industriales de México.* XI, Número 1, 1959.

————. "The Role of Government Enterprises in the Economic Development of Underdeveloped Regions: Mexico, a Case Study." Unpublished doctoral dissertation, The University of Texas, Austin, Texas, 1955.

GOLDSMITH, RAYMOND W. *Financial Intermediaries in the American Economy Since 1900.* Princeton, N. J.: Princeton University Press, 1958.

————. *A Study of Savings in the United States.* 3 volumes. Princeton, N. J.: Princeton University Press, 1955.

GORDON, WENDELL C. *The Economy of Latin America.* New York: Columbia University Press, 1950.

GOUVEA DE BULHOES, OCTAVIO. *Función de los precios en el desarrollo.* México: Centro de Estudios Monetarios Latinoamericanos, 1961.

GURLEY, JOHN G. "The Influence on Prices of Changes in the Effective Supply of Money," in *Employment, Growth and Price Levels,* Hearings before the Joint Economic Committee, 86th Congress, 1st Session. Washington: Government Printing Office, 1959.

———— and SHAW, EDWARD S. *Money in a Theory of Finance.* Washington: The Brookings Institution, 1960.

HAMMOND, BRAY. *Banks and Politics in America from the Revolution to the Civil War.* Princeton, N. J.: Princeton University Press, 1957.

HANSEN, ALVIN H. *A Guide to Keynes.* New York: McGraw-Hill Book Company, 1953.

HARVARD UNIVERSITY INTERNATIONAL PROGRAM IN TAXATION. *Taxation in Mexico.* Boston: Little, Brown and Company, 1957.

HERNÁNDEZ DELGADO, JOSÉ. *Nacional Financiera como coayudante de la industrialización.* México: Nacional Financiera, 1961.

HIGGINS, BENJAMIN. *Economic Development.* New York: W. W. Norton and Company, Inc., 1959.

KEYNES, J. M. *The General Theory of Employment, Interest and Money.* New York: Harcourt, Brace and Company, 1936.

Legislación sobre el Banco de México. México. Departamento de Gráficas de la Secretaría de Hacienda y Crédito Público, 1958.

LERNER, MAX (ed.). *The Portable Veblen.* New York: The Viking Press, 1958.

LEWIS, W. ARTHUR. *The Theory of Economic Growth.* Homewood, Ill.: Richard D. Irwin, Inc., 1955.

Leyes y Códigos de México, Código Agrario y leyes complementarias. Seventh edition. México: Editorial Porrua, 1961.

Leyes y Códigos de México, Legislación Bancaria. Second Edition; México: Editorial Porrua, 1960.

Ley orgánica y estatutos del Banco de México, S. A., y otras disposiciones legales. México: Editorial Información Aduanera de México, 1959.

LÓPEZ MALO, ERNESTO. *Ensayos sobre localización de la industria en México.* México: Universidad Nacional Autónoma de México, Dirección General de Publicaciones, 1960.

LÓPEZ MATEOS, ADOLFO. *The Economic Development of Mexico During a Quarter of a Century (1934–1959).* México: Nacional Financiera, 1959.
LÓPEZ ROMERO, ADOLFO. *Plan México.* México: Libro-Mex Editores, 1958.
LÓPEZ ROSADO, DIEGO. *Banca Central: Cursos de mejoramiento del personal de Banco de México, S. A.* México, Banco de México, 1954.
———. *Ensayos sobre historia económica de México.* México: Imprenta Universitaria, 1957.
MANERO, ANTONIO. *La reforma bancaria en la revolución constitucionalista.* Biblioteca del Instituto Nacional de Estudios Históricos de la Revolución Mexicana, 1958.
———. *La revolución bancaria en México, 1865–1955.* México: Talleres Gráficos de la Nación, 1957.
MARTÍNEZ BAEZ, ANTONIO, et al. *La Constitución de 1917 y la economía mexicana.* México: Universidad Nacional Autónoma de México, Escuela Nacional de Economía, 1958.
México: Cinquenta años revolución. 4 volumes. México: Fondo de Cultura Económica, 1960–1962.
MINTS, LLOYD W. *A History of Banking Theory in Great Britain and the United States.* Chicago: University of Chicago Press, 1945.
MOORE, O. ERNEST. *Evolución de las instituciones financieras en México.* México: Centro de Estudios Monetarios Latinoamericanos, 1963.
MORA ORTIZ, GONZALO. *El Banco Nacional de Comercio Exterior.* México: Editorial Ruta, 1950.
NACIONAL FINANCIERA, S. A. *La Nacional Financiera, S. A. en el progreso económico de México, Documentos para la historia de un gobierno.* México: Editorial la Justicia, 1959.
———. *Quince años de vida, 1934–1949.* México: Nacional Financiera, 1949.
———. *Un sexenio de trabajo, 1952–1958.* México: Nacional Financiera, 1958.
———. *Fondo de garantía y fomento de la industria mediana y pequeña.* México: Editorial Cultura, 1958.
———. *Fondo de garantía y fomento del turismo.* México: Editorial Cultura, 1958.
NAVARRETE, IFIGENIA M. DE. *La distribución del ingreso y el desarrollo económico de México.* México: Instituto de Investigaciones Económicos, Escuela Nacional de Economía, 1960.
ORIVE ALBA, ADOLFO. *La política de irrigación en México.* México: Fondo de Cultura Económica, 1960.
ORTIZ MENA, RAÚL, et al. *El desarrollo económico de México y su capacidad para absorber capital del exterior.* México: Nacional Financiera, 1953.
PANI, ALBERTO J. *Los orígenes de la política crediticia: con la réplica y las contraréplicas suscritadas.* México: Editorial Atlante, 1951.
POTASH, ROBERT A. *El Banco de Avío de México: El fomento de la industria 1821–1846.* México: Fondo de Cultura Económica, 1959.

Ross, Standford G., and Christensen, John B. *Tax Incentives for Industry in Mexico.* Cambridge: Law School of Harvard University, 1959.
Ryan, John Morris. *Handbook for the Foreign Investor in Mexico.* Second Edition; Mexico: John Morris Ryan, 1961.
Sánchez Cuen, Manuel. *El crédito a largo plazo en México, reseña histórica y El Banco Nacional Hipotacario Urbano y de Obras Públicas, S. A.* México: Gráfica Panamericana, 1958.
Schumpeter, J. A. *Business Cycles.* Volume I. New York: McGraw-Hill Book Company, 1939.
———. *Capitalism, Socialism and Democracy.* Third Edition; New York: Harper and Brothers, 1950.
———. *The Theory of Economic Development.* Cambridge: Harvard University Press, 1934.
Secretaría de Hacienda y Crédito Público, Dirección General de Crédito. *Legislación Bancaria.* México: Secretaría de Hacienda y Crédito Público, 1957.
Shaw, Edward S. "Money Supply and Stable Economic Growth," in *United States Monetary Policy.* New York: The American Assembly, 1958.
Siegel, Barry N. *Inflación y desarrollo: Las experiencias de México.* México: Centro de Estudios Monetarios Latinoamericanos, 1960.
Silva Herzog, Jesus. *El agrarismo mexicano y la reforma agraria: Exposición y crítica.* México: Fondo de Cultura Económica, 1959.
———. *El Mexicano y su morada y otros ensayos.* México: Ediciones Cuadernos Americanos, 1960.
Tamagna, Frank. *La banca central en América Latina.* México: Centro de Estudios Monetarios Latinoamericanos, 1963.
Tucker, William P. *The Mexican Government Today.* Minneapolis: University of Minnesota Press, 1957.
Urquidi, Victor L. *Trayectoria del mercado commun latinoamericano.* México: Centro de Estudios Monetarios Latinoamericanos, 1960.
Veblen, Thorstein. *The Engineers and the Price System.* New York: The Viking Press, Inc., 1921.
———. *Imperial Germany and the Industrial Revolution.* New York: The Viking Press, Inc., 1915.
———. *The Theory of Business Enterprise.* New York: Charles Scribner's Sons, 1904.

Index

Aggregate demand. *See* Demand, aggregate
Aggregated model. *See* Model, aggregated.
Aggregated model, modified. *See* Model, modified aggregated
Agricultural Bank. *See* National Agricultural Bank
Agricultural credit, Mexican: pre-1940, 41–43; and Sinaloa Regional Bank, 56; and government intermediaries, 57; and regional credit banks, 57; and local credit societies, 57
Agricultural Development Bonds, 69n
Agricultural production. *See* Production, agricultural
Agriculture, Mexican, 44. *See also* Production, agricultural
Alhadeff, David A., 133
Allocation decisions, financial sector, 114–18, 136
Allocation function of intermediaries, 4
Almacenes Nacionales de Depósito, 43
Appropriability, 25
Assets, financial. *See* Financial assets
Authority, financial. *See* Financial authority
Authority, monetary. *See* Monetary authority
Ayres, C. E., 4

Banco de México: established, 41; functions of, 41, 46; public works financing, 43–44; as commercial bank, 44n; Charter Law, 1941, 45; control of private intermediaries, 52–53; and Coordinating Committee, 58; statistics published, 61–66 *passim;* sources and uses of funds, 66–70; importance, 66–70 *passim;* compared with Federal Reserve, 66–68; owners, 68; loan maturities, 68n; debt to intermediaries, 70; long-term ratio, 126; share of business and individual financing,

127–28 *passim;* and financial innovation, 135; mentioned, 49, 51
Banco de Pequeño Comercio, 57
Banco Nacional Cinematográfico, 55
Banco Nacional de Comercio Exterior. *See* National Foreign Commerce Bank
Banco Nacional de Crédito Agrícola y Ganadero. *See* National Agricultural Credit Bank
Banco Nacional de Crédito Ejidal. *See* National Ejido Credit Bank
Banco Nacional de Fomento Cooperativo, 44, 55
Banco Nacional del Ejército y la Armada, 58
Banco Nacional de Transportes, 55
Banco Nacional Hipotecario Urbano y de Obras Publicas. *See* National Mortgage Bank
Banco Nacional Obrero de Fomento Industrial, 44, 55
Banco Provincial de Sinaloa, 55–56
Bancos de ahorro y préstamo para la vivienda familiar. *See* Savings and loan banks, home
Bancos de depósito. *See* Deposit banks
Bank, central. *See* Central bank
Bank credit. *See* Loans; Securities, primary
Bank of Mexico. *See* Banco de México
Bank reserves, 23, 26, 59–60. *See also* Reserve requirements
Banks, commercial: as traditional intermediaries, 28; in traditional economy, 22–23; number of Mexican, 44; and Mexican Revolution, 44n; mentioned, 1, 3. *See also* Deposit banks; Deposit and savings banks
Banks, deposit. *See* Deposit banks
Banks, deposit and savings. *See* Deposit and savings banks
Banks, equipment loan, 44
Banks, government. *See* Government intermediaries

economy, 23n; control by Minister of Finance, 51; held by Banco de México, 69–70, 108; held by monetary intermediaries, 79; held by government intermediaries, 87; held by financial sector, 92, 93; statistical definition, 102; trends in Mexican holdings, 104–5

Foreign investment. *See* Investment, foreign

Foreign loans, 54, 56

Foreign sector. *See* Rest-of-world sector

Foreign securities. *See* Securities, foreign

Full employment. *See* Employment, full

Funds, flow of. *See* Flow-of-funds

Funds, pension, 62

Funds, sources of. *See* Sources of funds

Funds transfers. *See* Flow-of-funds

Funds, uses of. *See* Uses of funds

Gold. *See* Foreign exchange

Goods and services, 8

Government. *See* Government sector

Government banks. *See* Government intermediaries

Government consumption, trends in, 101

Government deficit financing: in traditional economy, 23; trends in Mexican, 105–7; importance of Mexican, 123; and Mexican innovation financing, 127. *See also* Policy, fiscal; Securities, government

Government enterprise investment. *See* Investment, government enterprise

Government income. *See* Income, government

Government intermediaries: and Mexican economic development, 5, 129; assumptions concerning, 11–12; Carranza's views, 39–40; importance in Mexico, 45, 87–89 *passim;* established in Mexico, 41–44; description of Mexican, 54–58; proposed budgets, 58–59; board of directors meetings, 59; Mexican defined, 61–62; sources and uses of funds, 87–89; government financing by, 107; and demand for loanable funds, 116–17; long-term ratio of, 126; and business and individual financing, 127–28 *passim;* and financial innovation, 128–29, 135–36; funds from rest-of-world sector, 129; trend in long-term ratio,

131; and Mexican interest rates, 133; and Mexican innovation financing, 138; nonfinancial activities of Mexican, 138; and Mexican inflation, 139; mentioned, 7, 37. *See also* Banco de México; Government nonmonetary intermediaries

Government investment. *See* Investment, government

Government loans of financieras, 48

Government nonfinancial enterprises: defined, 7; sources and uses of funds, 8–9; and Mexican economic development, 113; mentioned, 62

Government nonmonetary intermediaries, Mexican: defined, 62; sources and uses of funds, 70–73; importance of, 70–73, 127–28 *passim;* specialization of, 112; long-term ratio, 126, 128; and long-term finance, 134

Government sector: defined, 7; sources and uses of funds, 9; assumptions concerning, 10–11; in aggregated model, 12; in traditional economy, 23; in transitional economy, 26, 31; —Mexican: defined, 62; sources and uses of funds, 99–102; and economic development, 113; importance of, 113; and financial innovation, 135–36

Government securities. *See* Securities, government

Government services, 25

Government spending, Mexican, 101

Government transfers. *See* Transfers, government

Gross national product, real Mexican: statistical use, 65–66; growth rate of, 110, 121. *See also* Income, real national; Output

Guaranty companies, Mexican, 62

Gurley-Shaw model. *See* Model, aggregated

Gurley-Shaw theory: and underdeveloped countries, viii, 35; and market imperfections, 1–2; and present theory, 1–3; and control of financial sector, 2; and intermediary budget restraint, 2; social accounting framework, 6–10; review by Patinkin, 12–15; and full-employment assumption, 12n; and financial innovations, 25–26, 33; and intermediary funds allocation, 35; and intermediary special-

savings banks, 75–76; and Mexican inflation, 118

Reserves: of banks in traditional economy, 23, 26; 100 per cent, 59–60; statistical treatment of capital and surplus, 63

Rest-of-world sector: in social accounting framework, 9; in transitional economy, 26, 27; and innovation financing, 26, 27

—Mexican: sources and uses of funds, 62, 102–5; financing Mexican development, 107–8; and investment financing, 109–10; relative importance, 113–14 *passim;* and innovation financing, 123; and financial innovation, 135; trend in innovation financing, 137

Retained earnings: in traditional economy, 24; in transitional economy, 28; statistical treatment of government enterprises', 101; as source of investment financing, 109–10; mentioned, 22. *See also* Profits, reinvested

Returns, diminishing, 23–24

Revolution, Mexican, of 1910–1917: and continuing institutional change, 38; described, 38–39; and financial institutions, 39–40; financing of, 44n; and financial innovation, 135

Saving: ex ante, 31; planned, 34; Mexican domestic, 109–10

—forced: in transitional economy, 30–35 *passim;* defined, 31; and financial planning, 35; and Mexican financial policy, 139

—rate: effect of inflation on, 3; in aggregated model, 12n; in traditional economy, 22–25 *passim. See also* Propensity to save

Savings and loan banks, home: number of, 49; functions of, 49; control of, 50–53 *passim;* mentioned 46, 61, 62

Savings Association, National, 58

Savings banks, Mexican: number of, 47; functions of, 47; control of, 50–53 *passim;* mentioned, 46. *See also* Deposit and savings banks; Private nonmonetary intermediaries

Savings bonds, Mexican, 47

Savings certificates, Mexican, 46–47

Savings deposits. *See* Deposits, savings

Schumpeter, Joesph A., 4, 35–36

Sectors: nonfinancial, 2; of Mexican economy, 8–9

Securities: foreign, 9; in transitional economy, 25–26; fixed-interest, 63; statistical definition of Mexican, 63–64; government enterprise, 101

—business and individual: in transitional economy, 25–26; Banco de México's, 68–69; government nonmonetary intermediaries', 72; deposit and savings banks', 75; private nonmonetary intermediaries', 78; monetary intermediaries', 79–81 *passim;* nonmonetary intermediaries', 81–83 *passim;* private intermediaries', 84–86 *passim;* government intermediaries', 87–89 *passim;* financial sectors', 91–93 *passim;* trends in outstanding, 98–99, 108; owned by businesses and individuals, 99; rest-of-world sector's, 104–5; as source of investment financing, 109–10; demand for, 133–34. *See also* Bonds; Loans; Securities, primary

—government: issues of, 9; in transitional economy 25–26; Banco de México's, 69; government nonmonetary intermediaries', 72; deposit and savings banks', 75–76; private nonmonetary intermediaries', 78; monetary intermediaries', 79–81 *passim;* nonmonetary intermediaries', 81–83 *passim;* private intermediaries', 86–87; government intermediaries', 87–89 *passim;* financial sector's, 92, 93; foreign owned, 102, 104–5, 108; trends in outstanding, 102; as investment financing, 109–10. *See also* Securities, primary

—indirect: public's preferences, 2; as intermediaries' assets, 2–3; requiring particular assets, 3; defined, 7; in social accounting framework, 8; as financial policy target, 11–12; in aggregated model, 12; in modified aggregated model, 15–19 *passim;* in disaggregated model, 19–22; in transitional economy, 30, 31; stock of Mexican, 31n; diversification of, 33; assumed luxury good, 34; and intermediary specialization, 115–18 *passim;* diversification of Mexican, 117, 134; and inflation, 124. *See also* Money; Securities, nonmonetary indirect

THE FINANCIAL SECTOR AND
ECONOMIC DEVELOPMENT:
THE MEXICAN CASE

BY ROBERT L. BENNETT

        designer: Edward King
      compositor: Monotype Composition Co.
       typefaces: Perpetua, Times Roman
         printer: John D. Lucas Printing Co.
          paper: Perkins and Squier GM
         binder: Moore and Co.
  cover material: Columbia Riverside Linen